HOW DO FAMILIES COPE WITH CHRONIC ILLNESS?

Family Research Consortium: Advances in Family Research

The Family Research Consortium was established to improve the quality of research and the breadth of collaboration in the field of family research. It has held five summer institutes for experienced researchers. The consortium designed and ran a multi-site postdoctoral training program in family process and mental health and initiated a number of collaborative research programs among its members. The consortium had 10 members: Elaine Blechman, PhD (Colorado), Robet Cole, PhD (Rochester), Philip Cowan, PhD (Berkeley), John Gottman, PhD (University of Washington), Mavis Hetherington, PhD (University of Virginia), Sheppard Kellam, MD (Johns Hopkins University), Ross Parke, PhD (University of California Riverside), Gerald Patterson, PhD (Oregon Social Learning Center), David Reiss, MD (George Washington University), and Irving Sigel, PhD (Educational Testing Service).

The work of the consortium was supported by two NIMH grants: a research grant, 1R01MH40357 and a training grant, 1T32MH18262. Joy Schulterbrandt was project officer and played a major role in stimulating the current congress and future ones as well.

This volume is based on the third summer institute, *How Do Families Cope With Chronic Illness? An Integration of Research on Chronic Physical and Mental Disorder*. Other volumes in the Family Research Consortium series include:

Patterson, G.R. (Ed.) *Aggression and Depression in Family Interactions* (1990)

Cowan, A., & Hetherington, E.M. (Eds.) *Family Transitions* (1991)

Hetherington, E.M., & Blechman, E. (Eds.) *Stress, Coping, and Resiliency in Children and the Family* (*in preparation*)

Parke, R., & Kellam, S. (Eds.) *Exploring Family Relationships with Other Social Contexts* (*in preparation*)

HOW DO FAMILIES COPE WITH CHRONIC ILLNESS?

Edited by
Robert E. Cole
University of Rochester Medical Center
David Reiss
George Washington University Medical Center

Routledge
Taylor & Francis Group
LONDON AND NEW YORK

First published 1993 by Lawrence Erlbaum Associates, Inc.

2 Park Square, Milton Park, Abingdon, Oxon OX14 4RN
711 Third Avenue, New York, NY 10017, USA

Routledge is an imprint of the Taylor & Francis Group, an informa business

First issued in paperback 2016

Library of Congress Cataloging-in-Publication Data

How do families cope with chronic illness? / edited by Robert E. Cole, David Reiss.
p. cm.
Proceedings of the Third Summer Institute of the Family Research Consortium.
Includes bibliographical references.
ISBN 0-8058-1111-7 (cloth)
1. Chronically ill children—Family relationships—Congresses.
I. Cole, Robert E. II. Reiss, David, 1937- . III. Family Research Consortium. Summer Institute (3rd : 1988 : Hilton Head, S.C.)
RJ380.H69 1992
155.9'16—dc20 91-44421
CIP

Publisher's Note
The publisher has gone to great lengths to ensure the quality of this reprint but points out that some imperfections in the original may be apparent.

ISBN 978-0-8058-1111-7 (hbk)
ISBN 978-1-138-97204-9 (pbk)

Contents

Introduction

Robert E. Cole
University of Rochester
David Reiss
George Washington University Medical Center

This volume, and the conference proceedings it reports, is a major effort to examine the family's response to chronic illness in one or more of its members. The conference brought together researchers in three areas: family responses to chronic psychiatric disorders, family responses to chronic medical disorders, and family responses to early childhood anomalies that may lie on the border between these two. The conferees asked whether there were important connections among the data these three groups of researchers had collected. If there were common threads how might they inform us about processes of family adjustment to chronic illness? How might they illumine the impact of family process on the pathogenesis and course of chronic disorders? Could they help us understand how these disorders might influence the development and maintenance of the family system? Can they shape the long-term care of chronically ill patients and their families?

These questions are posed at a critical point in the history of medical and psychiatric practice. First, there is an accumulating body of research in all three areas of inquiry, cited earlier, that has used careful methods and yielded intriguing, although preliminary, findings.

Second, recent data are revising our notions of the disorders themselves. What they have in common is becoming more apparent. For example, evidence is mounting that chronic psychiatric disorders reflect, in part, abnormalities of brain structure and function. In this sense they are, in part, "medical" disorders. On the other hand a number of medical disorders produce a broad range of psychological symptoms and are exquisitely sensitive to psychosocial influences. Moreover, careful longitudinal data are now revealing early, preclinical forms of both medical and psychiatric disorders that enable researchers to examine the interaction of both physical and psychosocial forces that shape these subtle prodromes into conspicuous syndromes.

Finally, and perhaps most importantly, chronic disorder is becoming an ordinary feature of family life and development; it is no longer an exotic catastrophe. Three major features of contemporary medical practice make this so. First, a major impact of medical progress is to save desperately ill patients from certain death. However, we still cannot protect many of those saved from a life burdened with severe, chronic disabilities. This is true early in life, for example, for congenital heart disease and cystic fibrosis, in adolescence for head and spinal cord injury, and in adulthood for a variety of organ failures, particularly the heart and kidney. Second, a combination of economics and ideology has emptied our psychiatric hospitals; most of the discharged chronic patients are living with their families. Finally, pure economics is sharply curtailing the use of the hospital for the care of the chronic medical disorders; again, the family is taking over.

Thus, the problem of chronic illness and the family is no longer a concern limited to subspecialties within medicine and psychiatry and affecting a minority of families. Rather it is likely that, if current trends continue, almost all families will have, for a significant phase of their development, to deal with chronic illness. Thus, all researchers and clinicians must take the mutual relationship between family and chronic illness into account.

The chapters in this book are intended to sharpen our focus on this ubiquitous problem. We have ordered them in a way we hope best achieves our integrative aims. The first three chapters concern the family's response to disorders that are distinctly "medical," although the disorders themselves have important psychological components. The first two chapters of this set focus on childhood diabetes that has been the object of a broad range of psychosocial studies, many of them summarized in these two chapters. The third chapter in this first set focuses on children with a chronic illness that affects the brain: cerebral palsey.

The next three chapters focus on the family's response to "grey zone" disorders or anomalies that appear early in life. The first of these three concerns children who show many minor physical anomalies such as multiple hair whorls, high palates, asymmetries of the ears, and single palmar creases. These anomalies have been observed and studied for years and are part of the trisomy-21 syndrome, although they are widely distributed in the general population. They are nonheritable anomalies that probably reflect intrauterine influences and may be associated with anomalies of the central nervous system.

The second and third chapters in this set focus on "communication handicaps." This is a broad category of developmental delays in both productive or receptive language function that often become apparent when the child enters school. Their relationship to brain dysfunction is as murky as the minor physical anomalies. The minor physical anomalies seem to be associated with disorders of behavior self-regulation; the communication handicaps with difficulties in learning and school performance. Further, the children with communication handicaps are distinct from those with anomalies: They have been diagnostically labeled before the researcher enters the scene. Thus, child and family know the child is, in some way, "different." The minor physical anomalies are usually not apparent to child or family, are certainly not labeled or diagnosed, and do not influence the child's attractiveness.

Thus, these two early starting, "grey zone" conditions give us a chance to examine: (a) the family's response to a mild disorder, probably brain-based, early in the affected member's development; (b) the effects of early diagnostic labeling, and (c) the impact of a mild deficit or anomaly on the family without their awareness of its presence.

Chapter 7 focuses on an explicit and major psychiatric syndrome: schizophrenia. As is self-evident, this is a syndrome labeled and treated by mental health professionals and, in this sense, is clearly a "psychiatric disorder." However, a range of new investigative techniques—from brain imaging to receptor-specific pharmacologic agents—is suggesting significant brain dysfunction for many patients with these disorders. By the time they enter research projects, these patients have suffered from these disorders for years, and their families are dramatically different than those in the preceding chapters. The patients have probably had some developmental aberrations from early childhood. In this limited sense, these patients may be similar to some of those with physical anomalies or communication handicaps. Typically, they received their diagnosis of schizophrenia years before entry into the study and have shown both bizarre and withdrawn behavior and have been hospitalized many times.

Data on these patients give special emphasis to the term *chronic*. In studies of these patients we are learning about families who have dealt with a series of strains, stresses, and crises for a long time. Although it is distinctly possible that schizophrenia is a unique burden to families, it is equally possible that we can learn something from it of much more general importance. Data from these studies may give us a glimpse of the long-term adaptation to chronic illness of many varieties and suggest, for future study, more rigorous comparisons between families dealing with the early phases of chronic disorder and those still surviving much later in course of illness.

Finally, chapter 8 reflects an effort to develop a model based on experience of the researchers with both psychiatric and medical illness. Results are reported from family process studies of alcoholism, chronic renal disease in adults, and a broad range of neurological and non-neurological chronic medical disorders in adolescence.

Are there threads that connect these separate studies in the eight chapters? We think there may be and that they are worth attending to now as guides to future research. One set of common themes concerns emerging concepts about the family's response to chronic illness.

COMMON THEMES IN FAMILIES FACED WITH CHRONIC ILLNESS

It is possible to follow some of the concepts common to these studies using a simple four-step scheme: (a) features of the illness that determine its impact on the family; (b) the family's shared conception of the illness, which can be assessed or measured independently from these more objective features; (c) the family's response to the initial and unfolding patterns of disorder; and (d) concepts relating to the outcome—for the illness, for the patient, and for the family.

Characteristics of the Illness. A great variety of chronic medical and psychiatric disorders afflict patients and their families. We are not able to proceed efficiently in this field unless we are guided by some general dimensions of illness that are critical for their impact on families. We cannot have a separate family science for each illness. Nonetheless, few studies have systematically sampled illnesses, a point to which we return later. Thus, we need to cull from less systematic comparisons some early trends to use as a basis for constructing future studies. In this section, mainly for illustrative purposes, we identify one dimension that distinguishes among illnesses and that may be critical for understanding their impact on families: brain involvement.

A repeated theme in several of the chapters and in the conference discussion was the importance of distinguishing those illness that involve the brain and those that do not. Chapter 3 reviews most of the literature in this area and chapter 8 provides new data consistent with this review. What we know is that those chronic illnesses that have significant impact on the brain have long-term negative consequences for development from childhood, through adolescence, and possibly well into adulthood. As chapter 3 emphasizes, we still have not identified a unique role of the family in this often replicated finding. Chapter 3 examines one self-reported family variable—cohesion—as an exemplar of analyses that are crucial here. These analyses determine whether deficits in cohesion mediate the effect of brain damage on psychological development and whether brain-damaged children are uniquely sensitive to low cohesion in their families. The analyses argue against both hypotheses, but also provide an analytical format for examining these same questions with a much greater range of both self-report and observational measures of family process.

The Family's Shared Conception of the Illness. A family's beliefs about illness and about what constitutes an appropriate response, also serve to shape its actions. The characteristics of many diseases are clear and the patient's symptomatology and behavior are understood to be illness driven and beyond his or her control. For other diseases, and for many chronic conditions, the boundaries of illness are less clear and the family must develop some understanding of what behavior is actually symptomatic, what behavior is not, which responses are appropriate, and which are not. Certain behaviors are easy to accept as symptomatic: pain, nausea, and fatigue, for example. Others are less easy to accept: irritability, irresponsibility, and odd mannerisms. These are more likely to be interpreted as willful or hostile and to be met with anger or resentment. Chapter 7 discusses the impact of family beliefs on family interaction and the gradual learning process that occurs in the context of schizophrenia. Chapter 5 discusses the relationships between beliefs and behavior more generally.

The Unfolding Pattern of the Disorder. These illnesses and conditions are not static over time and the families' responses are not constant. Illnesses progress through several stages as do the families' level of understanding, their ability to predict important events and changes in course, and their ability to manage an accumulating and often unrelenting stress. Clearly, some of these difficulties abate and some become more challenging.

Chapters 1 and 2 provide an important contrast with chapters 7 and 8. The first two focus on the family's response to the onset of a chronic illness. These chapters review data from the first months after the diagnosis is made to somewhat later in the course of illness. However, compared to the life span of this illness, all these data refer to the patient and the family relatively early in the course of the disease.

These data suggest that in the early phases many families focus on the illness, become more cohesive, and feel more self-reliant. Where they are able to communicate clearly and effectively with one another, the medical course for the affected member goes more smoothly. Indeed, taken together these data suggest a clear focus, by the family group, on the emerging illness, a focus that may have, for the short term, positive adaptive consequences.

However, even in these early phases there are signs of potential trouble for many families. As chapter 1 points out, those families that lack effective communication skills may contribute to a stormy course of the illness and, secondarily, to even more stress for themselves. One might imagine a downward spiral for these families with serious negative consequences for the patient and other family members.

Even in well-functioning families there may be seeds of difficulty. Note in chapter 2, for example, that children–in these earliest phases–are expressing reservations about the effectiveness of their families in dealing with their illness. We do not know if these expressed reservations reflect a more general tendency of adolescents to view their family more negatively than do their parents; sibling comparisons will be crucial for future studies. However, in chapter 7, one of the clinical vignettes points to the transactional significance of these complaints by patients about the families. From the clinical observations reported in this chapter, these complaints appear to be part of a process by which the families become "hooked" by the illness; they may, over time, become unduly centered on its problems and consequences out of a continuing anxiety about its outcome and by feelings of overresponsibility fed by subtle but continuing complaints from the patient.

Chapters 7 and 8 give some very early clues about very long-term adaptation to chronic illness. Some of these adaptational strategies may arise from the family's sheer exhaustion from centering its activities around the actual and perceived demands of the illness. It is possible, of course, that for many families, an early and effective adjustment to lifelong illness is possible. The family, in time, can return to its "ordinary business," with the illness relatively in the background and under as good medical and psychological control as possible. However, because of the burdens of the illness or a persistent pattern of over focus on the illness, some families may never reach the equilibria they had before the onset of illness. These two chapters suggest longer term adaptational strategies for these families.

For example, the data in chapter 7 are consistent with an adaptational strategy we might label *reduced expectations.* After a prolonged period of stress in dealing with chronic schizophrenia, the family permanently lowers its expectations for the patient. Chapter 7 suggests that family problem-solving discussions in these families go more smoothly when the patients are most symptomatic, particularly for those with the most extensive history of hospitalizations. Over time, families expect their patients to have many symptoms and poor functioning and where patients, for whatever reasons, show more effectiveness, the family's previously successful adaptation to the illness is disrupted.

Thus, in these families, the patient and family may be implicitly cooperating to put the patient at the margin of family affairs. The patient's poorer functioning is "accepted" at the price of not involving the patient in the more demanding and challenging events of family life.

The preliminary data in chapter 8 suggest a more advanced phase of this adaptational process. Here, the data concerns chronic renal patients. Thus, the sequence we are mapping here may be a general one. The data in chapter 8 suggest that, after years of stress, when all else fails, the patient and family may "arrange" for the patient to be excluded altogether from the ongoing life of the family. For medical patients, chapter 8 suggests this may be one mechanism that contributes to death in chronically ill patients. In the case of psychiatric patients, this progressive "marginalization" of the patient may have led families to support permanent hospitalization of the patient, when this was available. The equivalent for some families may now be permanent homelessness.

Concepts Related to Outcome. Given the dynamic and changing nature of how families respond to chronic illness over time and the complex and often unrelenting burden placed on families, simple models relating "appropriate" family behavior to "good" patient outcomes must be revisited. Both chapters 7 and 8 present data that at first seem counterintuitive. What we understand to be adaptive family functioning seems to be related to the relapse and rehospitalization of family members with chronic schizophrenia and to the death of those with renal disease. Chapter 7 describes the conflict between the reduced expectations and protective behavior of those families who have struggled with schizophrenia and the desire for success and independent function by a subset of relatively high functioning patients. In these families, conflict and a lack of support are related to relatively high levels of patient function. Chapter 8 describes the synergy between the family's need to maintain itself against the persistent demands of renal disease and the patient's own desire not to burden his or her family.

Our existing models of family adaptation to the stress of chronic illness and the relationship between family behavior and the course of illness needs further elaboration. Current models are often too simple to accommodate the complexity we observe. By the juxtaposition of several lines of inquiry and the search for common and contrasting ideas, we hope to facilitate this process.

CHAPTER 1

Family Communication and Type 1 Diabetes: A Window on the Social Environment of Chronically Ill Children

Elaine A. Blechman
University of Colorado at Boulder

Alan M. Delamater
Wayne State University

Successful adaptation to the discovery that a child has diabetes demands radical family reorganization. The medical regimen for the newly diagnosed Type 1 diabetic child complicates every aspect of daily life and childrearing. Meals and exercise must be planned, insulin administered, and blood glucose levels monitored. Depending on the glucose test results and the advice of the health-care team, changes in food, exercise, and insulin must be introduced. The redeployment of attention, time, money, and community linkages required for success with this complex regimen inevitably affects every family member. Despite the difficulties, prospective studies indicate that more than 90% of children (Kovacs, Feinberg et al., 1985) and parents (Kovacs, Finkelstein et al., 1985) newly confronted with the diagnosis of diabetes in a child have a successful psychological adaptation 9 months later.[1] It is clear, however, that many children who have satisfactory overall psychological adjustment may not cope so well with the regimen, as compliance problems are common even among newly diagnosed patients (Delamater, 1990).

How do effective families cope? Our purpose in this chapter is to begin to answer this question. We do this by examining conventional wisdom about families of diabetic children, presenting a contrarian

[1]These data are consistent with those reported in chapter 2.

model, reviewing the literature on family factors and diabetic youths, and illustrating the model with data collected in our laboratories.

DOMINANT BELIEFS IN FAMILY RESEARCH

Knowledge about how the successful majority of families of diabetic children cope (and of the coping strategies of families caring for children with other chronic illnesses and handicaps) is limited because of a deficit-oriented belief system that permeates family research. In this section, we acknowledge these dominant beliefs. Later, we present a contrarian model.

Hypothesis Testing is More Important Than Description. The deficit hypothesis, derived from Minuchin's theory of the "psychosomatic family," asserts that the diabetic child's poor metabolic control is the product of dysfunctional family interaction (Minuchin, Rosman, & Baker, 1978; Rosman & Baker, 1988). Tests of this hypothesis (beginning with Minuchin's own reports) dominate the family-research literature. Descriptive data contrary to the deficit hypothesis seem to be viewed as unworthy of dissemination. It is particularly difficult to find detailed descriptions of families of physically hardy, diabetic children (those who maintain good metabolic control even when confronted with psychological stress) (Blechman & Brownell, 1988).

Dysfunctional Families are More Interesting Than Effective Families. Consistent with the deficit hypothesis, family research has focused on the unsuccessful minority of families with children in poor metabolic control, ignoring the effective families that produce resilient, physically hardy (albeit diabetic) children. Although studies often compare dysfunctional and "normal" control families, these "normals" are distinguished by their lack of clinically judged maladaptation rather than by objective evidence of successful coping. Some recent exceptions to this trend are presented here (Blechman, Carr, Chanler, & Saenger, 1989; Hanson, Henggeler, Harris, Burghen, & Moore, 1989).

"Psychosomatic" Family Processes Directly Stress the Diabetic Child. The direct-stress hypothesis, central to Minuchin's "psychosomatic" family theory, contends that exposure to dysfunctional family discussions causes, in the short run, elevated production of stress hormones in the diabetic child; in the long run, brittle or uncontrolled diabetes. Although it is widely believed that Minuchin's research supports the direct-stress hypothesis, Coyne and Anderson (1988, 1989) have shown that Minu-

chin's research is fatally flawed and that the data cannot support the direct-stress hypothesis. Reviewing other studies of the direct-stress hypothesis, Goetsch (1989) concluded that support is equivocal because most studies have employed faulty research methods.

Well-controlled laboratory studies of physiological effects of acute psychological stress (Delamater, Bubb et al., 1988; Gilbert, Johnson, Silverstein, & Malone, 1989) critically tested and found no support for the direct-stress hypothesis. However, in a recent correlational study using self-report methods, a direct effect of stress (including family stress) upon metabolic control was shown in adolescent patients (Hanson, Henggeler, & Burghen, 1987a). Metabolic control may also be obstructed by avoidant coping responses (Delamater, Kurtz, Bubb, White, & Santiago, 1987) and/or insufficient regimen adherence (both of which may be indirectly fostered by family stress). Other studies similarly suggest that a multiplicity of pathways lead to poor control and a multitude of child and family skills are required for good control (Delamater, Smith, Kurtz, & White, 1988; Hanson et al., 1987a).

Homeostasis Maintains Diabetic Symptoms and Prevents Family Change. Central to Minuchin's structural family therapy (Minuchin, 1974; Minuchin & Fishman, 1981) is the widely accepted belief that dysfunctional families resist change (especially during treatment) because of inherent pressures to maintain the status quo. These same pressures maintain the diabetic symptoms initially caused by stress.

> Structural therapists place great emphasis on the strength of a family's homeostatic mechanisms which they describe in terms of rules governing how family members interrelate. These rules, viewed as beyond the awareness of family members, must change in order for the family's structure and thus the symptomatic behaviors of family members to change. (Anderson & Stewart, 1983, p. 18)

Recast in social-learning terms, the homeostasis hypothesis may involve a two-stage reinforcement process. First, family members attend to symptomatic behavior, strengthening (via positive reinforcement) symptomatic behavior and weakening (via extinction and punishment) healthy, nonsymptomatic behavior. Second, family members ignore all but illness-related problems, strengthening (via negative reinforcement) an ineffective communication process ridden with avoidance, denial, and unacknowledged conflict about "nonexistent" problems of marital dissatisfaction and sibling strife.

Stated this way, the homeostasis hypothesis sounds at first like a reasonable account of the conditions that maintain symptoms and family dysfunction. On closer inspection, it is clearly an inadequate and logically flawed perspective. Prima facie evidence confirming the homeostasis hypothesis does not emerge each time a family does not want treatment or does not change during treatment. The therapist or the intervention may be ineffectual or mismatched to the family. The diabetic child cannot be judged "symptomatic" without carefully collected, objective measures of metabolic control. Family processes cannot be judged dysfunctional without independent and objective corroboration that these processes reliably and substantially discriminate between families of diabetic children in good and poor metabolic control.

Prima facie evidence that ineffective communication causes the diabetic child's poor metabolic control does not emerge simply because the two conditions are observed together. The child's poor metabolic control may have stressed the family beyond its limits of tolerance or a third variable such as poverty may have caused both poor metabolic control (via inability to get good medical care and resources for regimen adherence) and family disorganization. Poor metabolic control and ineffective family communication may also be maintained by (and contextually appropriate in response to) a health-care system that holds parents responsible for whatever happens to the diabetic child, provides inadequate training for the job of parental paramedic, and chides parents for worry and overinvolvement (Coyne & Anderson, 1989).

A CONTRARIAN, COMPETENCY MODEL

We believe that preventative interventions for families of newly diagnosed diabetic children must be informed by descriptions of how families with well-controlled diabetic children communicate.

Blechman (1990b) proposed a social-learning model of effective family communication to describe the promotion of competence (and the diminution of psychopathology) in family members. The propositions are: (a) A good mood signals prolonged contact with pleasurable consequences and optimal preparedness for learning and performance. (b) Effective family communication promotes good moods in all family members. (c) Family members who are often in good moods are primed for physical hardiness and competence and shielded from psychopathology, despite cultural, biological, and socioeconomic handicaps. We have expanded the third proposition to include the construct of physical hardiness and address the problem central to this chapter.

In the following section, we repeat the operational definitions of key constructs, define physical hardiness, and consider the expanded third proposition in light of data from the research literature and our laboratories.

A Model of Effective Family Communication

Proposition 1: A Good Mood Signals Prolonged Contact With Pleasurable Consequences and Optimal Preparedness for Learning and Performance

The functional properties of a good mood are summed up in vernacular phrases like, "I'm on a roll." "I'm ready to take on the world." "Everything's coming up roses." A good mood signals that biological, cognitive, and behavioral processes involved in learning and performance are optimal. A bad mood signals that functioning is suboptimal. Actions undertaken during a good mood should have numerous positive consequences that reinforce successful functioning along with efforts to stay in a good mood and keep others in a good mood. Actions undertaken during a bad mood should have numerous negative consequences that obstruct successful functioning, and perpetuate own and others' bad moods.

This proposition predicts that a diabetes educator would be most likely to succeed in teaching skills to the newly diagnosed diabetic child and family if all family members are in good moods during the teaching session (or at least not in bad moods). Later on, child and family would be most likely to perform their newly acquired skills when they are in good (or neutral) moods.

Moods. Moods are summary statements about the individual's response to the environment. Moods, defined this way, are readily assessed by asking, "How are you?" or, by daily administration of a mood adjective checklist and an inventory of daily hassles (Wills, 1990). A good mood ("I feel great!") is a statement that every aspect of individual interaction with physical and psychological self and physical and social environment is successful and that the consequences are highly reinforcing. A bad mood ("Don't ask!") is a statement that every aspect of individual interaction with self and environment is unsuccessful and that the consequences are punishing. Cognitive processes underlying learning and performance such as attention, perception, and memory are suboptimal in a bad mood and optimal in a good mood (Dumas, 1990; Hatfield & Rapson, 1990; Jouriles & O'Leary, 1990; Leventhal & Tomarken, 1986).

Preparedness for Learning and Performance. Preparedness for learning and performance can be assessed by observation of behavioral and physiological responses to stressful stimulation. Attentive, exploratory behavior that keeps the individual in maximal contact with important features of the current environment signals optimum opportunities for learning and performance; behavior that escapes or avoids the current environment signals minimal opportunities.

New Information Questions. A prime behavioral index of preparedness for learning and performance, useful as soon as a child can talk, can be based on the frequency with which the individual asks new information questions during challenges (Plutchik & Plutchik, 1990). New information questions are counted only if they elicit answers (and thereby put the individual in contact with important features of social and nonsocial tasks). The index excludes unanswered questions, questions that were asked and answered earlier in the same conversation (showing inattentiveness), and "why" questions about motives ("Why do you always ignore what the doctor tells you to do?"). Motivational and ad hominem "why" questions are usually answered with irritation or anger, whereas scientific "why" questions elicit new information.

Beginning with the announcement of the diagnosis of diabetes, the diabetic child and the family are confronted with a series of challenges. One such challenge to the child might be summed up as, "Figure out how to eat food you like, that other kids eat, that your parents can afford, and still get good blood-glucose readings." The frequency with which child and family ask each other and the medical team relevant new information questions in response to this challenge should predict successful coping with the challenge and accompanying good moods. Families that ask few new information questions may instead engage in mutual blaming (in the form of motivational "why" questions) or avoidant coping (denying that any dietary problem exists). The likely outcome is poor metabolic control.

Mood Regulation. Mood is maintained and intensified through actions that contact consequences congruent with the mood. Mood is shifted through actions contacting mood-incongruent consequences. The child who "whistles a happy tune" despite sadness has a pleasant impact on other people; their actions help dispel the child's sadness. In our model, mood regulation is an indirect product of modification of one's behavior and of other's behavior rather than a direct product of modification of thoughts (e.g., by saying "I have a lot of good reasons to be happy") and feelings (e.g., by imagining happy events). Notice that the process of mood regulation envisioned in this model is one of interpersonal communication. In the process, the child's mood is modified and others' moods are affected as well.

Some people are particularly skilled at shifting themselves and others into good moods despite contrary circumstances. The emotion-regulation skills required to shift from a bad mood to a good one are gradually developed (Kopp, 1989). The acquisition of these skills is influenced by the child's innate reactivity threshold (Saarni & Crowley, 1990). These skills are learned through communication with parents, beginning with the parents' first attempts to soothe their crying newborn (Lindahl & Markman, 1990) and culminating in parents' responses to their adolescents' complaints (Wills, 1990). Unarmed with emotion-regulation skills, children are at risk for social incompetence (Parke & Asher, 1983) and for drug use in adolescence as an artificial method of mood regulation (Wills, 1990).

Mood regulation may be particularly difficult for chronically ill children. Confronted with an illness that marks them as different and interferes with all their activities, it is not surprising that diabetic and asthmatic children score higher on depression than healthy children (Nelms, 1989). In a recent study of 50 diabetic adolescents, the learned helplessness attributional style was found to be a significant predictor of both depression and poor metabolic control (Kuttner, Delamater, & Santiago, in press). Diabetic children, in particular, may have difficulties with mood regulation that have a physiological basis. Illness symptoms may be misperceived as signs of a bad (anxious or sad) mood. Diabetic children in poor metabolic control may be caught in a positive feedback loop with hyperglycemia potentiating stress responsiveness and punishing the child's erratic efforts to relax and feel better.

In summary, the skill of emotion regulation (getting yourself up when you are feeling down) is learned gradually in the course of child development. Because a good mood is a prerequisite for optimum learning and performance under tough circumstances, diabetic children and the family need this skill to ensure the child's survival, longevity, and physical hardiness.

Proposition 2: Effective Family Communication Promotes Good Moods in all Family Members

Effective family communication hinges on the exchange of information about feelings with self and others. The most basic communication process, information exchange, is also a medium for emotional regulation. Information exchange allows family members to understand their own and the others' points of view; to be seen as empathic, sensitive, and cooperative; to influence each other's moods and behavior; and to solve mutual problems collaboratively. Effective family communication promotes good moods because it is an intrinsically pleasurable and tension-defusing process and because it permits family members to achieve important outcomes that would otherwise be difficult or impossible to reach. Effective family communication is a group coping strategy that enables family members to confront and do something about the unpleasant facts of life. For the diabetic child and family, effective communication permits tension-free and productive exchanges about the child's illness and the medical regimen.

When communication is ineffective, family members are likely to engage in avoidance of each other. When forced to be together, they are likely to deny problems and avoid discussing them, resorting instead to wishful thinking (the problem does not exist) and stonewalling (other family members do not exist); alternatively they may engage in openly hostile and conflictual interactions.

Effective Family Communication. In any episode of effective communication, the impact of people's spontaneous and symbolic, verbal and nonverbal behavior matches their intentions (Blechman, 1990a). Engaged in effective communication, participants act on their social environment in a predictable and powerful manner. Effective communication involves three kinds of interpersonal impact: sending a message, influencing behavior, and solving a problem.

The three types of impact can be viewed as tiers in a communication pyramid with information exchange at the base. In the first tier, *information exchange,* one person sends a message about personal experience to another person(s) who gets the message. ("Ma, I don't feel so good." "You're feeling sick?" "Yeah, like I have a cold"). In the second tier, *behavior management,* one person sends a message requesting behavior change and a second person is influenced. ("Go get the thermometer and take your temperature." "O.K."). In the third tier, *problem solving,* two (or more) people acknowledge a mutual problem and plan a collaborative future solution. ("What should I do when you're busy and I don't feel good and want to talk to you?" "Well, what worked for us last time that happened?"). Any directly observed human interaction can be reliably coded by trained observers to yield quantitative information about these dimensions of effective communication (Dumas, Blechman, & Prinz, 1990).

The capacity to exchange messages about personal experience (perceptions of affect, cognition, and behavior) is the cornerstone of effective family communication. Information exchange is a prerequisite for behavior management because it is impossible to influence a listener who is unresponsive to one's words and actions. A combination of information exchange and behavior management are prerequisites for problem solving because it is impossible to reach a compromise about a mutual problem with a partner who is unwilling to make concessions.

Information exchange, a process that in and of itself may be experienced as relaxing and nurturing, permits control and collaborative problem solving within the family. In a family with a diabetic child, information exchange would promote openness to new information from sources outside the family and collaboration with medical experts. Chronic ineffective communication severs the diabetic child and family from all these benefits. As a result, in any particular family there can be multiple psychosocial pathways to poor metabolic control, including: high perceived stress, low perceived familial support, a lack of understanding about the nature of problems as seen by other family members, a lack of expert information about common solutions for similar problems, tendencies to avoid aversive contact with family members and experts, an inability to persuade others of one's own point of view, and an inability to negotiate mutually agreeable solutions to joint problems.

In summary, effective family communication is the gateway to a good mood for diabetic child and family. Although the acquisition of mood-regulation skill poses a problem for all children, particularly for the diabetic child, the family skilled at effective communication is best equipped to promote the child's skill acquisition and buffer other family members stressed by the burden and uncertainty of caregiving. The family skilled at effective communication prior to the diagnosis of diabetes would be most likely to bounce back quickly, recovering from the shock of the diagnosis, and reorganizing family life to promote good metabolic control without making illness the family's central feature.

Multiproblem families, unskilled at communication prior to diagnosis, are least likely to recover and most likely to struggle unsuccessfully with the spiral of problems associated with poor metabolic control (Blechman, 1990a). Ineffective communication in the multiproblem family is not the direct cause of the diabetic child's poor control. In a multitude of ways (differing between multiproblem families), ineffective communication obstructs good moods, the acquisition of mood-regulation skill, and readiness to learn and perform components of the diabetic medical regimen under even the toughest circumstances.

Proposition 3: Family Members Who are Often in Good Moods are Optimally Prepared for Competence and Physical Hardiness

When family communication is effective, family members' frequent good moods signal that they are primed for competence and physical hardiness despite cultural, biological, and socioeconomic handicaps. When family communication is ineffective, family members' frequent bad moods signal that they are disposed to little physical hardiness and much incompetence and psychopathology despite cultural, biological, and socioeconomic advantages. Multiple pathways from mood to physical hardiness in the diabetic child have been considered previously. The key mechanism presumably affecting physical hardiness is readiness for learning and performing elements of the diabetic's medical regimen. According to the proposed model, good mood telegraphs such readiness. In an alternative mechanism, bad moods associated with stress would impact directly on metabolic control via counterregulatory (i.e., glucose elevating) hormones.

Competence. Measures of social and achievement competence represent the bottom-line success of an individual's response to challenges in interpersonal relationships, at school, and on the job (Blechman & Brownell, 1988; Blechman, McEnroe, & Carella, 1985; Blechman, Tinsley, Carella, & McEnroe, 1985). An individual who is socially competent is liked by others despite the differences of opinion and preference that characterize human relationships. An individual who is high on achievement competence does well at school and on the job, despite the inadequacies and hardships of these settings. Emotional competence (or resilience) describes the outcome of prolonged adaptive coping with the regulation of emotional arousal (Blechman & Tryon, in press; Lindahl & Markman, 1990; Saarni & Crowley, 1990). An individual who is emotionally competent overcomes depression and anxiety despite circumstances that put most other people in lingering bad moods.

Physical Hardiness. A physically hardy, diabetic child is one who is in relatively good metabolic control compared to diabetic peers of the same age and gender (Blechman & Brownell, 1988). Metabolic control of diabetic patients is most often defined by measures of long-term average blood glucose levels obtained generally by glycosylated hemoglobin assay. Besides acceptable levels of glycosylated hemoglobin, physical hardiness in this context may also be reflected by normal physical growth and development, by the child's regular attendance at school and social activities, and by avoidance of hospitalizations for hypoglycemia ("insulin reactions") and extreme hyperglycemia (diabetic ketoacidosis).

From Communication to Physical Hardiness. The central thesis of the family communication model is that effective family communication optimizes family members' physical hardiness and competence despite their biological, cultural, and socioeconomic handicaps. Elsewhere evidence of the relationship between communication and competence has been discussed (Blechman, 1990b; Blechman & McEnroe, 1985; Blechman, McEnroe, & Carella, 1985; Blechman, Tinsley et al., 1985; Blechman & Tryon, in press). Here, we review the literature on family factors and diabetes and present findings about the relationship between communication and physical hardiness in the diabetic child.

FAMILY FACTORS, REGIMEN COMPLIANCE, AND METABOLIC CONTROL

Considerable research has focused on family factors in relation to regimen compliance and metabolic control of diabetic youths. In this section we review studies utilizing self-report methods and direct observations of family interactions of children with established diabetes. We then consider family factors in studies of newly diagnosed children and in interventions to improve regimen compliance and metabolic control.

Self-Report/Rating Methods. Initial studies showed that families with children in good metabolic control had less conflict, fewer financial problems, greater cohesion and stability, and more distinct boundaries between family members than families of children in poor metabolic control (Anderson, Miller, Auslander, & Santiago, 1981; Koski & Kumento, 1977; Swift, Seidman, & Stein, 1967). As pointed out in reviews of this topic (Anderson & Auslander, 1980; Delamater, 1986; Johnson, 1980), a number of studies suggest the importance of these family factors despite methodological problems such as reliance on self-report ratings of global, nondisease-related family factors and inconsistent measurement of metabolic control.

Later clinical studies have generally supported these initial findings. For example, in a study of adolescents selected for chronically poor metabolic control, Orr and colleagues (Orr, Golden, Myers, & Marrero, 1983) found significant family dysfunction and psychosocial problems, including isolation, depression, and excessive school absences. Similarly, in a retrospective review of 30 youths selected for recurrent hospitalizations due to ketoacidosis, White, Kolman, Wexler, Polin, and Winter (1984) found chronic family conflict, inadequate parenting, lack of family involvement in the treatment regimen, and financial difficulties for the majority of families. Although these reports are limited by small samples and nonblind ratings, they do support previous findings and the common clinical belief that stress in families is a key factor in many cases of poor metabolic control.

It is worth noting that, despite the methodological limitations of the studies reviewed earlier, a consistent picture of the family of youths with metabolic control problems has emerged from clinical and empirical studies using self-report and rating methodologies. The variable of greatest importance seems to be family stress in the form of interpersonal conflict and limited personal and financial resources.

Family interactions specific to the regimen were investigated by Schafer, Glasgow, McCaul, and Dreher (1983). These investigators found that ratings of disease-specific nonsupportive behavior was associated with low rates of compliance to both glucose testing and diet. The only general measure of family functioning related to adherence was family conflict, which was associated with poor glucose-testing compliance. Similarly, Kurtz and Delamater (1984) found low rates of disease-specific supportive behavior to be associated with glucose-testing compliance problems.

Recent work by Hanson and colleagues (Hanson et al., 1987a) has helped to clarify the role of family factors in regimen compliance and metabolic control. In a study of 93 patients, standardized psychosocial measures and multiple regression analyses were used to specify a model of associations among psychosocial, behavioral, and metabolic measures. Direct associations were found between stress and metabolic control and between regimen adherence and metabolic control. (It is important to note that the measure of stress used in this study, the Adolescent-Family Inventory of Life Events and Changes, could be considered a measure of family stress.) Further, family relations (including general measures of cohesion, adaptability, and marital satisfaction, and disease-specific measures of support and knowledge) were found to have an indirect relationship with metabolic control, via its effects on regimen adherence. Another study by these investigators has shown that parental support of the regimen is associated with improved regimen adherence and that social competence (of the adolescent) buffers the relationship between stress and metabolic control (Hanson, Henggeler, & Burghen, 1987b). Recent work by Hanson and colleagues (Hanson et al., 1989) suggests that the relationship between family factors and metabolic control of adolescents is mediated by duration of diabetes: Under conditions of short duration, relationships are strong, while they weaken with longer duration.

A study by Mittl, Delamater, Vogler, and Santiago (1989) utilized structural equation modeling to test a causal model specifying that adaptive functioning would predict regimen adherence and metabolic control in adolescents. The sample consisted of 50 patients from two-parent, mostly middle-class families. The latent variable "adaptive functioning" was created from patient- and mother-completed standardized measures of behavior problems, marital adjustment, and parent-teen distress. Results showed significant direct paths connecting adaptive functioning with metabolic control and dietary adherence with metabolic control, with higher levels of each associated with better metabolic control. At a univariate level the strongest predictor of metabolic control was the measure of parent–teen relationship distress.

Direct Observations of Family Interactions. Relatively few studies have employed direct observation methodologies to investigate family interactions and communication skills in families with diabetic youths. Bobrow, AvRuskin, and Siller (1985) studied mother–daughter communication skills in relation to regimen compliance of 50 adolescent girls. The dyads were audiotaped while they discussed three problematic situations (for 5 minutes each) and their interactions were coded according to the Hill Interaction Matrix and the Beavers-Timberlawn Family Evaluation Scale (modified for the study). Results showed that better compliance was associated with more effective communication (i.e., information exchange, behavior management, problem solving); poor compliance was associated with more confrontative, emotionally charged, and negative interactions.

In a study of the relationship between parent–adolescent interactions and regimen compliance, Kurtz and Delamater (1987) compared self-report ratings and direct observations of family interactions in 15 adolescent–mother dyads. Both general, nondisease-related and specific, diabetes-related situations were investigated. The dyads completed questionnaires concerning their interactions in both situations and they were videotaped while discussing general and diabetes-related situations in which they had disagreements (as determined by questionnaire). The patients were classified as high or low on measures of blood glucose testing and dietary compliance. When using self-report ratings, there was little evidence of relationships between family relationships and regimen compliance. However, analyses of the data obtained from direct observations (using the Interaction Behavior Code) showed significant differences in communication skills of patients in the high and low compliance groups. Regardless of the type of disagreement the dyads attempted to resolve (i.e., nondisease-related or diabetes-specific), mother–adolescent dyads in the high compliance group demonstrated significantly better communication skills than dyads in the low compliance group, as indicated by more positive problem-solving skills and effectiveness, more friendliness, and fewer negative problem-solving skills and putdowns.

Another study that used direct observations of family interaction was conducted recently by Blechman and colleagues (Blechman et al., 1989). These investigators studied 29 Type 1 diabetic youths and their families with an interest in the relationship between effective family communication and the child's metabolic control. The children were diabetes clinic patients at an inner-city and a suburban hospital.

Each family came to the lab and performed three challenging tasks that have been used in previous studies of family communication (Blechman & McEnroe, 1985; McEnroe, Blechman, & Ruff, 1988). These tasks are best performed by families in which members score high on emotional, achievement, and social competence, and low on behavior problems/psychopathology. In data analysis, the scores achieved by the entire family are the units of analysis. Two of the tasks have definite right or wrong, better or worse, outcomes: tower building (TB) and 20 questions (TQ). One task has no right or wrong answer: plan-something-together (PST).

In TQ, family members as a group try to guess a common household object known only to the experimenter. As a group, they have 20 questions to use up before guessing the correct answer. This task appears to be a task requiring the communication skill of information exchange. Family members need to be able to ask good questions of the experimenter and to listen to each other's questions and to the experimenter's answers.

In TB, family members, each with a uniquely colored set of wooden blocks, repeatedly attempt to build a joint tower. TB appears to be a task requiring the communication skill of behavior management. Family members need to be able to influence each other to cooperate so that someone will have a chance to win.

In PST, family members have 15 minutes to arrive at a plan for how to spend $500 on a hypothetical week-end vacation. PST appears to be a task requiring the communication skill of problem solving. Family members need to be able to view the plan as a mutual problem and to work at devising a plan satisfactory to all members.

Consistent with a pattern of effective family communication identified in previous research, some families showed skills at all tasks: They built taller towers in TB, guessed more answers on TQ, and spent more time discussing the solution to PST. In these families (contrary to previous findings), family members rated lower satisfaction with their PST plan. Children with good metabolic control (as expected) came from families showing the pattern of effective communication just described. Good metabolic control was also significantly related to parental education, income, and fathers' participation in the study (for two-parent families). Regression analyses identified time spent on PST, child's satisfaction with the PST solution, correct TQ answers, and family income as the strongest predictors of metabolic control. Number of parents was the strongest single predictor of metabolic control but was redundant with respect to the variables just mentioned (leaving the equation as soon as they entered).

Studies of Newly Diagnosed Children. Several studies with newly diagnosed children have identified psychosocial patterns of functioning and predictors of regimen compliance and metabolic control. Hauser and colleagues (Hauser, Jacobson, Wertlieb, Brink, & Wentworth, 1985) found significantly more organization and recreational activities in families of newly diagnosed children compared with medical control families. Wertlieb, Hauser, and Jacobson (1986) tested the hypothesis that family factors mediated the psychological adaptation of children to diagnosis. Although there were no differences in behavior problems or family environment between diabetic and control groups, a different pattern emerged for the groups in correlating behavior problems with family environment. For diabetics, behavior problems increased with family conflict and decreased with organization and control, whereas for the medical control group problems increased with organization and control and decreased with cohesion. Based on these findings, the authors suggest that families of newly diagnosed children must deal with issues of control, limits, and rules differently than in nondiabetic families where control is more related to behavior problems in youths.

Direct observations of family interaction were used in a study by Hauser et al. (1986) to determine the impact of diagnosis on family functioning. Subjects were studied approximately 6 months after diagnosis and compared with a medical control group. Results showed better communication (i.e., more enabling speech, as indicated by active understanding, focusing, and problem solving) in patients and mothers, and more constraining (i.e., judgmental, indifferent, devaluing) interactions among fathers of diabetics compared with the control families.

Although there are only a few studies in the literature, psychosocial factors have been studied as predictors of later regimen compliance and metabolic control. Jacobson et al. (1987) found compliance to worsen over the first 18 months of diabetes. Better compliance during the second 9 months was associated with younger age, increased self-esteem and social competence, fewer behavior problems, internal locus of control, and better overall adjustment to diabetes. Age and social competence accounted for the majority of the variance in compliance. A recent prospective study of 36 children by Delamater and colleagues (Delamater, Schmidt et al., 1990) found regimen-compliance problems to be common in newly diagnosed children over the first 2 years of diabetes; however, psychosocial factors (including behavior problems, family environment and diabetes-specific support) were not predictive of compliance rates.

Shouval, Ber, and Galatzer (1982) reported better compliance associated with a highly organized family environment. These investigators also found that cohesiveness, independence, and expressiveness were associated with better metabolic control. In a prospective study of 43 newly diagnosed children, Sargent, Rosman, Baker, Nogueira, and Stanley (1985) found that positive family interactions at diagnosis were associated with improved metabolic control 3 years later. However, a recent study of 85 children, ages 8–13, failed to find any relationships between family functioning (as rated by mothers) and short- or longer-term metabolic control (Kovacs, Kass, Schnell, Goldston, & Marsh, 1989).

Demographic variables such as socioeconomic status (SES) and race have also been studied as predictors of metabolic control in newly diagnosed children. The few studies to address this issue have indicated that children of low SES (Fishbein, Faich, & Ellis, 1982; Hamman et al., 1985) and those from Black and single-parent families (Auslander, Anderson, Bubb, Jung, & Santiago, 1990) are at higher risk for subsequent metabolic control problems.

Interventions With Families. A recent review of compliance interventions for children with diabetes indicates that relatively few controlled studies (14 randomized group designs and 4 single-case studies) have been conducted (Delamater, in press). All four of the single-case studies and six of the group studies employed family interventions. Results from single-case studies have shown that parent-administered point reinforcement systems (Carney, Schechter, & Davis, 1983; Lowe & Lutzker, 1979) and behavioral contracts (Gross, 1982; Schafer, Glasgow, & McCaul, 1982) were effective in improving regimen compliance. In only two of these studies (Carney et al., 1983; Schafer et al., 1982), however, was there evidence of improved metabolic control.

Family-based behavioral self-management interventions (including contingent praise, goal-setting, communication skills, and behavioral contracts) were investigated in several group studies (Delamater et al., in press; Epstein et al., 1981; Gross, Magalnick, & Richardson, 1985). Although metabolic control of patients did not improve in these studies, regimen compliance did improve as a result of the family interventions. Another salutory effect was decreased regimen-related family conflict (Gross et al., 1985) and improved parent–teen relationships (Delamater et al., in press).

The other three group studies provide evidence of family interventions producing improvements in both regimen compliance and metabolic control (Anderson, Wolf, Burkhart, Cornell, & Bacon, 1989; Delamater, Bubb et al., 1990; Satin, La Greca, Zigo, & Skyler, 1989). Anderson et al. (1989) evaluated peer-group problem solving and simultaneous parent groups focusing on negotiating appropriate levels of involvement in the regimen and reinforcement of regimen compliance. Sixty pre-adolescent patients were followed over 18 months, with treatment sessions held at quarterly outpatient clinic visits. Patients in the intervention group reported significantly better regimen compliance and metabolic control, suggesting that this type of intervention may prevent the deterioration of metabolic control typically observed during early adolescence.

The effects of a 6-week multifamily group intervention and simulation of diabetes was investigated by Satin and colleagues (1989) in a study of 32 adolescent patients. Results showed improved metabolic control in patients participating in the multifamily plus parent simulation group compared with the untreated control group at the conclusion of treatment and at 6-month follow-up. Compliance was also rated as improved, although this was measured by just one retrospective, global rating. Presumably, the parent simulation intervention facilitated parental empathy, understanding, and support for the daily management tasks faced by the adolescents, improving family communication and moods.

In a study of family-based self-management training with 36 newly diagnosed children, Delamater, Bubb, et al. (1990) found significantly improved metabolic control 2 years after diagnosis in patients who participated in a seven-session program held in the first 4 months after diagnosis, relative to patients treated conventionally. There was also evidence of improved dietary compliance. The self-management training incorporated behavioral principles and emphasized utilization of blood glucose monitoring for solving daily diabetes management problems. Thus, the intervention focused on improving family communication and problem solving. These results suggest that this type of intervention during the first few months after diagnosis may prevent the worsening in metabolic control typically seen during the first 2 years after diagnosis.

SUMMARY AND CONCLUSIONS

Relatively little is known about how the successful majority of diabetic children and families cope with the demands of daily disease management. Most of our knowledge is based on studies of those children and families who do not adapt well. This focus on dysfunction has provided some useful information, however. Demographic factors such as SES, psychological factors such as coping styles, and familial factors all have some impact on diabetes management. For example, studies of demographic factors suggest that youths of lower SES and/or from single-parent homes are at risk for metabolic control problems. Studies of psychological factors indicate that youths in poor metabolic control have a learned helplessness attributional style, employ maladaptive coping responses to stress, and are more likely to have some psychosocial problems. Although the concept of "psychosomatic families" has not received empirical support, there is evidence that family stress (in terms of conflict, limited personal and financial resources) is associated with poor metabolic control. Conversely, good metabolic control has been related to less family conflict, fewer financial problems, greater cohesion and stability, more distinct boundaries between family members, and greater levels of overall adaptive functioning.

We have presented a competency model of family functioning that proposes that (a) good moods signal pleasurable consequences and optimal preparedness for learning and performance, (b) effective family communication promotes good moods in family members, and (c) family members in good moods are optimally prepared for competence and physical hardiness. This model has received considerable empirical support in studies of children without chronic illness.

We believe that this model holds promise for understanding how family factors operate in chronic illnesses such as childhood diabetes. Although the model has not been fully tested with diabetic samples, our review of the literature on family factors and diabetes indicates that portions of the model can already be supported by empirical studies. For example, the model proposes that effective family communication (consisting of information exchange, behavior management, and problem-solving skills) leads to good moods that promote competence and physical hardiness. In the case of diabetes, competence and physical hardiness translate to high levels of regimen compliance and metabolic control. Several studies have shown that ratings of disease-specific supportive family interactions are associated with improved regimen compliance. Furthermore, results from three studies employing direct observation methods indicate that youths who cope well (i.e., have better compliance and metabolic control) evidence more effective communication skills when interacting with their mothers to resolve disagreements.

Another way to show how effective family communication promotes adaptation to diabetes can be seen in results from family intervention studies. Although the interventions incorporated a variety of techniques, they each had the essential components of effective family communication, including information exchange (discussing regimen goals, parent simulation of diabetes management tasks), behavior management (use of contingent reinforcement, behavioral contracts), and problem solving (identifying problems, generating solutions, negotiation, discussion and plan making). Improvements in regimen compliance and metabolic control, as well as improved parent–child relationships and decreased regimen-related conflict, have been documented in controlled studies.

Ultimately, studies of communication patterns in families with diabetic children can inform clinicians about strategies to use at diagnosis to facilitate adaptation and prevent psychosocial, regimen compliance, and metabolic control problems. Several prospective studies with newly diagnosed patients, including one family-based intervention study, suggest the important role of family factors in the adaptation of diabetic children.

In conclusion, it is clear that family factors play a significant role in how children cope with diabetes, in terms of psychosocial adaptation, as well as regimen compliance and metabolic control. The family communication model provides a useful framework for understanding the role of the family in the process of diabetes management and also for guiding empirical research.

REFERENCES

Anderson, B. J., & Auslander, W. (1980). Research on diabetes management and the family: A critique. *Diabetes Care, 3,* 696–702.

Anderson, B. J., Miller, J. P., Auslander, W. F., & Santiago, J. V. (1981). Family characteristics of diabetic adolescents: Relationship to metabolic control. *Diabetes Care, 4,* 586–594.

Anderson, B. J., Wolf, R. M., Burkhart, M. T., Cornell, R. G., & Bacon, G. E. (1989). Effects of peer-group intervention on metabolic control of adolescents with IDDM: Randomized outpatient study. *Diabetes Care, 12,* 179–183.

Anderson, C. S., & Stewart, S. (1983). *Mastering resistance: A practical guide to family therapy.* New York: Guilford Press.

Auslander, W., Anderson, B. J., Bubb, J., Jung, K. C., & Santiago, J. V. (1990, May). Risk factors to health in diabetic children: A prospective study from diagnosis. *Health and Social Work,* 133–142.

Blechman, E. A. (1990a). Effective communication: Enabling the multi-problem family to change. In P. Cowan & M. Hetherington (Eds.), *Advances in family research* (Vol. 2, pp. 219–244). Hillsdale, NJ: Lawrence Erlbaum Associates.

Blechman, E. A. (1990b). A new look at emotions and the family: A model of effective family communication. In E. A. Blechman (Ed.), *Emotions and the*

family: For better or for worse (pp. 201–224). Hillsdale, NJ: Lawrence Erlbaum Associates.
Blechman, E. A., & Brownell, K. D. (1988). Competence and physical hardiness. In E. A. Blechman & K. D. Brownell (Eds.), *Handbook of behavioral medicine for women*. New York: Pergamon Press.
Blechman, E. A., Carr, R., Chanler, A., & Saenger, P. (1989, October-November). *Communication skill in families of IDDM youth*. Paper presented at the third joint meeting of the European Society for Pediatric Endocrinology, Jerusalem, Israel.
Blechman, E. A., & McEnroe, M. J. (1985). Effective family problem solving. *Child Development, 56*, 429–437.
Blechman, E. A., McEnroe, M. J., & Carella, E. T. (1985). Childhood competence and depression. *Journal of Abnormal Psychology, 95*, 223–227.
Blechman, E. A., Tinsley, B., Carella, E. T., & McEnroe, M. J. (1985). Childhood competence and behavior problems. *Journal of Abnormal Psychology, 94*, 70–77.
Blechman, E. A., & Tryon, A. S. (in press). Familial origins of affective competence and depression. In B. L. Bloom & K. Schlesinger (Eds.), *Depression and clinical psychology: The Boulder symposium*. Hillsdale, NJ: Lawrence Erlbaum Associates.
Bobrow, E. S., AvRuskin, T. W., & Siller, J. (1985). Mother–daughter interaction and adherence to diabetes regimens. *Diabetes Care, 8*, 146–151.
Carney, R., Schechter, D., & Davis, T. (1983). Improving adherence to blood glucose testing in insulin-dependent diabetic children. *Behavior Therapy, 14*, 247–254.
Coyne, J. C., & Anderson, B. J. (1988). The "psychosomatic family" reconsidered: Diabetes in context. *Journal of Marital and Family Therapy, 14*, 113–123.
Coyne, J. C., & Anderson, B. J. (1989). The "psychosomatic family" reconsidered II: Recalling a defective model and looking ahead. *Journal of Marital and Family Therapy, 15*, 139–148.
Delamater, A. M. (1986). Psychological aspects of diabetes mellitus in children. In B. B. Lahey & A. E. Kazdin (Eds.), *Advances in clinical child psychology* (Vol. 9). New York: Plenum.
Delamater, A. M. (1990). Adaptation of children to newly diagnosed diabetes. In C. S. Holmes (Ed.), *Neuropsychological and behavioral aspects of diabetes*. New York: Springer-Verlag.
Delamater, A. M. (in press). Compliance interventions for children with diabetes and other chronic diseases. In N. Krasnegor, S. B. Johnson, L. Epstein, & S. Jaffe (Eds.), *Developmental aspects of health compliance behavior*. Hillsdale, NJ: Lawrence Erlbaum Associates.
Delamater, A. M., Bubb, J., Davis, S. G., Smith, J. A., Schmidt, L., White, N. H., & Santiago, J. V. (1990). Randomized prospective study of self-management training with newly diagnosed diabetic children. *Diabetes Care, 13*, 492–498.
Delamater, A. M., Bubb, J., Kurtz, S. M., Kuntze, J., Smith, J. A., White, N. H., & Santiago, J. V. (1988). Physiologic response to acute psychological stress in adolescents with Type 1 Diabetes Mellitus. *Journal of Pediatric Psychology, 13*, 69–86.

Delamater, A. M., Kurtz, S. M., Bubb, J., White, N. H., & Santiago, J. V. (1987). Stress and coping in relation to metabolic control of adolescents with Type 1 diabetes. *Developmental and Behavioral Pediatrics, 8,* 136–140.

Delamater, A. M., Schmidt, L., Bubb, J., Santiago, J. V., Smith, J. A., & White, N. H. (1990, June). *Regimen adherence of children with newly diagnosed Type I diabetes mellitus.* Paper presented at First International Congress of Behavioral Medicine, Uppsala, Sweden.

Delamater, A. M., Smith, J. A., Bubb, J., Davis, S. G., Gamble, T., White, N. H., & Santiago, J. V. (in press). Family-based behavior therapy for diabetic adolescents. In J. H. Johnson & S. B. Johnson (Eds.), *Advances in child health psychology: Proceedings of the Florida Conference.* Gainesville, FL: University of Florida Press.

Delamater, A. M., Smith, J. A., Kurtz, S. M., & White, N. H. (1988). Dietary skills and adherence in children with Type 1 Diabetes Mellitus. *The Diabetes Educator, 14,* 33-36.

Dumas, J. E. (1990). Contextual effects in mother-child interaction: Beyond an operant analysis. In E. A. Blechman (Ed.), *Emotions and the family: For better or for worse.* Hillsdale, NJ: Lawrence Erlbaum Associates.

Dumas, J. E., Blechman, E. A., & Prinz, R. J. (1990). *INTERACT/BLISS: A computer coding system to assess small group communication.* Unpublished manuscript.

Epstein, L., Beck, S., Figueroa, J., Farkas, G., Kazdin, A. E., Daneman, D., & Becker, D. (1981). The effects of targeting improvements in urine glucose on metabolic control in children with insulin dependent diabetes. *Journal of Applied Behavior Analysis, 14,* 365–375.

Fishbein, H. A., Faich, G. A., & Ellis, S. E. (1982). Incidence and hospitalization patterns of insulin dependent diabetes mellitus. *Diabetes Care, 5,* 630–633.

Gilbert, B. O., Johnson, S. B., Silverstein, J., & Malone, J. (1989). Psychological and physiological responses to acute laboratory stressors in insulin-dependent diabetes mellitus adolescents and nondiabetic controls. *Journal of Pediatric Psychology, 14,* 577–592.

Goetsch, V. L. (1989). Stress and blood glucose in diabetes mellitus: A review and methodological commentary. *Annals of Behavioral Medicine, 11,* 102–107.

Gross, A. (1982). Self-management training and medication compliance in children with diabetes. *Child and Family Behavior Therapy, 4,* 47–55.

Gross, A., Magalnick, L. J., & Richardson, P. (1985). Self-management training with families of insulin-dependent diabetic children: A controlled long-term investigation. *Child and Family Behavior Therapy, 7,* 35–50.

Hamman, R. F., Cook, M., Keefer, S., Young, W. F., Finch, J. L., Lezotte, A., McLaren, B., Orleans, M., Klingensmith, G., & Chase, H. P. (1985). Medical care patterns at the onset of insulin-dependent diabetes mellitus: Association with severity and subsequent complications. *Diabetes Care, 8*(Suppl.1), 94–100.

Hanson, C. L., Henggeler, S. W., & Burghen, G. A. (1987a). Model of associations between psychosocial variables and health-outcome measures of adolescents with IDDM. *Diabetes Care, 10,* 752–758.

Hanson, C. L., Henggeler, S. W., & Burghen, G. A. (1987b). Social competence and parental support as mediators of the link between stress and metabolic control in adolescents with insulin dependent diabetes mellitus. *Journal of Consulting and Clinical Psychology, 55,* 529–533.

Hanson, C. L., Henggeler, S. W., Harris, M. A., Burghen, G. A., & Moore, M. (1989). Family system variables and the health status of adolescents with Insulin-Dependent Diabetes Mellitus. *Health Psychology, 8,* 239–253.

Hatfield, E., & Rapson, R. (1990). Emotions: A trinity. In E. A. Blechman (Ed.), *Emotions and the family: For better or for worse.* Hillsdale, NJ: Lawrence Erlbaum Associates.

Hauser, S. T., Jacobson, A. M., Wertlieb, D., Brink, S., & Wentworth, S. (1985). The contribution of family environment to perceived competence and illness adjustment in diabetic and acutely ill adolescents. *Family Relations, 34,* 99–108.

Hauser, S. T., Jacobson, A. M., Wertlieb, D., Weiss-Perry, B., Follansbee, D., Wolfsdorf, J., Herskowitz, R. D., Houlihan, J., & Weydert, J. A. (1986). Children with recently diagnosed diabetes: Interactions with their families. *Health Psychology, 5,* 273–296.

Jacobson, A. M., Hauser, S. T., Wolfsdorf, J. I., Houlihan, J., Milley, J. E., Herskowitz, R. A., Wertlieb, D., & Watt, E. (1987). Psychologic predictors of compliance in children with recent onset of diabetes mellitus. *Journal of Pediatrics, 110,* 805–811.

Johnson, S. B. (1980). Psychosocial factors in juvenile diabetes: A review. *Journal of Behavioral Medicine, 3,* 95–116.

Jouriles, E. N., & O'Leary, K. D. (1990). Influences of parental mood on parent behavior. In E. A. Blechman (Ed.), *Emotions and the family: For better or for worse.* Hillsdale, NJ: Lawrence Erlbaum Associates.

Kopp, C. B. (1989). Regulation of distress and negative emotions: A developmental view. *Developmental Psychology, 25,* 343–354.

Koski, M. L., & Kumento, A. (1977). The interrelationship between diabetic control and family life. *Pediatric and Adolescent Endocrinology, 3,* 41–45.

Kovacs, M., Feinberg, T., Paulauskas, S., Finkelstein, R., Pollock, M., & Crouse-Novak, M. (1985). Initial coping responses and psychosocial characteristics of children with insulin dependent diabetes mellitus. *Journal of Pediatrics, 106,* 827–834.

Kovacs, M., Finkelstein, R., Feinberg, T. L., Crouse-Novak, M., Paulauskas, S., & Pollack, M. (1985). Initial psychologic responses of parents to the diagnosis of insulin dependent diabetes mellitus in their children. *Diabetes Care, 8,* 568–575.

Kovacs, M., Kass, P., Schnell, T., Goldston, D., & Marsh, J. (1989). Family functioning and metabolic control of school-aged children with IDDM. *Diabetes Care, 12,* 409–414.

Kurtz, S. M., & Delamater, A. M. (1984). Family interactions, adherence, and metabolic control in IDDM. *Diabetes, 33*(Suppl. 1), 78A.

Kurtz, S. M., & Delamater, A. M. (1987, June). *Multimethod assessments of parent-child interactions and adherence in IDDM.* Paper presented at XII Congress of the International Diabetes Federation, Madrid, Spain.

Kuttner, M., Delamater, A. M., & Santiago, J. V. (in press). Learned helplessness in diabetic youths. *Journal of Pediatric Psychology.*

Leventhal, H., & Tomarken, A. J. (1986). Emotions: Today's problems. *Annual Review of Psychology, 37,* 565–610.

Lindahl, K. M., & Markman, H. J. (1990). Communication and negative affect regulation in the family. In E. A. Blechman (Ed.), *Emotions and the family: For better or for worse.* Hillsdale, NJ: Lawrence Erlbaum Associates.

Lowe, K., & Lutzker, J. (1979). Increasing compliance to a medical regime with a juvenile diabetic. *Behavior Therapy, 10,* 57–64.

McEnroe, M. J., Blechman, E. A., & Ruff, M. H. (1988). Inner-city families: Competence, depression, and communication.

Minuchin, S. (1974). *Families and family therapy.* Cambridge, MA: Harvard University Press.

Minuchin, S., & Fishman, H. C. (1981). *Family therapy techniques.* Cambridge, MA: Harvard University Press.

Minuchin, S., Rosman, B. L., & Baker, L. (1978). *Psychosomatic families: Anorexia nervosa in context.* Cambridge, MA: Harvard University Press.

Mittl, V., Delamater, A. M., Vogler, G., & Santiago, J. V. (1989, March). *Adaptive functioning and metabolic control in adolescents with diabetes.* Paper presented at 10th annual meeting of the Society of Behavioral Medicine, San Francisco, CA.

Nelms, B. C. (1989). Emotional behavior in chronically ill children. *Journal of Abnormal Child Psychology, 17,* 657–668.

Orr, D., Golden, M., Myers, G., & Marrero, D. (1983). Characteristics of adolescents with poorly controlled diabetes referred to a tertiary care center. *Diabetes Care, 6,* 17–175.

Parke, R. D., & Asher, S. R. (1983). Social and personality development. *Annual Review of Psychology, 34,* 465–510.

Plutchik, R., & Plutchik, A. (1990). Communication and coping in families. In E. A. Blechman (Ed.), *Emotions and the family: For better or for worse.* Hillsdale, NJ: Lawrence Erlbaum Associates.

Rosman, B. L., & Baker, L. (1988). The "psychosomatic family" reconsidered: Diabetes in context—a reply. *Journal of Marital and Family Therapy, 14,* 125–132.

Saarni, C., & Crowley, M. (1990). The development of emotion regulation: effects on emotional state and expression. In E. A. Blechman (Ed.), *Emotions and the family: For better or for worse.* Hillsdale, NJ: Lawrence Erlbaum Associates.

Sargent, J., Rosman, B., Baker, L., Nogueira, J., & Stanley, C. (1985). Family interaction and diabetic control: A prospective study. *Diabetes, 34*(Suppl. 1), 77A.

Satin, W., La Greca, A., Zigo, M., & Skyler, J. (1989). Diabetes in adolescence: Effects of multifamily group intervention and parent simulation of diabetes. *Journal of Pediatric Psychology, 14,* 259–276.

Schafer, L., Glasgow, R., & McCaul, K. (1982). Increasing the adherence of diabetic adolescents. *Journal of Behavioral Medicine, 5,* 353–362.

Schafer, L., Glasgow, R., McCaul, K., & Dreher, M. (1983). Adherence to IDDM regimens: Relationship to psychosocial variables and metabolic control. *Diabetes Care, 6,* 493–498.

Shouval, R., Ber, R., & Galatzer, A. (1982). Family social climate and the social adaptation of diabetic youth. In Z. Laron (Ed.), *Psychological aspects of diabetes in children and adolescents.* Basel: Karger.

Swift, C., Seidman, F., & Stein, H. (1967). Adjustment problems in juvenile diabetics. *Psychosomatic Medicine, 29,* 555–571.

Wertlieb, D., Hauser, S., & Jacobson, A. M. (1986). Adaptation to diabetes: Behavior symptoms and family context. *Journal of Pediatric Psychology, 11,* 463–479.

White, K., Kolman, M., Wexler, P., Polin, G., & Winter, R. (1984). Unstable diabetes and unstable families: A psychosocial evaluation of diabetic children with recurrent ketoacidosis. *Pediatrics, 73,* 749–755.

Wills, T. A. (1990). Social support and the family. In E. A. Blechman (Ed.), *Emotions and the family: For better or for worse.* Hillsdale, NJ: Lawrence Erlbaum Associates.

CHAPTER 2

The Family and the Onset of Its Youngster's Insulin-Dependent Diabetes: Ways of Coping

Stuart T. Hauser
Massachusetts Mental Health Center
Harvard Medical School, and
Joslin Diabetes Center

Alan M. Jacobson
Massachusetts Mental Health Center
Harvard Medical School, and
Joslin Diabetes Center

Robin Bliss
Janet Milley
Joslin Diabetes Center

Maria Ann Vieyra
Joslin Diabetes Center

John B. Willett
Chari Cole
Joslin Diabetes Center
Harvard Graduate School of Education

Joanne DiPlacido
Boston University

Elizabeth Paul
Boston University
Wellesley College

Philip Lavori
Harvard Medical School

Joseph I. Wolfsdorf
Ramonde D. Herskowitz
Joslin Diabetes Center
Harvard Medical School

Donald Wertlieb
Tufts University

Families of children and adolescents with newly diagnosed insulin-dependent diabetes are touched by this chronic illness in many ways (Patterson, 1988; Rolland, 1988). Large issues—family members' visions of the youngster's unfolding life and longevity—and more mundane concerns, such as mealtime routines, daily bodily care, the use of the family car, and being on one's own at parties, are all affected. After feelings of fear, panic, and guilt subside, some families begin to realize the youngster's death is not imminent. Family members may accept the presence of this new illness, not singling out the child or adolescent with diabetes as special or implicitly defective, in need of special protection, or special monitoring. At the other extreme are those families overwhelmed by the transformation of a formerly healthy younger member into one who now has a chronic incurable illness. Feeling helpless, family members may then deny the problem, acting as if the diabetes never occurred, forgetting about diet precautions or minimizing restrictions (Hauser & Solomon, 1985). Successful management of their child's diabetes may require parents to reconsider shared assumptions about how to best care for their children, redistribute responsibilities, reorganize daily routines, and renegotiate family roles.

So broad a spectrum of demands and responses leads to many questions about what underlies successful and unsuccessful family adaptation to the advent of this new illness. Although we are increasingly aware of the continuing strains experienced by families with a diabetic youngster, we do not yet know of the specific ways such families handle these strains and—most important—what distinguishes families that competently handle these difficulties from those who are thrown off, or collapse, under the new daily pressures and long-term fears.

Our research program focuses on both of these gaps in our understanding of how families deal with chronic illness. In order to consider the primary question of how families with a diabetic youngster differ from other families, we consistently include comparison families differing in terms of the youngster's health status. In our earliest studies, this comparison group consisted of families whose children had no medical or psychiatric diagnosis (Hauser, Jacobson, Noam, & Powers, 1983; Hauser, Powers, Houlihan, Jacobson, & Noam, 1985). We found that these youngsters differed from those with diabetes along a number of lines (self-image complexity, ego development). But these results left us in the dark as to whether the differences were based on the new experience with diabetes or whether they might be consequences of the, usually sudden, introduction of a medical team into the life of the youngster and family. To be sure, the unbidden entry of new health-care providers and institutions can have many and varied repercussions. As a way of disentangling these "medical effects" from "diabetes-specific effects," our current strategy is to follow families with preadolescent or early adolescent members who were recently diagnosed with insulin-dependent diabetes and families with youngsters of the same age who were recently diagnosed with a serious acute illness, one that was neither life-threatening nor trivial. By selecting this sample for comparison, we can ensure that both sets of families had some meaningful contact with a health-care provider and that we could control for the impacts that a new medical intervention might have on the youngster and family. If we studied a more conventional comparison group (e.g., no illness), we would be unable to trace consequences of medical interventions from those connected with the onset of a youngster's diabetes. Although this new step cannot fully clarify what is unique to families with a diabetic youngster (we have not included comparisons with other serious chronic illnesses, such as epilepsy or asthma), it does move us toward discerning how the medical encounter itself may influence the child and family.

Clinical observations and theoretical arguments converge in suggesting that most families are not rendered severely dysfunctional when a child or adolescent member is diagnosed as suffering from diabetes (Jacobson, Hauser, Powers, & Noam, 1983; Stein, 1989). In fact, some of our findings suggest the opposite. We have seen indications of enhanced family cohesion and organization, and greater attentiveness of family members to one another's needs soon after the preadolescent or early adolescent family member has been diagnosed as having diabetes (Hauser et al., 1986, 1989). Based on these observations we expected to find that an important way that such families would cope with the youngster's diabetes would be through strategies emphasizing coordination and acknowledgment of feelings. But there is also a darker side. In observing family interactions, we found indications of strains between parents and youngster, such as more indifference and judgmental behaviors from fathers toward other family members (Hauser et al., 1986). Thus, we expected to find coping strategies reflective of these greater strains, such as avoidance and mechanically using past experiences to guide ways of handling new problems. Before reviewing our approach to family coping, and what we found, it is helpful for us to first consider the clinical and intellectual roots of these new explorations.

THEORETICAL AND EMPIRICAL PATHS TO FAMILY COPING

Family Processes and Insulin-Dependent Diabetes

A growing number of theoretical and empirical contributions, including several from our ongoing program of research, address the complex interplay between family processes and psychological features of adolescents with insulin-dependent diabetes (Anderson & Auslander, 1980;

Anderson, Miller, Auslander, & Santiago, 1981; Baker, Minuchin, Milman, Liebman, & Todd, 1970; Benoliel, 1977; Bobrow, Asruskin, & Siller, 1985; Crain, Sussman, & Weil, 1966; Delamater, in press; Hanson, Henggler, & Burghen, 1987; Hauser, Jacobson, Wertlieb, Brink, & Wentworth, 1985; Hauser et al., 1986; Koski, Ahlas, & Kumeto, 1976; Wertlieb, Hauser, & Jacobson, 1985).

Two directions of work can be distinguished in this burgeoning literature. There are those contributions tracking how the family may influence the adjustment and metabolic control of the diabetic child or adolescent. Much of this research follows the mother–child relationship, and its effect on the young patient's adjustment (Anderson & Auslander, 1980; Mattson, 1979; Pond, 1979; Vandenbergh, 1971). Recently, attention has turned to how the family as a unit may influence the diabetic youngster, with investigations citing the importance of maladaptive parenting styles (Stein, 1989), parental self-esteem (Grey, Genel, & Tamborlane, 1980), marital satisfaction (Hanson, Henggler, Harris, Burghen, & Moore, 1989), as well as specific family orientations and relationships (Hanson et al., 1987; Hauser, Jacobson et al., 1985b; Hauser et al., 1989; Mendlowitz, 1983).

A second set of investigations considers impacts of the youngster's diabetes on the relationship between parents (Crain et al., 1966); the relationship between parent and child (Pond, 1979); and overall aspects of family functioning, such as coping and problem solving (D'Onofrio, 1979; Hauser, 1990; Hauser, 1988; Powers, Dill, Hauser, Noam, & Jacobson, 1984). This second line of inquiry is most relevant to the studies of coping we report in this chapter, comparing the coping strategies used by families with a diabetic child with those of families with an acutely ill child.

The concept of coping is closely related to that of stress. Both constructs are embedded in a long tradition of theoretical and empirical work. Although it is beyond the scope of this chapter to review this extensive literature, a brief excursion into the most germane aspects of this work sets the stage for a clearer understanding of our probes into the relatively uncharted area of family coping.

Stress and Coping: Individual and Family Perspectives

The influences of stress upon psychological and physiological functioning have been studied by numerous investigators in the biological and social sciences (cf. Selye, 1956). However, the very concept of stress can be a confusing and vague one. *Stress* is most often defined in the literature as a perceived imbalance between the capacities or resources of the person and the demands of the environment. The ways in which an individual or family is affected by a given stressor depends on many interacting factors, including the type of stress, the coping processes used in handling the stress, developmental stage, and sociocultural forces (Lazarus & Folkman, 1984; Silver & Wortman, 1980). Not all stressors lead to problematic outcomes. There is currently much interest in the question of why some individuals and families fare better than others when facing adversity. In fact, a number of recent investigations consider resilient outcomes, unexpectedly robust adaptations to clearly adverse circumstances (Garmezy & Rutter, 1983; Hauser & Bowlds, 1990; Hauser, Vieyra, Jacobson, & Wertlieb, 1985; Werner & Smith, 1977).

Such striking variability in the impacts of stressful events has prompted investigators to take a closer look at intermediate connections between these events and adaptation. One key link involves *coping processes,* those attempts to alter the "mismatch" between the person and his or her environment (Hauser & Bowlds, in press; Rutter, 1981); those "cognitive and behavioral efforts made to master, tolerate, or reduce demands that tax a person's resources (Kessler, Price, & Wortman, 1985, p. 550). These efforts include alteration of environmental demands, individual or family resources or capacities, or individual or family needs, goals, and preferences (Menaghan, 1983). Coping efforts do not by definition lead to favorable outcomes. Some may increase the risk of maladaptation, whereas others facilitate adjustment to stress (Hauser & Solomon, 1985; Lazarus & Folkman, 1984).

Coping processes have usually been studied in terms of individual strategies or processes (e.g., Haan, 1977; Kessler et al., 1985; Lazarus & Folkman, 1984). With the advent of family systems theory and a growing number of investigators observing family interactions (e.g., Grotevant & Cooper, 1985, 1986; Hauser et al., 1984; Reiss, 1981), there has evolved a deepened interest in understanding how families cope with stress (Hauser, 1990; Menaghan, 1983; Reiss & Oliveri, 1980). From this vantage point, in order to understand a family's handling of stress one must study the family as a unit because the family is considered to be more than the sum of its individual members (Kantor & Lehr, 1975; Lewis, Beavers, Gossett, & Phillips, 1976; Minuchin, 1985; Minuchin, Rosman, & Baker, 1978). This line of reasoning leads to new conceptualizations and assessments of how families cope with acute stresses and chronic strains (McCubbin & Patterson, 1981a; Menaghan, 1983; Reiss & Oliveri, 1980). Our research program, then, represents further efforts to more precisely characterize profiles of family coping.

Family coping refers to those perceptions, attitudes, and behaviors expressed by family members in their attempts to master the effects of stressful events on their family group. Such responses include ways of observing, acting, and expressing feelings (Hauser et al., 1988). Notable in this conceptualization of family coping is our emphasis on the family group as the target of family member's coping efforts, in contrast to family member's description of coping strategies addressed to mastering immediate or ongoing difficulties they are experiencing as individuals (a distinction also made by Reiss & Oliveri, 1980). Similar to Stone and Neale (1984), we deliberately narrow (and thereby sharpen) our definition by excluding certain dimensions: processes that the family is completely unaware of (e.g., total denial); and simple reactions to situations that are apparently not intended to contribute to the family's handling or controlling a given situation or its effects. This definition is at the core of our efforts to identify and assess family coping strategies. As is soon apparent, to minimize theoretical confusion, as well as to avoid a premature restriction of perspectives, our definitions and linked empirical scales build upon prior clinical and theoretical studies of family coping (e.g., Menaghan, 1983; McCubbin & Patterson, 1981a, 1981b; Minuchin et al., 1978; Olson, Sprenkle, & Russell, 1979; Reiss & Oliveri, 1980) and individual coping (e.g., Lazarus & Folkman, 1984). In other words, we include a broad spectrum of coping strategies that may be available to families as they respond to stressful events.

Other research groups have presented theoretically guided approaches to assessing family coping (McCubbin & Patterson, 1981a, 1981b; Reiss & Oliveri, 1980). For the most part, these approaches focus on either how family coping may promote adaptive outcomes or on how such processes can lead to individual and family dysfunction. Rarely does one find discussion of how family coping strategies may contribute to adaptive and dysfunctional individual or family outcomes. In addition, many family investigations are based on self-reports obtained from family members, thereby reflecting the individual's perceptions of how his or her family copes. Our method, the Family Coping Coding System (FCCS; Hauser et al., 1988), based on family systems, family stress, and ego psychology perspectives, is characterized by three features that together distinguish it from other family coping approaches:

1. A broad range of coping variables are defined conceptually and empirically. These dimensions are expected, on theoretical and clinical grounds, to be associated with adaptive as well as problematic functioning of families.

2. The method focuses on the coping strategies of the family as a unit, as revealed in family discussions of the events surrounding the onset of a family member's (preadolescent or adolescent) illness; the

unfolding of shared family perspectives and problem-solving efforts during the course of stressful circumstances (e.g., the diagnosis of their child's chronic illness). This approach, strongly influenced by Reiss and Oliveri (1980), represents a distinct departure from methods that assess family coping through pooling separate written self-reports of family members (e.g., McCubbin & Patterson, 1981b).

3. Coping strategies are grouped into three conceptually distinct categories. This tripartite classification parallels earlier classifications elaborated by Lazarus and Folkman (1984) and Pearlin and Schooler (1978). Similar categories have been referred to as family perceptions, resources and adaptation (McCubbin, Boss, Wilson, & Lester, 1979), configuration, coordination and closure of family paradigms (Reiss, 1981), cohesion and adaptability (Olson et al., 1979), and enmeshment and rigidity (Minuchin et al., 1978).

OBSERVING AND MEASURING FAMILY COPING

Observations of Family Narratives

We generate observations about family coping through a semistructured family interview, the Family Life Events Interview, developed by Reiss and Oliveri (1980) from individual life events measures constructed earlier by Holmes and Rahe (1967) and Dohrenwend and Dohrenwend (1974). At the heart of this interview are the ways that a recent major event (e.g., the advent of an adolescent's diabetes or acute illness) has interrupted or changed the usual activities of the family group. After family members review either the onset of the child's diabetes or recent acute illness, the interviewer inquires about when and how the diagnosis was made, the circumstances surrounding the diagnosis. The interviewer probes sequential phases of the family's response: the family's framing of the problem and search for information; how the family organized its approach and handling of the problem; emotional reactions to the event; the family's overall response and resolution of the initial event and its sequelae. Questions are designed to elicit the family members' narratives of this experience, not answers to forced choice questions about specific strategies or responses.

The family interviewers are students with a bachelors degree in psychology, graduate students in psychology, and other health professionals who have had clinical experience working with families. All interviewers are carefully trained before conducting this semistructured interview with the families. The family discussions generated by these interviews are then audiotaped and transcribed to permit analysis with the FCCS by experienced raters, trained to reliability through the rules, definitions, and examples found in the FCCS manual (Hauser et al., 1988).

Analyzing Family Narratives: The FCCS

In first constructing this approach to analyzing the family coping discussions, we developed conceptual and empirical definitions for over 40 coping strategies, based on theoretical, clinical, and empirical studies (Hauser et al., 1988). Fifteen of these strategies were eventually dropped from the system because adequate interrater reliability could not be achieved despite redefinitions, clearer examples, and extensive discussions among the coders. The remaining 32 family coping strategies represent the appraisal, problem-solving, and emotion management areas.

Because the overall domain of interest is family coping, speeches must refer to the whole family or another member of the family to be scored as indicators of these strategies. In other words, individual "I" statements do not qualify as representing components of family coping. Some examples should clarify this basic distinction. When an adolescent boy says "I handled things well, and now I know how to give my own shots," his speech is not scored as a family coping one, because he is describing his individual coping. On the other hand, a description by an adolescent girl with diabetes expresses an aspect of family coping: "It's hard and we're not expert at everything yet; but I know how to give shots and my parents do, too." In this instance, she has included herself and her parents, rather than only herself.

Family coordination is reflected by an adolescent's description of the family's schedules: "We have very different schedules, and it's hard to get us all together. But we eat together as much as possible, and my mom and my sister help me with my shots." In contrast, a family's noncoordination is described by the teen-ager's declaration of how he benefits by independent management of his insulin schedule: "It's better if I just give the shots and do the testing myself. When my mother and father try to get involved, we always lose track of who's doing what, and I end up losing a meal or missing a shot." In all of these examples we hear the adolescent describing coping efforts that include the family. One important exception to this emphasis on referring to the entire family or another family member is our treatment of emotion management strategies, as is described later. The interested reader can find brief definitions of all 30 family coping strategies, together with illustrative excerpts from family interviews, in the appendix to this chapter.

We include family coping strategies from three conceptual areas.

Appraisal-focused coping strategies refer to the family's cognitive assessment or interpretation of the stressful situation. "Appraisal is the cognitive process through which an event is evaluated with respect to what is at stake and what coping resources are available" (Folkman & Lazarus, 1980, p. 223). The importance of these strategies is based on the assumption that a family's view or understanding of its situation is a significant factor in effective family functioning during a period of stress (Hill, 1958; Reiss, 1981).

Problem-focused coping strategies refer to the planning or taking of actions by the family to deal with the stressful situation at hand. In this domain, the emphasis is on behavioral efforts, rather than the kinds of cognitive or interpretive activities included within the appraisal-focused category. The function of this set of family coping strategies is considered to be the management or alteration of the problem in the environment that is leading to the family's stressful situation.

The last set of family coping processes, *emotion-management* strategies, refer to family members' efforts to contain or regulate problematic feelings. These strategies deal with expression of affect, within and outside the family. This is the only family coping category in which individual responses are assessed because preliminary coding trials by our group revealed that family members rarely describe their feelings or their regulation from a family perspective. Moreover, when such descriptions were offered, they appeared as abstract and usually awkward constructions—"We never express anger as a family"—that were not responded to as meaningful communications by other family members. Consequently, in order to preserve important data about feelings and their significance in terms of the family's response to stressful events, this set of family coping strategies was conceptually and empirically defined in terms of individuals' descriptions of the ways they dealt with their emotional reactions to a given stressful situation. We assume that these individually based strategies reflect ways that the family group handles emotions elicited by stressful events.

Using the conceptual and empirical definitions, further amplified by examples, trained raters scored every speech expressed by each family member during the course of the family coping discussion. In each speech, all instances of any of the 32 coping strategies (e.g., family mastery) are scored for their presence. Then, scores on each strategy are summed over all speeches to generate 32 coping scores for each person.[1] In the analyses presented here, many of the 32 coping scores were

[1]An earlier scoring method was based on a 0 to 2 rating of members for the whole discussion. However, this system did not lead to the more sensitive intensity index we were interested in obtaining, and was then abandoned in favor of this frequency score.

markedly skewed with modal value zero; therefore scores were dichotomized prior to analysis, each score thereby depicting whether a given coping strategy was observed during the family discussion. The interested reader can learn more about the details of this coding system through a recent chapter (Hauser, 1990) and unpublished coding manual (Hauser, Paul, DiPlacido, Rufo, & Spetter, 1990), available from the first author.

There have now been 106 one- and two-parent family coping discussions coded by two coders trained to reliability. Additional coders participated in earlier trials of sets of five transcripts. These smaller trials provided the basis for consensus discussions between the coping teams and the senior author (STH), leading to subsequent refinement of definitions and examples used for coding. Further details about specific reliabilities can be found in our earlier report of the FCCS (Hauser et al., 1988).

COPING STRATEGIES USED BY FAMILIES OF YOUNGSTERS WITH RECENTLY DIAGNOSED DIABETES AND ACUTE ILLNESS

The family coping strategy scores of the family members participating in the discussion (parents and patient), were the dependent variables in all of our analyses. The analyses that we present here compare these family members, whose youngster was recently diagnosed with diabetes, and those families with an acutely ill child, in their handling of the new illness.

Sample

For this first full comparative study of these two illness groups (in contrast to the previous case study; Hauser et al., 1988), we include 79 two-parent families drawn from our larger overall sample of 123 families. Coders were blind to the research questions, hypotheses, and findings. There were 42 diabetic families and 37 acute illness families. Specific demographic characteristics of the two subsamples are given in Table 2.1. There is a higher proportion of upper middle-class families in the acute illness group so all of our analyses include social class as a covariate.

TABLE 2.1
Demographic and Speech Characteristics of the Families With Diabetic and Acute-Illness Youngsters

	Diabetes	*Acute Illness*
Number of families	42*	37**
Socioeconomic Status		
upper middle	24	23
middle class	9	11
working/lower	9	3
Gender of patient		
male	20	19
female	22	18
Age of patient[a]	12.59 (1.99)	12.88 (1.78)
Speeches[b]		
Mother	63.62	49.16[c]
Father	45.57	36.51[d]
Adolescent	48.29	52.89

*Two of these families have mothers with stepfathers

**One family has a mother with a stepfather; one family has a father with a stepmother; one family has two adoptive parents; one child lives in a joint arrangement, part-time with mother, part-time with father and stepmother.

[a]Mean and (standard deviation)

[b]Mean number of speeches

[c]$t = 2.43$; $p < .02$

[d]$t = 2.04$; $p < .04$

Preliminary Analyses

Preliminary analyses explored possible differences between one- and two-parent families in a smaller set of families ($n = 71$) who had been reliably coded. Three multivariate analyses of covariance (MANCOVAs) were used to compare the family coping scores of these one- and two-parent families. These analyses indicated highly significant multivariate main effects for number of parents (one vs. two) for each area of family coping (i.e., appraisal, problem solving, and emotion management). Consequently, the findings presented in this chapter include only those 79 two-parent families who participated in the family coping discussion soon after the diagnosis of the youngster's diabetes or acute illness. Thirteen additional two-parent families were not included because either they did not participate in the family discussion ($n = 11$), or their tapes were not transcribable ($n = 2$). Comparisons of the entire set of two-parent families with missing family coping data ($n = 13$) with patients and families who provided all family data revealed no differences in terms of social class, gender, age, ego development (parents or youngsters), self-esteem, or behavioral symptoms.

A final set of preliminary analyses compared the "diabetic" and "acute" families in terms of how much each family member spoke during the discussions. Parents of youngsters with diabetes spoke more often, in contrast to no differences between the youngsters (see Table 2.1). Consequently, in all of the analyses described here, the family members' number of speeches was included as a covariate.

Coping Strategies Analyses

Three sets of MANCOVAs were carried out to compare the two sets of families in terms of appraisal, problem-solving, and emotion-management coping strategies.[2] In all analyses, illness type was the predictor and social class and number of speeches were the covariates. When significant multivariate effects were obtained, follow-up univariate analyses of covariance were carried out on the separate coping variables. Because an important research question concerns whether family members in different roles have varied perceptions of family coping strategies, all analyses are carried out separately for each member (mothers, fathers, adolescents).

Appraisal-Focused Strategies

Mothers. There was a significant multivariate effect for illness type [$F(13, 63) = 3.07; p < .001$]. Follow-up univariate analyses of covariance revealed that, compared with mothers of youngsters who had been re-

[2]Recall that scores on each of the 32 coping strategies were dichotomized prior to analysis, each dichotomy then indicating whether the particular coping strategy was observed (or not) during the entire family discussion. For the purposes of this chapter, we have treated these dichotomies as dependent variables in our analyses of covariance in the spirit of the *linear probability model* (Goldberger, 1964). One advantage to this approach is that the estimated means reported in Tables 2.2 through 2.4 can be interpreted as the adjusted *proportions* of respondents demonstrating each coping strategy, broken down by family-type (diabetic or acute). Unfortunately, our use of dichotomous outcome variables violates the distributional assumptions underpinning our analyses. However, we believe that our results are credible for two reasons. First, estimates of the differences between diabetic and acute families (and estimated slopes associated with the covariates) are still unbiased (Aldrich & Nelson, 1984, p. 13). Second, although standard errors are typically inflated when dichotomies are treated as outcomes in parametric analyses (Aldrich & Nelson, 1984, p. 18), such inflation offers a measure of "protection" to our findings. If the distributional assumptions were satisfied, standard errors would decline and the statistical significance of our findings would be improved. This suggests that the differences between acute and diabetic families that we report in this chapter would remain, and be strengthened, under more advantageous measurement conditions.

cently diagnosed as having an acute illness, mothers of youngsters with diabetes were more likely to see their family as a consensual unit. Moreover, these mothers perceived their families as holding a clear construction (family theory) of their experience, one not driven so strongly by past experience (cf. Table 2.2).

Fathers. There was a significant multivariate effect for illness type [F (13, 63) = 5.34; p < .0001]. Follow-up univariate analyses of covariance revealed that, compared with fathers of youngsters who had been recently diagnosed as having an acute illness, fathers of youngsters with diabetes were more likely to see their family as having mastery over the current situation and less likely to blame others for their difficulties. Similar to their wives, these men perceived their families as a consensual unit and as having a clear view of their situation (cf. Table 2.2).

Adolescents. There was a significant multivariate effect for illness type [F (13, 63) = 2.59; p < .006]. Follow-up univariate analyses of covariance revealed that youngsters with recently diagnosed diabetes were more likely to describe their families as a consensual unit and—consistently—less likely to see this unit a simply as collection of individuals. They also saw their families as expressing more avoidance of their problems (see Table 2.2).

Problem-Focused Strategies

Mothers. There was a significant multivariate effect for illness type [F (10, 66) = 5.66; p < .0001]. Follow-up univariate analyses of covariance revealed that, compared with mothers of youngsters with a recent acute illness, mothers of recently diagnosed diabetic youngsters described their families as seeking support, pursuing alternate rewards, and trying out new responses. In addition, they also described their families as being more self-reliant (see Table 2.3).

Fathers. There was a significant multivariate effect for illness type [F (10, 66) = 2.19; p < .03]. Follow-up univariate analyses of covariance revealed that, for the most part, the fathers of youngsters with diabetes closely paralleled their wives in their perceptions of how the family dealt with the youngster's onset of the illness. Like their spouses, fathers describe their families as pursuing alternative rewards, seeking support, and trying out new responses. Although they also described their families as more self-reliant, these differences were not as marked as they were for their wives (see Table 2.3).

TABLE 2.2
Appraisal-Focused Family Coping Strategies of Family Members with Diabetic and Acute-Illness Youngsters (With Social Class and Number of Speeches Covaried): Adjusted Means

Coping Strategy	*Diabetes*	*Acute Illness*	*F value*
	Mothers		
Avoidance	.01	.01	.00
Blaming	.37	.45	.56
Cognitive flexibility	.60	.54	.21
Family as collect.	.20	.17	.11
Consensual unit	.67	.38	6.55**
Family theory	.63	.12	26.85****
Helplessness	.33	.31	.04
Mastery	.45	.31	1.68
Opinionated	.09	.11	.13
Optimism	.08	.07	.00
Curr/experience	.21	.11	1.28
Past/determinant	.50	.76	5.43*
Pessimism	.02	.00	.86
	Fathers		
Avoidance	.03	.00	1.47
Blaming	.19	.43	5.04*
Cognitive flexibility	.51	.32	2.85[t]
Family as collect.	.16	.22	.50
Consensual unit	.70	.26	17.04****
Family theory	.55	.05	32.27****
Helplessness	.43	.33	.78
Mastery	.46	.07	17.91****
Opinionated	.04	.11	1.33
Optimism	.13	.07	.90
Curr/experience	.09	.14	.56
Past/determinant	.44	.66	3.82[t]
Pessimism	.02	.00	.69
	Adolescents		
Avoidance	.26	.06	6.64**
Blaming	.10	.21	1.66
Cognitive flexibility	.05	.08	.16
Family as collect.	.04	.23	7.48***
Consensual unit	.26	.05	6.70*
Family theory	.12	.06	.97
Helplessness	.05	.05	.00
Mastery	.09	.06	.31
Opinionated	.20	.20	.00
Optimism	.00	.06	2.57
Curr/experience	.09	.08	.02
Past/determinant	.20	.34	2.14
Pessimism	.02	.00	.53

$^{t}p < .08$; $^{*}p < .05$; $^{**}p < .01$; $^{***}p < .008$; $^{****}p < .0001$.

TABLE 2.3
Problem-Focused Family Coping Strategies of Family Members with Diabetic and Acute-Illness Youngsters (With Social Class and Number of Speeches Covaried): Adjusted Means

	Diabetes	*Acute Illness*	*F Value*
Mothers			
Alternative Rewards	.41	.10	10.43***
Coordination	.89	.78	1.81
Noncoordination	.10	.05	.61
Established ways	.36	.24	1.16
Funct. impotence	.14	.08	.73
Seeking info	.97	.89	1.93
Rejecting info	.01	.01	.00
Seeking support	.61	.17	23.00****
Rejecting support	.01	.01	.00
Self-reliance	.59	.22	11.46***
Trials/new resps	.86	.53	12.04****
Fathers			
Alternative Rewards	.31	.03	11.03***
Coordination	.74	.62	1.64
Noncoordination	.07	.09	0.15
Established ways	.24	.14	1.24
Funct. impotence	.10	.05	.57
Seeking info	.86	.89	.11
Rejecting info	.04	.03	.02
Seeking support	.29	.06	7.07**
Rejecting support	00	00	00
Self-reliance	.39	.21	2.77^t
Trials/new resps	.57	.38	2.95^t
Adolescents			
Alternative Rewards	.10	.02	2.76^t
Coordination	.42	.26	2.17
Noncoordination	.03	.08	1.16
Established ways	.19	.11	.87
Funct. impotence	.12	.03	2.99^t
Seeking info	.47	.73	5.81*
Rejecting info	.10	.03	1.59
Seeking support	.22	.03	6.99**
Rejecting support	.08	.02	1.02
Self-reliance	.33	.03	12.88****
Trials/new resps	.39	.37	.04

$^t p < .10$; *$p < .05$; **$p < .01$; ***$p < .006$; ****$p < .0009$.

Adolescents. There was a significant multivariate effect for illness type [F (11, 65) = 3.46; $p < .0008$]. Follow-up univariate analyses of covariance revealed that, compared with their counterparts, youngsters with diabetes described their families as seeking more support, being more self-reliant, and seeking alternative rewards. On the other hand, they clearly characterized their families as being less involved in seeking information about their current difficulties (see Table 2.3).

Emotion-Management Strategies

Mothers. There was a significant multivariate effect for illness type [F (6, 70) = 3.87; $p < .002$]. Follow-up univariate analyses of covariance revealed that, compared with mothers of acute illness youngsters, a strikingly higher percentage of mothers of youngsters with diabetes expressed their feelings to others outside of their families and described more impulsive expression of their feelings (cf. Table 2.4).

Fathers. There was a significant multivariate effect for illness type [F (6, 70) = 3.68; $p < .003$]. Follow-up univariate analyses of covariance revealed that, compared with fathers of acute illness youngsters, fathers of youngsters with diabetes were more likely to express their feelings within the family as well as to others outside the family (see Table 2.4).

Adolescents. There was a significant multivariate effect for illness type [F (6, 70) = 4.34; $p < .0009$]. Follow-up univariate analyses of covariance revealed that, compared with acute illness youngsters, those with diabetes more often expressed their feelings to others outside the family and modulated their feelings. In addition, these youngsters were less likely to minimize their awareness of their own and other family members' feelings (see Table 2.4).

DISCUSSION

Summary and First Interpretations

We find, then, that the families with diabetic youngsters differ from the comparison group with respect to many coping strategies. When compared with the families whose child has had a recent acute illness, they contrast most strikingly along the lines of their *appraisal* of the situation. Although we did not find direct indicators of more coordination or acknowledgment in these families, as we had predicted, we did see the families with diabetic youngsters more often expressing a "we're

TABLE 2.4
Emotion-Focused Family Coping Strategies of Family Members with Diabetic and Acute Illness Youngsters (with Social Class and Number of Speeches Covaried): Adjusted Means

	Mothers		
	Diabetes	*Acute illness*	*F value*
Acknowledgment	.91	.95	.50
Conscious restraint	.38	.33	.28
Displacement of feelings	00	00	00
Direct expression of feelings	.98	.95	.07
Direct expression to others	.50	.08	18.58****
Impulsive express	.05	.00	2.90^{t}
Minimization	.69	2.84	1.72
Modulation	00	00	00
	Fathers		
Acknowledgment	.90	.85	.34
Conscious restraint	.26	.14	1.52
Displacement	00	00	00
Direct expression of feelings	1.00	.87	5.63*
Direct expression to others	.42	.06	15.17****
Impulsiveness	.04	.01	.61
Minimization	.76	.79	.06
Modulation	00	00	00
	Adolescent		
Acknowledgment	.38	.35	.01
Conscious restraint	.10	.27	3.19^{t}
Displacement	00	00	00
Direct expression of feelings	1.00	1.00	00
Direct expression to others	.41	.19	4.99*
Impulsive expres.	.10	.00	3.09^{t}
Minimization	.43	.70	5.79*
Modulation	.14	00	5.95*

$^{t}p < .08$; $^{*}p < .05$; $^{**}p < .01$; $^{***}p < .005$; $^{****}p < .0007$.

all in this together" view, perceiving the illness as a problem for the entire family, not just for the child. These families also hold a shared view about the causes and consequences of the illness (family theory), as well as a greater sense of mastery, in which the family feels that it can deal successfully with its new difficulties. It is possible that the intrusive and complex demands accompanying the child's diabetes are most effectively handled—at first—through members viewing their group as a coherent "family team," believing that if they work together they can deal with anything, in this case the chronic illness—diabetes.

Families facing their children's diabetes daily confront new pressures in some of the most charged areas of personal and family life: meals, bodily care (giving shots), bodily fluids (blood, urine), regulation of independence. Moreover, they are more frequently reminded—at an earlier age than most families—of the precariousness of a young son or daughter's health and mortality. These families also report that they are more likely to use past experiences to help them assess their current situation. This may represent their drawing upon all available resources: past successful understandings as well as current supports.

At this early point in dealing with their youngster's diabetes, the families report more feelings of successfully dealing with the illness, as opposed to the acute illness families. The acute-illness families may not need to think so much in terms of successfully dealing with the illness, because the distressing events have already passed. Most of these families may conclude that they dealt with it reasonably and now the experience is over; there is little need to emphasize their perceptions of mastery or experiences of self-reliance. In contrast, members of families whose children have diabetes may find it helpful to cite any and all instances of successful handling of the illness. These explicitly recognized moments of self-reliance may promote greater hope for successful future coping with this chronic strain.

Along with these signs of experienced effectiveness are suggestions of more difficult moments. The youngsters describe more avoidance of the illness by their families, see their families as seeking less information than the acute-illness families, and allude to their families as experiencing more futility and frustration in handling the demands that they are now facing (functional impotence). Diabetes is an illness that requires a new lifestyle not only for the patient, but also for the family. There are many more demands placed on the family, demands not accompanying an acute illness. The child who has a broken arm or leg, or who has a transient serious infection, is not going to require sustained family cooperation and pervasive family changes. Given the multifold and continuous strains on the family, ones undoubtedly exacerbated by the era of development that the new patient is entering or in the midst of–adolescence, a time fraught with conflicts over independence and control (Hauser, Jacobson et al., 1990; Powers, Hauser, & Kilner, 1989), there is ample opportunity for mistakes and perceptions of failure.

In light of these demands, it is not surprising that parents and adolescents from the diabetic group described their families as seeking more support from others. Outside supports can buffer the family's strains in handling the new difficulties–the new relationships within the family and with new caregivers, the strong and often unpredictable feelings triggered by the child's frightening illness. Consistently, members of these families describe expressing their feelings to others outside the family as well as within it.

Finally, we see that the parents of the diabetic youngsters portray their families as having discovered new rewards as they deal with their new problems, and deliberately experimenting with new routines. The youngster's diabetes is an illness that must be handled in some way for the rest of the patient's life; and thus becomes incorporated into the daily family experience. Discovering new gratifications and alternate ways of handling the diabetes represents a favorable adaptation compared, for instance, with futily trying to salvage old routines: unchanged meals, no new monitoring of body changes, or medications. The comparison families perceive the acute illness as but a passing disruption in their normal lives, and hence do not treat it as something meriting alternative rewards or new routines. The illness has a beginning and an end. Once the acute illness is over with the family can and does return to its everyday routine.

A consistent observation across all three coping realms involved how differently the adolescents perceived their families, in contrast to much similarity between the two parents. For example, these young patients perceive their families as expressing more avoidance and as being less likely to seek new information. And–again differing from their parents–see themselves as modulating their feelings to others outside the family and as being more aware of their own and others' feelings within the family. These clear generational differences are important, and caution us against generalizing about members of the "family" as having uniform perceptions of the youngster's illness or ways of coping.

Family Coping, Family Interactions, and the Course of Diabetes

Now that we know more of how the two sets of families differ in their coping strategies, we are in a better position to address important questions about links between these coping strategies and aspects of the patient's diabetes and socioemotional development. For instance: What specific family coping strategies, or combinations of them, contribute to adolescents' adherence with diabetes management? Are certain family coping strategies more likely to be associated with the young patient's socioemotional development? And how does change in the level of parent and adolescent socioemotional development affect family coping strategies and the young patient's adherence? We can no longer assume that family processes function only as determinants of diabetes status and individual development (Hauser & Solomon, 1985). Longitudinal data from our project will certainly allow us to discern which family coping strategies are related to more optimal diabetes adherence (Hauser, Jacobson et al., 1990) and also how changing individual family member development (e.g., ego development; Hauser, 1976) influences family coping patterns.

There are compelling reasons for us to clarify these links with the patients' development because most of them are in–or about to enter–adolescence, a volatile time, with a rapidly changing child encountering and struggling with complex issues involving pubertal transformations, separation and individuation (cf. Powers et al., 1989). This period is made even more complex for adolescents (and their families) who have been recently diagnosed with diabetes because the illness introduces new strains into the family, disrupting or seriously altering many aspects of family life: meals, exercise patterns, monitoring of bodily fluids, relations between parent and child with respect to bodily care. These changes are perhaps most unwelcome during this phase of the life cycle, as they intensify already present family conflicts over autonomy, separation, dependence, and protection.

In terms of change, there are many reasons to expect that family coping strategy patterns may not remain stable through the years of adolescence. As the child struggles for more independence and autonomy, the family coping patterns that are first seen at the onset of the diabetes may not be expressed later on. For instance, during the first year of her diabetes, Judy was one of the most adherent patients. So too, her family appeared to be coping with her diabetes in adaptive ways, for example dealing with the disease as a "team" (consensual unit). Yet 4 years later we find a strikingly different picture. Judy is now one of the least adherent patients. Have her family's coping strategies shifted from self-reliance, mastery, or working together as a unit? Did such family shifts precede or follow Judy's deteriorating adherence?

At another level of observation, we are following family interaction patterns (Hauser et al., 1986; Stein, 1989). Through our assays of family interactions–The Constraining and Enabling Coding System–we identify developmentally relevant ways in which parents and youngsters speak to one another during family discussions. We distinguish two kinds of interaction styles: constraining interactions, through which family members inhibit or constrain the thoughts or feelings of each other; and enabling interactions, in which members support and encourage expression of more independent thoughts and perceptions.

Because the young patient's needs for continued support and autonomy are prevalent during the onset and early years of this illness, there are likely important ties between these interactions and the ways the patient and his or her family cope with the illness. We expect that constraining styles will be related to coping strategies of helplessness, avoidance, pessimism, and functional impotence. In contrast, enabling styles are likely linked with more adaptive family coping strategies, such as, mastery, self-reliance, conceiving of the family as a unit, coordination, and cognitive flexibility. To be sure, we do not know yet whether what we intuitively and clinically consider to be "adaptive" coping (e.g., mastery, support seeking) is indeed related to successful family adaptation to the illness, and whether "negative" coping (e.g., support rejection, blaming others, avoidance) is linked to unfavorable adaptation. Through our longitudinal analyses we may discover that certain supposedly negative coping strategies may actually be functional for certain families.

Although we have not yet systematically tested these predictions, results from previous constraining and enabling analyses (Hauser et al., 1986), together with the new family coping strategies findings in this chapter, point toward likely connections. Specifically, our family interaction observations indicated that, when compared with families of acute illness youngsters, families of the diabetic youngsters expressed more enabling speeches (focusing, problem solving, active understanding). At the same time, these family members were more devaluing toward one another, and fathers were more judgmental and indifferent. These findings are indeed reminiscent of our observations of the family strategies. In terms of their appraisal strategies, the families with a diabetic youngster describe themselves as dealing with the stress as a family (solving the problem together) and hold a shared family theory. They also report experiencing mastery in dealing with the new strains introduced by the illness. In contrast, the youngsters in these families cite the family's avoidance.

One way to think about these seemingly paradoxical findings is that the advent of this chronic illness at first promotes considerably more engagement among the members of a family with a diabetic youngster (as can be seen in the higher levels of enabling interactions and conceiving of the family as a working group [consensual unit]). Within these families of newly diagnosed diabetic children an initial spirit of hope and optimism prevails ("We'll fight this together." "We're all in this together Judy—you're not alone."). These hopeful responses emerge in our observations of coping strategies and family interactions. Family members' perceptions of the family environment in the months after the onset of the young patient's diabetes also point to experiences of enhanced family collaboration and cooperation (Hauser et al., 1989). The families with diabetic youngsters describe higher levels of organization and greater emphasis on recreational activities in their family.

Yet alongside this upbeat coping response are more disquieting feelings not so easily expressed. Dismay, discomfort, sadness, anger, and guilt are among the dysphoric responses often triggered in many families of diabetic patients as reported by several clinical observers. These feelings can lead to the traces of difficulties that we first see in these early moments following onset of the illness, functional impotence as well as conflicts about restraining feelings.

Future Directions

Throughout this chapter, and especially in our long discussion, we have pointed to unsettled theoretical and empirical questions, ones opened up by our new studies, ones not yet pursued. We conclude with those that we consider most noteworthy.

Components of Family Coping. In this first set of explorations our analyses and discussion have largely focused on the family unit. Yet we know from our other studies that family members may at times respond differentially to the onset and continued presence of diabetes (Hauser et al., 1986, 1989). It is likely that there are parental and adolescent differences with respect to family coping strategies, differences that could be coupled with the phase of the illness, as well as (or in concert with) generational differences. A father, for instance, may participate very differently in the family's appraisal of the illness at the onset of the diabetes than at a point several years later. Along similar lines, we need to clarify how the adolescent's gender and physical (pubertal) development may influence family and individual coping, a direction of work we have begun to explore in other ongoing family studies (Safyer et al., 1990; Stein, 1989).

A second set of questions about components of family coping involve relations among the coping realms, especially emotion management. In this latter domain we followed individual strategies. What, if any, are the relations between these strategies and the family's other coping strategies? And, does this relation vary for different family members and over time?

Family Diversity. For these comparative analyses the entire set of two-parent families with diabetes was analyzed as a group. But we know, clinically, that there is much diversity among families and family members. Some families respond to this new event with seeming calm and competence, whereas others experience major disruptions in their functioning. Can these differences in family responses be assessed through the Family Coping Coding System? Is such variation influenced by the developmental levels of the parents or by their medical or psychiatric histories? We deliberately restricted one-parent families from these first analyses, so we do not yet know about the impacts of family structure on family coping. It will be important to discover how, if at all, the one-parent families differ from those with both parents present; and to clarify how duration and severity of illness may influence such differences.

Family Coping Over Time: The Interplay of Diabetes Outcomes and Family Functioning. There is the possibility that the course of a patient's diabetes may contribute to his or her family's coping strategies. Patients with unstable metabolic control, or those who are minimally adherent, may elicit very different coping strategies from their families than those youngsters whose course of illness is more stable. Our assumption in the preceding discussion was that the coping strategies would contribute to differences in adherence and metabolic outcomes. Because the studies we reported were cross-sectional, there was no way to empirically determine direction of effects. In future analyses, we will be able to use our repeated measures of family coping and diabetes-specific functioning (e.g., metabolic control, early complications) to explore this important causal question. In addition, these longitudinal data will lead to our tracing the extent to which family coping strategies change over time, and how such changes may be connected with other aspects of family functioning, such as family interactions, conflict, and perceived environment.

APPENDIX: FAMILY COPING STRATEGIES: BRIEF DEFINITIONS

Appraisal-Focused Coping Strategies

Opinionated. Speaker presents inflexible, set ideas about the situation and disregards others' ideas and viewpoints. For example, as the adolescent expresses his desire to go to the local pediatrician, the father interrupts stating, "You're wrong. The Joslin was the best place to go."

Optimism. Speaker expresses a hopeful outlook regarding the outcome of the stressful event for the family. For instance, "I know that things will work out. I have that feeling and I think the kids do too."

Pessimism. Speaker views the stressful event as one that will have a negative impact on the family or family members. For example, "When we found out it was diabetes we were devastated. All we could think about was a lifetime of doctors and illness."

Helplessness/Family as a Victim. Speaker sees the family as incapable of managing the current situation. Statements indicating lack of control over what happens or showing a "why us" or victimized attitude. For instance, "Our family is so disorganized as it is, we never thought we'd be able to handle all the changes we'd have to make;" and "My mother always says 'why does this have to happen to us?' "

Mastery. Family views themselves as able to handle the stressor competently. For example, "I think we'll be able to continue to handle the illness well."

Family as Consensual Unit. Family member views the event as a family matter; "we're all in it together" is the main emphasis of the speech. For example, "We all think that what has happened to Susie is terrible. We understand that this is really something that she will have to deal with for the rest of her life; we just try to make her understand that we're behind her 100% in anything that she decides."

Family as a Collection of Individuals. Speaker views the stress as happening to individual family members and not to the family as a whole. For instance, "I'm out of the house at work most of the time, and his sister is rarely home, so Doug really has to deal with the diabetes himself. In our family, everyone needs to solve their problems on their own."

Current Experiences as Key. Family member stresses that it is the elements of the present situation, its pressures and their current understanding that determine how the family plans to handle the given stress or life event. For instance, "We think about it, but we just stick to today . . . not the next day."

Past as the Major Determinant. There is a strong emphasis on past events as providing the framework for how to understand and handle the present situation. For instance, "I told her that we had come through many problems; we had come through a divorce together; we had come through orthopedic surgery together, and we'd come through this the same way."

Family Theory. Speaker reflects a clear, or rigidly held, family construction of the event or shared expectations about its progress. For example, "We weren't surprised about the diabetes. Every fifth kid in the family gets it. My dad's the 10th kid and has it, my sister's the 5th kid and she has it, and I'm the 10th, so I got it too."

Cognitive Flexibility. Speaker indicates that the family values open-minded consideration of different possibilities prior to drawing conclusions about the stressor, its causes, and its consequences. For example, "The stomach problem, which may or may not be due to dairy products or some other food allergy . . . it might be nerves."

Avoidance. Speaker does not consider or discuss the specific member's or family's stressful circumstances despite direct references by other family members or interviewer. For example, a mother asks her son: "Why don't you want them to know that you're sick? They should know, don't you think, if you had a problem sometime?" The adolescent avoids the subject and does not answer the question.

Blaming. Speaker explains the family's view that various factors (people, events) have caused or exacerbated the severity of the illness or stressful event. For instance, "It was our fault that Judy got sick. We were just putting too much faith in what the doctor told us."

Problem-Focused Coping Strategies

Self-Reliance. Speaker emphasizes family success (competence, capability) at dealing with the stressful event. For example, "We seem to have succeeded in achieving many of the things we are trying to do. It worked better than I ever thought it would."

Functional Impotence. Speaker indicates that dealing with the stressor has been a real problem for the family. For example, "We get really nervous and become all thumbs when it comes to administering the insulin. We're really afraid of those needles. None of us wants to have the responsibility of giving the shots, so its becoming a real problem."

Coordination/Integration. Family member stresses the importance of coordinated efforts from the family in order to successfully manage the stressful event. For example, "Everybody has pitched in and helped with the various aspects of treatment."

Noncoordination. Speaker emphasizes the family's lack of coordination and describes difficulties in working together at solving problems related to the stressor. For instance, "It's better if I just give the shots and do the testing myself. When my mother and father try to get involved, we always lose track of who's doing what and I end up losing a meal or missing a shot."

Seeking Information. Speaker encourages the gathering of information related to the stressor in an effort to find out how the stressor can be best understood or most successfully managed. For example, "I have learned a lot in just the brief time we have been exposed to the problem. My wife made calls to people while Timothy was in the hospital. If you're unsure of something, you should probe to seek the answer, that's how we achieve success."

Information Rejection. Speaker actively discourages or rejects the family's obtaining new information about the stressful event. For example, "You can only learn so much . . . after that it just clouds what you already know."

Support Seeking. Speaker encourages the family's turning to institutions, agencies, and individuals outside the family specifically for support (financial, material, emotional assistance). For instance, "I felt that especially at his age, the stress was the main thing that it would be very helpful to all of us if we could talk about it with someone else. We felt that by establishing something here at Joslin, Tom would always have someplace to come and to call."

Support Rejection. Family discourages and refuses assistance and support from individuals and agencies. For example, "Initially we didn't want to join the Joslin family support group. We just didn't think we needed their help at that time."

Alternative Rewards. Speaker describes how new rewards or incentives have emerged as incidental consequences of the given stressor or related coping strategies. For example, "We're very happy that Paul went to diabetes camp. Now he is able to take care of himself. What is even more important is that he has become a much more responsible person overall. This is something that's had an important effect on just about every aspect of his life."

Emotion-Management Coping Strategies

Direct Expression of Feelings. Speaker shows that he or she believes that verbally expressing feelings is a positive way to deal with stressful circumstances. Speaker may express his or her own emotions, may encourage others to express their feelings, or may state a belief in this strategy.

Acknowledgment of Other's Feelings. Speaker shows an awareness, recognition, or sensitivity to the feelings expressed by other family members. For example, "I think you were also uneasy for a while just telling people you have diabetes and this added to it. This year you've gotten more comfortable with it."

Displacement of Feelings. Speaker describes the expression of his or her feelings about the stressful event as directed toward other family members or individuals outside the family. For instance, "Since Barbara has been diagnosed as having diabetes, I think I have let her get away with a whole lot more. Unfortunately, I take out my anger on her brother instead."

Conscious Restraint of Feelings. Speaker shows an awareness of his or her feelings or emotions, but controls their expression within the family. For example, "I just told everyone to shut up about it. I'm sick of hearing about it and talking about it won't make it go away."

Minimization of Feelings. Speaker shows a curtailed awareness or minimization of his/her or other member's feelings about the event. For example, in response to the father's description of his son's diabetes as an "emotionally trying experience," the adolescent states, "Oh Dad, I really think you're exaggerating. It's only as big a deal as you make it."

Direct Expression of Feelings to Others. Speaker expresses feelings about the stressful event to individuals outside the family. For example, "I can remember telling my friend Mary how upset the family was about Tom's illness."

Modulation of Feelings to Outsiders. Speaker modulates or minimizes his or her strong feelings about the stressful situation to those outside the family. For instance, "It's not that we're made of steel or anything. It's just that my husband and I don't think that being emotional in front of others is always the most appropriate response."

ACKNOWLEDGMENTS

The research reported in this chapter was supported by a Grant from the NIH (#R01-AM27845) and an NIMH Research Scientist Award (#5K-03 70178). Extremely important contributions to the final analyses were made by Julie McCarter.

REFERENCES

Aldrich, J. H., & Nelson, F. D. (1984). *Linear probability, logit and probit models* (Sage University Paper series on Quantitative applications in the social sciences, 07–045). Beverly Hills, CA: Sage.

Anderson, B. J., & Auslander, W. (1980). Research on diabetes management and the family: A critique. *Diabetes Care, 3,* 696–702.

Anderson, B. J., Miller, J., Auslander, W., & Santiago, J. (1981). Family characteristics of diabetic adolescents: Relationships to metabolic control. *Diabetes Care, 4,* 586–594.

Baker, L., Minuchin, S., Milman, L., Liebman, R., & Todd, T. (1970). Psychosomatic aspects of juvenile diabetes mellitus: A progress report. *Diabetes in Juveniles: Modern Problems in Pediatrics, 17,* 332–343.

Benoliel, J. Q. (1977). Role of the family in managing young diabetics. *Diabetes Educator, 5,* 8.

Bobrow, E., Asruskin, T., Siller J. (1985). Mother–daughter interaction and adherence to medical regimens. *Diabetes Care, 8,* 146–155.

Crain, A. J., Sussman, M. B., & Weil, W. B. (1966). Effects of a diabetic child on mental integration and related measures of family functioning. *Journal of Health and Human Behavior, 7,* 122–127.

Delamater, A. M. (in press). Adaptation of children to newly diagnosed diabetes. In C. Holmes (Ed.), *Neuropsychological and behavioral aspects of insulin and non-insulin dependent diabetes.* New York: Springer-Verlag.

Dohrenwend, B. S., & Dohrenwend, B. P. (Eds.). (1974). *Stressful life events: Their nature and effects.* New York: Wiley.

D'Onofrio, J. C. (1979). A comparison of verbal interaction patterns in families with an asthmatic, diabetic, and non-disabled child. *Dissertation Abstracts International, 40,* 4477-B.

Folkman, S., & Lazarus, R. S. (1980). An analysis of coping in a middle-age community sample. *Journal of Health and Social Behavior, 21,* 219–239.

Garmezy, N., & Rutter, M. (Eds.). (1983). *Stress, coping and development in children.* New York: McGraw-Hill.

Goldberger, A. S. (1964). *Econometric theory.* New York: Wiley.

Grey, M. J., Genel, M., & Tamborlane, W. V. (1980). Psychosocial adjustment of latency-aged diabetics: Determinants and relationship to control. *Pediatrics, 65,* 69–73.

Grotevant, H. D., & Cooper, C. R. (1985). Patterns of interaction in family relationships and the development of identity exploration in adolescence. *Child Development, 56,* 415–428.

Grotevant, H. D., & Cooper, C. R. (1986). Individuation in family relationships. *Human Development, 29,* 82–100.

Haan, N. (1977). *Coping and defending: Processes of self-environment organization.* New York: Academic Press.

Hanson, C. L., Henggeler, S. W., & Burghen, G. A. (1987). Social competence and parent support as mediators of the link between stress and metabolic control in adolescents with insulin-dependent diabetes mellitus. *Journal of Clinical and Consulting Psychology, 55,* 529–533.

Hanson, C. L., Henggeler, S. W., Harris, M., & Burghen, G., & Moore, M. (1989). Family system variables and the health status of adolescents with insulin-dependent diabetes mellitus. *Health Psychology, 8,* 239–253.

Hauser, S. T. (1976). Loevinger's model and measure of ego development: A critical review. *Psychological Bulletin, 83,* 928–955.

Hauser, S. T. (1990). The study of families and chronic illness: Ways of coping and interacting. In G. Brody & I. Sigel (Eds.), *Methods of family research* (Vol. 2, pp 59–86). New York: Plenum.

Hauser, S. T., & Bowlds, M. K. (1990). Stress, coping and adaptation within adolescence: Diversity and resilience. In S. Feldman & G. Elliot (Eds.), *At the threshold: The developing adolescent. The Carnegie Foundation Volume on Adolescence* (pp. 388–413). Cambridge, MA. Harvard University Press.

Hauser, S. T., Jacobson, A. M., Lavori, P., Wolfsdorf, J. I., Herskowitz, R. D., Milley, J. E., & Bliss, R. (1990). Adherence among children and adolescents with insulin-dependent diabetes mellitus over a four-year longitudinal follow-up: II. Immediate and long-term linkages with the family milieu. *Journal of Pediatric Psychology, 15,* 527–542.

Hauser, S. T., Jacobson, A. M., Noam, G., & Powers, S. I. (1983). Ego development and self-image complexity in early adolescence: Longitudinal studies of psychiatric and diabetic patients. *Archives of General Psychiatry, 40,* 325–332.

Hauser, S. T., Jacobson, A. M., Wertlieb, D., Brink, S., & Wentworth, S. (1985). The contribution of family environment to perceived competence and illness adjustment in diabetic and acutely ill adolescents. *Family Relations, 34,* 99–108.

Hauser, S. T., Jacobson, A. M., Wertlieb, D., Weiss-Perry, B., Follansbee, D., Wolfsdorf, J. I., Herskowitz, R. D., Houlihan, J., & Rajapark, D. C. (1986). Children with recently diagnosed diabetes: Interactions within their families. *Health Psychology, 5,* 273–296.

Hauser, S. T., Jacobson, A., Wertlieb, D., Wolfsdorf, J., Herskowitz, R., Vieyra, M., & Orleans, J. (1989). Family contexts of self-esteem and illness adjustment in diabetic and acutely ill children. In C. Ramsey (Ed.), *The science of family medicine* (pp. 469–484). New York: Guilford Press.

Hauser, S. T., Paul, E., DiPlacido, J., Rufo, P., & Spetter, L. D. (1990). *Family coping process manual.* Unpublished manuscript, Harvard Medical School, Boston, MA.

Hauser, S. T., Paul, E., Jacobson, A. M., Weiss-Perry, B., Vieyra, M., Rufo, P., Spetter, D., DiPlacido, J., Wolfsdorf, J., & Herskowitz, R. (1988). How families cope with diabetes in adolescence: An approach and case analysis. *Pediatrician, 15,* 80–94.

Hauser, S. T., Powers, S. I., Houlihan, J., Jacobson, A. M., & Noam, G. (1985, May). *The contribution of family processes to the course of development of normal, diabetic, and psychiatrically ill adolescents.* Paper presented at annual meeting of the American Association for the Advancement of Science (AAAS), Los Angeles.

Hauser, S. T., Powers, S., Noam, G., Jacobson, A., Weiss, B., & Follansbee, D. (1984). Familial contexts of adolescent ego development. *Child Development, 55,* 195–213.

Hauser, S. T., & Solomon, M. L. (1985). Coping with diabetes: Views from the family. In P. Ahmed & N. Ahmed (Eds.), *Coping with diabetes* (pp 234–266). Springfield, IL: Thomas.

Hauser, S. T., Vieyra, M., Jacobson, A., & Wertlieb, D. (1985). Vulnerability and resiliency in adolescence: Views from the family. *Journal of Early Adolescence, 5,* 81–100.

Hill, R. (1958). Generic features of families under stress. *Social Casework, 49,* 139–150.

Holmes, T. H., & Rahe, R. H. (1967). The social readjustment rating scale. *Journal of Psychosomatic Research, 11,* 213–218.

Jacobson, A. M., Hauser, S. T., Powers, S., & Noam, G. (1983). Ego development in diabetics: A longitudinal study. In A. Laron, & A. Galatzer (Eds.), *Psychological aspects of diabetes in children and adolescents.* Karger: Basel.

Kantor, D., & Lehr, W. (1975). *Inside the family.* San Francisco: Jossey-Bass.

Kessler, R. C., Price, R. H., & Wortman, C. B. (1985). Social factors in psychopathology: Stress, social support, and coping processes. *Annual Review of Psychology, 36,* 531–572.

Koski, L., Ahlas, A., & Kumeto, A. (1976). A psychosomatic follow-up study of childhood diabetics. *Acta Paedopsychiatrica, 42,* 12–25.

Lazarus, R. S., & Folkman, S. (1984). *Stress, appraisal, and coping.* New York: Springer.

Lewis, J. M., Beavers, W. R., Gossett, J. T., & Phillips, V. A. (1976). *No single thread: Psychosocial health in family systems.* New York: Brunner-Mazel.

Mattson, A. (1979). Juvenile diabetes: Impacts on life stages and systems. In B. Hamburg & G. Inoff (Eds.), *Behavioral and psychosocial issues in diabetes.* Washington DC: Government Printing Office.

McCubbin, H. I., Boss, P., Wilson, L., & Lester, G. (1979). Developing family invulnerability to stress: Coping strategies wives employ in managing separation. In *Trost, Proceedings: World Congress of Sociology.* Beverly Hills, CA: Sage.

McCubbin, H. I., & Patterson, J. M. (1981a). *Systematic assessment of family stress resources and coping: Tools for research, education, and clinical intervention.* St. Paul: University of Minnesota, Family Social Science.

McCubbin, H. I., & Patterson, J. M. (1981b). Broadening the scope of family strengths: An emphasis on family coping and social support. In N. Stinnett, J. DeFrain, K. King, P. Knaub, & G. Rowe (Eds.), *Family strengths 3: Roots of well-being.* Lincoln: University of Nebraska Press.

Menaghan, E. (1983). Individual coping efforts and family studies: Conceptual and methodological issues. In H. I. McCubbin, M. B. Sussman, & J. M. Patterson (Eds.), *Social stress and the family: Advances and developments in family stress theory and research.* New York: Haworth Press.

Mendlowitz, D. (1983). The relationship between level of metabolic control in children with juvenile onset diabetes and dimensions of family functioning. *Dissertations Abstracts International, 44.*

Minuchin, P. (1985). Families and individual development: Provocations from the field of family therapy. *Child Development, 56,* 289–302.

Minuchin, S., Rosman, B. L., & Baker, L. (1978). *Psychosomatic families.* Cambridge MA: Harvard University Press.

Olson, D. J., Sprenkle, D. H., & Russell, C. S. (1979). Circumplex model of marital and family systems: 1. Cohesion and adaptability dimensions, family types, and clinical applications. *Family Process, 18,* 3–28.

Patterson, J. (1988). Chronic illness in children and the impact on families. In C. Chilmas, E. Nunnaly, & F. Cox (Eds.), *Chronic illness and disability*. Beverly Hills: Sage.

Pearlin, L. I., & Schooler, C. (1978). The structure of coping. *Journal of Health and Social Behavior, 17,* 2–21.

Pond, H. (1979). Parental attitudes toward children with a chronic medical disorder: Special reference to diabetes mellitus. *Diabetes Care, 2,* 425–431.

Powers, S., Dill, D., Hauser, S., Noam, G., & Jacobson, A. (1984, October). *The coping strategies and psychological resources of seriously ill adolescents.* Paper presented at the Family Systems and Health pre-conference workshop, National Council on Family Relations, San Francisco, CA.

Powers, S., Hauser, S. T., & Kilner, L. (1989). Adolescent mental health. *American Psychologist, 44,* 200–208.

Reiss, D. (1981). *The family's construction of reality.* Cambridge, MA: Harvard University Press.

Reiss, D., & Oliveri, M. E. (1980). Family paradigm and family coping: A proposal for linking the family's intrinsic adaptive capacities to its responses to stress. *Family Relations, 29,* 431–444.

Rolland, J. S. (1988). A conceptual model of chronic and life-threatening illness and its impact on the family. In C. Chilmas, E. Nunnaly, & F. Cox (Eds.), *Chronic illness and disability.* Beverly Hills: Sage.

Rutter, M. (1981). Stress, coping, and development: Some issues and some questions. *Journal of Child Psychology and Psychiatric Allied Disciplines, 22,* 323–356.

Safyer, A., Hauser, S., Jacobson, A., Bliss, R., Milley, J., Wolfsdorf, J., & Herskowitz, R. (1990). *Family environments and diabetes adjustments: The role of gender and pubertal development.* Manuscript submitted for publication.

Selye, H. (1956). *The stress of life.* New York: McGraw-Hill.

Silver, R. L., & Wortman, C. B. (1980). Coping with undesirable life events. In J. Garber, & M. E. P. Seligman (Eds.), *Human helplessness: Theory and applications* (pp. 279–375). New York: Academic Press.

Stein, J. (1989). *Family interaction and adjustment, adherence, and metabolic control in adolescents with insulin-dependent diabetes.* Unpublished doctoral dissertation, Boston University, Boston, MA.

Stone, A. A., & Neale, J. M. (1984). New measures of daily coping: Development and preliminary results. *Journal of Personality and Social Psychology, 46,* 892–906.

Vandenbergh, R. L. (1971). Emotional aspects. In K. E. Sussman (Ed.), *Juvenile-type diabetes and its complications* (pp. 411–438). Springfield, IL: Thomas.

Werner, E. E., & Smith, R. S. (1977). *Kauai's children come of age.* Honolulu: University of Hawaii Press.

Wertlieb, D., Hauser, S. T., & Jacobson, A. (1985). Adaptation to diabetes: Behavior symptoms and family context. *Journal of Pediatric Psychology, 11,* 463–479.

CHAPTER 3

Psychiatric Sequelae of Brain Dysfunction in Children: The Role of Family Environment

Naomi Breslau
Henry Ford Hospital

Recent studies of childhood chronic conditions, such as cystic fibrosis or diabetes, have turned to psychosocial variables, among them the family environment, for explanations of the variability in children's adjustment. Family environment has been conceptualized to interact with children's disability, or to constitute an intervening mechanism that links disability to maladjustment. Almost all studies have used measures of psychopathology as indicators of the children's adjustment. Other psychological constructs, such as locus of control or self-concept, have also been used. Because the preponderance of the empirical evidence indicates that chronic conditions that do not involve brain dysfunction (e.g., cystic fibrosis in contrast to cerebral palsy) do not increase the affected children's risk for psychopathology, turning to family environmental factors to find explanations for psychiatric sequelae is not of compelling interest.[1] In contrast, the increased risk for psychopathology associated with conditions that involve the brain does warrant an inquiry into family factors as potentially influencing the outcomes in these children.

In this chapter I address this question. First, I summarize key findings from three epidemiologic studies that set the stage for recent empirical research (both epidemiologic and case-control studies) on

[1]However, family factors may still be of interest in this group. It may be that different family factors protect these non-neurologically ill children from psychopathology than protect healthy children. See chapter 2.

chronic illness and brain dysfunction as risks factors for psychopathology in children. I then discuss how family factors have been used in theoretical discussions and empirical studies about psychologic sequelae of children with brain dysfunction and report results of analysis designed to test alternative hypotheses concerning the role of family factors in explaining psychiatric sequelae of brain dysfunction in children.

EPIDEMIOLOGIC FINDINGS

There is strong evidence that cystic fibrosis, myelodysplasia, and other severe childhood chronic diseases have increased in prevalence in recent decades. The increased prevalence is due solely to improved survival, for the incidence of these childhood diseases have remained relatively stable (Gortmaker & Sappenfield, 1984). Children born with severe forms of spina-bifida or other congenital diseases are now more likely than in previous eras to survive beyond infancy. As a consequence, current cohorts of children with these conditions contain higher rates of severe handicap. Medical and surgical advances that contributed to the increased survival of severely handicapped children have also brought improvements in the health of other affected children. Medical complications of childhood chronic diseases can now be more effectively prevented and deterioration in physical functioning can often be halted until adolescence or even adulthood. Because the course of childhood chronic illness has been altered, the relevance of early reports on psychologic sequel of childhood chronic illness might be limited.

Estimates of the prevalence of psychiatric sequelae in disabled children were reported by Rutter, Tizard, and Whitmore (1970) for the total population of 9- to 11-year-old children residing on the Isle of Wight, England. The rate of psychiatric disorder in children with disabilities was considerably higher than in the general population of children, 17.2% versus 6.6%, respectively. However, the excess was accounted for mostly by the high rate of disorder in children with conditions that involved brain abnormality: The rate of psychiatric disorder in children with brain abnormalities (e.g., epilepsy or cerebral palsy) was 24%, whereas the rate of disorder in children with other chronic conditions (e.g., heart disease or asthma) was 9%. Compared to the general population of children, the relative risk of psychiatric disorder in children with brain abnormality was 3.64, whereas the relative risk in children with conditions that do not involve the brain was only 1.36, a finding of marginal statistical significance.

The coexistence of emotional, behavioral, and learning problems in children with neurologic abnormality had been long observed clinically. The Isle of Wight study clarified the specificity of brain abnormality as the cause of psychiatric disorder in the affected children. The findings indicated that the increased risk for psychiatric disorder was a direct effect of brain dysfunction, rather than a psychological response to having a physical handicap. The increased risk in children with brain dysfunction versus children with other handicaps could not be accounted for by differences in severity of handicap, intelligence, or social class, for the analysis showed that the increased psychiatric risk in children with brain dysfunction remained even after the effects of these factors had been statistically removed.

The slight excess in the prevalence of psychiatric disturbance among children with physical disabilities that do not involve the brain in the Isle of Wight provided little support for the hypothesis that life stress associated with physical handicap, increases the risk for psychiatric disorder in children.

Further evidence supporting the brain damage–psychiatric risk connection was reported by Seidel, Chadwick, and Rutter (1975) on the basis of a comparative study of all 5- to 15-year-old crippled children of normal intelligence residing in three London boroughs. Psychiatric disorder was found to be twice as common in children with brain dysfunction than in children with other chronic conditions, despite similar physical crippling and social background. More recently, Breslau (1985) and Breslau and Marshall (1985) found that children with conditions involving brain abnormality were at increased risk for severe psychopathology, whereas children with cystic fibrosis, a condition not involving the brain, were similar to the general population of children.

Estimates from another epidemiologic survey, conducted during the same period as the Isle of Wight study, were reported by Pless and Roghmann (1971) for Monroe County, New York. Rates of behavior problems were reported for chronically sick children as an aggregate and by type of disability (motor, sensory, cosmetic), duration (temporary vs. permanent), and severity of handicap (none or mild vs. moderate or severe). No distinction was made between conditions that involve brain abnormality and conditions that do not. In 6- to 10-year-old children, the overall prevalence of psychiatric disturbance was 23% in sick children versus 16% in controls. In 11- to 15-year-old children, the prevalence was 30% versus 13%, respectively.

The relative risk for psychiatric disturbance in younger children (i.e., children ages 6–10 years) was only slightly higher than that reported in the Isle of Wight for children with conditions that do not involve the brain, 1.43 versus 1.36, respectively. (All children in the Isle of Wight study were 9–11 years old.) If we take into account the fact that the group of disabled children in Monroe County included a small subset of children with brain abnormality, whose rate of psychiatric disturbance may have been higher than the rate in those without brain abnormality, then the results of the two studies on psychiatric sequelae of conditions with no brain involvement is very close indeed. The increased relative risk reported for the older group in Monroe County must be interpreted with caution, because it was (at least in part) a function of the lower rate of disturbance in older relative to younger controls (13% vs. 16%), a reversal of the general tendency for the prevalence of disturbance to rise with children's age (e.g., Offord et al., 1987).

Estimates of the prevalence of psychiatric disorder in children with chronic illness were reported recently from the Ontario Child Health Study, an epidemiologic survey of psychiatric disorder in the general population of children 4 to 16 years of age in Ontario, Canada (Cadman, Boyle, Szatimari, & Offord, 1987). Children with *disabling* chronic illness were far more likely than healthy children to have one or more psychiatric disorders. Among children with chronic illness *without disability,* the excess was attenuated. The Ontario Child Health Study was based explicitly on the assumption that the psychiatric impact of childhood chronic illness is unrelated to specific medical diagnoses (Cadman et al., 1986). Conditions that involved the brain were not distinguished from conditions that did not, thus inferences about the psychiatric risk associated specifically with either class of physical conditions cannot be drawn.

Several problems further limit the interpretation of the results of the Ontario survey. The list of chronic physical conditions included several vague and heterogeneous categories, most notably, the category of "speech problems," ascertained in 18% of the 528 chronically ill children (Cadman et al., 1986). Speech problems most probably represent developmental disorders, rather than physical disease, and are known to be strongly associated with psychiatric disorder (Rutter et al., 1970; Stevenson & Richman, 1978, 1985).

It should also be noted that in calculating the prevalence of psychiatric sequelae of chronic conditions, the authors have not taken into account the fact that the prevalence of chronic conditions was found in their study to be significantly higher in children from low income rather than high income families (Cadman et al., 1986). The report presents no information on whether or not the prevalence of childhood psychiatric disorders in Ontario varied across social classes. Existing evidence on the association of social class and psychiatric disorder in children is mixed, with the majority of studies (but not all) demonstrating social class differences in children of school age. (Rutter et al.,

1970; Stevenson & Richman, 1985.) The threat of a social class bias is exacerbated by the inclusion of developmental disorders (such as speech problems), previously demonstrated to be far more common in children of lower social classes.

PSYCHIATRIC SEQUELAE OF CONDITIONS INVOLVING THE BRAIN: THE ROLE OF FAMILY ENVIRONMENT

Two general hypotheses have been formulated about the mechanisms that might explain the increased prevalence of psychiatric disorder in children with brain abnormality. The first hypothesis postulates a direct disorganizing effect of brain abnormality on behavior. The likelihood of psychopathology, according to this hypothesis, might depend on the specific nature of the brain abnormality, including its locus or extent. Thus, for example, there is evidence that widespread damage is associated with greater psychiatric risk and that abnormal brain function, in contrast with a mere loss of function, confers a higher risk for psychopathology (Rutter et al., 1970).

The second hypothesis is that brain dysfunction increases the affected children's vulnerability to environmental stress. There are several reasons why this might be the case. Children with cerebral damage have lower IQ, even after children with mental retardation are excluded. Quite apart from their lower IQ, brain-damaged children are more likely than other children to have reading difficulties (Shaffer, 1985). These general and specific cognitive deficits may be the processes through which brain-damaged children are rendered more vulnerable to family stress (Shaffer, 1985; Seidel et al., 1975). Abnormal brain function may be associated also with shorter attention span and adverse temperamental characteristics that could impair a child's abilities to deal with challenging or stressful experiences.

The notion that factors in the family environment can cause childhood psychopathology is a dominant theme in the literature on diverse psychiatric disorders, ranging from conduct disorder to depression. Research on the effect of environmental stressors on children has focused primarily on ongoing conditions that have pervasive consequences for family life and affect children's environments in complex and variegated ways. Chronic adversities, such as prolonged family discord and chronic illness in a parent, have been found to increase the risk of all types of childhood psychopathology.

Studies on the effects of stressful family environments on children have typically ignored genetic contributions to the association between adverse family conditions and psychopathology in the children. The strong tendency toward family aggregation of psychopathology could account for such an association by mechanisms other than the postulated causal relationship. Children with psychiatric disorders are more likely to be exposed to family stressors, because their parents and other relatives are more likely than parents and relatives of other children to be psychiatrically ill themselves and thus at higher risk for early death, divorce, and other disruptive events. Nonetheless, despite reductions in the correlations when genetic confounding is controlled, the remaining associations with environmental factors suggest that the family environment does exert a causal influence on children's behavior, although the size of the influence is considerably smaller (Sines, 1987). Thus, if it were demonstrated that brain-damaged children were more vulnerable to family stress, their greater vulnerability could potentially explain their increased psychiatric risk.

Data suggesting that children with brain dysfunction might be more affected by family stress than other children were reported by Rutter et al. (1970). According to their report, psychiatric disorder in children with conditions involving the brain was associated with family disruption and parental illness. Similar findings were reported by Seidel et al. (1975). They showed that crowding, a broken home, marital discord, and mother's psychiatric disorder were more common in disabled children who were affected by psychiatric disorder than in disabled children who were free of disorder. On the basis of this evidence, Seidel et al. concluded that, although damage to the brain increases the risk of psychiatric disorder, whether or not disorder actually develops in a large degree depends on much the same psychosocial variables that are associated with psychiatric disorder in all children. They suggested that disorder is not caused directly by brain damage, but rather "develops as a result of a combination of increased biologic vulnerability and psychosocial hazard."

Neither of the studies by Rutter et al. and Seidel et al. subjected the vulnerability hypothesis to statistical test. Such a test requires evidence on whether or not the adverse effects of stressful events or circumstances are augmented in children with brain abnormality relative to other children. In statistical terms, support for the vulnerability hypothesis hinges on evidence of a significant interaction effect. The mere observation that brain-damaged children are more likely to develop psychiatric disorder if, say, there is marital discord in the family does not support the vulnerability hypothesis, unless the association of psychiatric disorder and marital discord in brain-damaged children is demonstrated to be significantly stronger than the corresponding association in the general population of children.

EMPIRICAL TEST OF ALTERNATIVE HYPOTHESES ON THE ROLE OF THE FAMILY: THE CLEVELAND STUDY OF DISABLED CHILDREN

In a large-scale study of children with a variety of physical disabilities, children with conditions involving the brain were found to be at increased psychiatric risk relative to children with physical conditions that did not involve the brain, as well as children who were physically healthy (Breslau 1985; Breslau & Marshall 1985). The purpose of the analysis summarized here was to test the vulnerability hypothesis as well as other hypotheses about the role of family environment in explaining the psychiatric risk associated with brain dysfunction (Breslau, 1990).

Methods

The study population included children with cerebral palsy, myelodysplasia, multiple physical handicaps and cystic fibrosis, and randomly selected healthy controls. The disabled children were patients of pediatric specialty clinics in two teaching hospitals in Cleveland, Ohio, whose caseloads were representative of area children with these conditions. The analysis summarized here is on children with cerebral palsy, myelodysplasia, and multiple physical handicaps, all conditions that involve the brain. Of the 351 children, ages 3 to 18, with conditions involving the brain, 292 (83%) complete interviews were obtained at initial assessment in 1978. For a control group, a three-stage probability sample was used to represent all Cleveland area children of comparable ages. From 530 children, ages 3 to 18, there were 454 (86%) complete interviews obtained at their initial assessment in 1979. Five years later, the two samples were reassessed, the disabled children, in 1983 and the controls, in 1984. At time of follow-up, the sample of 292 children with conditions involving the brain was reduced by death (n = 32) and relocation (n = 20) to 240, of whom 229 (95%) were re-evaluated. The sample of 454 controls was reduced by relocation to 424, of whom 360 (85%) were re-evaluated.

This report is on 157 children with brain dysfunction and 339 controls, for whom data were available from face-to-face diagnostic interviews. (Of the sample of 229 brain-damaged children for whom follow-up data from mothers were available, information from direct interviews was missing on 72 children, most of whom [n = 62] were unable to be interviewed because of moderate or severe mental retardation secondary to cerebral palsy or multiple physical handicaps.)

The two samples of children were similar in age, gender, and racial compositions. Verbal IQ, measured by the Peabody Picture Vocabulary Test, was markedly lower in the disabled children than in the controls, 83.2 ± 22 versus 99.7 ± 18, respectively, replicating earlier findings about IQ deficits associated with brain abnormality, even within brain-damaged children who are not mentally retarded. The sample of disabled children comprised 53 children with cerebral palsy, 61 with myelodysplasia, and 43 with multiple handicaps.

Interviews were conducted with mothers and children separately in their homes by trained lay interviewers. Data on children's psychopathology are from direct interviews with the children in which the NIMH-Diagnostic Interview Schedule for Children (DISC) was used (Costello, Edelbrock, Dulcan, Kalas, & Klaric, 1984). The DISC was designed to elicit information necessary to yield DSM-III diagnoses in children. It is a fully structured interview that specifies the exact wording and sequence of questions and provides a complete set of categories for classifying respondents' answers.

This analysis was performed on psychiatric syndromes as dimensional variables using symptom scales constructed by adding DISC items that inquire about criterial symptoms for specific DSM-III diagnoses. Each item is coded 0 if negative, 1 if probable, and 2 if positive. A Depression Scale, with 38 items, comprised four subscales, each measuring a clinically defined domain: affective (13 items, e.g., sadness, anhedonia, worthlessness, self-blame, irritability), cognitive (6 items, e.g., boredom, confusion, indecision), vegetative (7 items, e.g., loss of appetite, sleep disturbance, loss of energy, weight fluctuations), and suicidal (9 items, e.g., hopelessness, thoughts of death, suicidal thoughts, plans, and attempts). Additionally, the analysis covered data on scales measuring Overanxious Disorder (14 items), Separation Anxiety (22 items), Oppositional Disorder (14 items), Inattention (7 items), Impulsivity (8 items), and Hyperactivity (8 items).

The Peabody Picture Vocabulary Test–Revised (PPVT) (Dunn & Dunn, 1981) was administered to all the children as an estimate of general mental ability or intelligence.

The Family Environment Scale (FES; Moos & Moos, 1981) was used to elicit information from mothers about the social environment in the home and the family. The FES consists of 90 true–false questions covering dimensions of family relationship, personal growth, and family organization.

The hypothesis that children with conditions involving the brain are vulnerable to the effects of adverse family environments was tested as one of three alternative hypotheses about the potential role of the family environment in explaining psychiatric sequelae of brain dysfunction.

The first hypothesis postulates that the family environment is an *intervening* variable between brain dysfunction and psychopathology: The presence of a disabled child in the home may have adverse effects on the family social environment and the deteriorated family environment, in turn, may contribute to psychopathology in the child. The second hypothesis postulates that child disability interacts with family environment, enhancing the psychiatric effects of those adverse family conditions that are associated with psychopathology in all children. According to the third hypothesis, the effects of family environments are unrelated to brain dysfunction, exerting the same influence on psychopathology in brain-damaged children as they do in physically healthy children, that is, their effects are *additive.*

Results

A comparison of the samples of disabled children and controls on the symptom scales revealed significant differences in two areas, depression and inattention. Consequently, the analysis of the effects of family environment on psychopathology focused on these two domains.

To test the three hypotheses about the role of the family environment, hierarchical multiple regression analysis was used. Three successive regressions were performed. The first estimates the effects of disability on psychopathology, controlling for child's age, gender, and IQ. The second adds the family environment variable to the analysis. A comparison of the coefficients of the variable "sample" (disabled vs. controls) in the first and second regressions, that is, before and after family environment was added, can show whether or not family environment acts as an intervening variable between child disability and psychopathology. Evidence that the introduction of family environment in the second step reduced markedly the original association between child disability and psychopathology, as estimated in the coefficient for "sample" in the first regression, would support the hypothesis that the family environment is an intervening mechanism. In the third regression, a two-way interaction was added to test the vulnerability hypothesis.

The Family Cohesion subscale of the FES was used to measure family environment. Children's age, gender, and IQ were used as covariates to control for their effects.

The analysis of children's reports of symptoms of depression is presented in Table 3.1. In the first regression it can be seen that, when age, gender, and IQ are controlled, brain dysfunction, represented by the variable "sample" (coded 1 for disabled children and 0 for controls) was associated with a significant excess in depressive symptoms.

TABLE 3.1
Results From Successive Regressions for Depression

	1	*2*	*3*
Sample (disabled vs. controls)	2.26* (0.95)	2.18* (0.93)	–
Family cohesion	–	−1.22* (0.24)	–
Sample × Cohesion	–	–	0.01 (0.52)
R^2	.07	.12	.12

Adjusted for children's age, gender, and IQ.
Unstandardized partial regression coefficients; SE in parentheses.
*Coefficient exceeds twice its SE.

Children with conditions involving the brain scored, on the average, 2.26 higher on the depression scale than controls.

An examination of the second regression shows that family cohesion had a significant negative association with depression and increased by 5% the explained depression variance. A comparison of the results of the first and second regressions shows that the introduction of family cohesion did not reduce materially the association between brain dysfunction and depression: The coefficient of the variable "sample" remained significant and nearly unchanged, 2.26 versus 2.18, before and after family cohesion was introduced, respectively. The hypothesis that the family environment is an intervening variable between brain dysfunction and psychopathology was not supported.

The interaction hypothesis was tested by adding in the third step a product term, *sample times cohesion.* The results, which appear in the third column, provide no support for this hypothesis, in that the interaction term was not significant. The amount of variance explained by the interaction was less than 1%. In other words, the effect of family cohesion on depression in disabled children was not significantly stronger (or weaker) than its effect on depression in physically healthy controls.

The second and third regressions taken together indicate that family cohesion does have a significant effect on children's depression. It affected disabled children and healthy controls equally. The effects of family cohesion and brain dysfunction were additive, each contributing independently to children's depression. Thus, disabled children in adverse family environments were subject to the additive effects of both risk factors and were significantly more depressed than disabled children in beneficial family environments, who were subject only to the depressive effects of their physical condition.

The results of the inattention analysis are presented in Table 3.2. Controlling for children's age, gender, and IQ, brain dysfunction

TABLE 3.2
Results From Successive Regressions for Inattention

	1	*2*	*3*
Sample (disabled vs. controls)	0.73* (0.30)	0.72* (0.30)	–
Family cohesion	–	−0.20* (0.08)	
Sample × Cohesion	–	–	−0.35* (0.17)
R^2	.09	.10	.11

Adjusted for children's age, gender, and IQ.
Unstandardized partial regression coefficients; SE in parentheses.
*Coefficient exceeds twice its SE.

increased significantly children's symptoms of inattention. As in the depression regression, there is no support for the hypothesis that the family environment is the intervening mechanism through which psychiatric sequelae of brain dysfunction could be explained. The introduction of family cohesion in the second regression did not reduce markedly the association between child disability and inattention. As to the interaction hypothesis, the results show a significant interaction between brain dysfunction and family environment. However, brain dysfunction did not increase the power of family environment to cause inattention but instead it attenuated it, as can be seen from the sign of the interaction coefficient in the third column. The results indicate that, whereas the effect of family cohesion on inattention in the controls is significant, the corresponding effect in children with brain dysfunction was near zero. Thus, although the results show a significant interaction, they provide no support for the vulnerability hypothesis. With respect to symptoms of inattention, children with brain dysfunctions were less vulnerable to the effects of the family environment than physically healthy children.

These data provide no support for the hypothesis that the high risk for psychopathology associated with brain dysfunction is due to the children's vulnerability to family environment stress. When the family environment was found to be related to psychopathology in these children, the effect was additive. Nor do the results support the hypothesis that family adversity constitutes the mechanism that explains psychopathology in disabled children.

The different results on the effect of family cohesion on depression and inattention requires an explanation. It could be that depressive symptoms in children with brain dysfunction measure nonspecific psychologic distress associated with social devaluation and other negative experiences associated with being chronically ill or handicapped, as well as with general adversities that are unrelated to physical illness,

TABLE 3.3
Symptoms of Depression and Inattention in Children With Cystic Fibrosis and Brain Dysfunction and Controls

	Cystic Fibrosis (n=65)		*Brain Dysfunction (n=156)*		*Controls (n=338)*		
	mean	*(sd)*	*mean*	*(sd)*	*mean*	*(sd)*	*F*
Depression[a]	18.1	(7.2)	18.0	(9.9)	15.4	(9.2)	4.79*
Inattention[b]	3.1	(2.6)	4.6	(3.3)	3.3	(2.7)	11.09*

*$p < .05$

[a]Cystic fibrosis and brain dysfunction scored significantly higher than controls. Cystic fibrosis is not significantly different than brain dysfunction, according to Scheffe comparisons.

[b]Brain dysfunction scored significantly higher than cystic fibrosis and controls; cystic fibrosis is not significantly different from controls, according to Scheffe comparisons.

such as discord in the family. In contrast, inattention in these children might be more closely associated with their brain abnormalities. Further support for this interpretation comes from additional data, presented in Table 3.3, which show that children with cystic fibrosis, a condition that does not involve the brain, also manifested more depressive symptoms than controls, but not more symptoms of inattention. In other words, depressive symptoms appear to be children's psychologic reaction to stress associated with being chronically ill and affect children with conditions that involve the brain and those that do not involve the brain.

CONCLUSIONS

The empirical literature and the findings presented here do not support the hypothesis that family environments are the mechanisms through which children with brain dysfunction develop psychopathology. Moreover, they do not support the hypothesis that increased psychopathology in these children is due to the children's greater vulnerability to adverse family environments. Nevertheless, the findings do not contradict the general observation that family environments are important factors in the development of depressive symptoms in children, those who are disabled and those who are physically healthy. The data suggest that in children with brain dysfunction certain types of psychopathology (i.e., inattention) might occur as a direct effect of brain abnormality and might be relatively immune from the effects of adverse family environments. However, children with brain dysfunction, as children with conditions that do not involve the brain, are more depressed than healthy children. Additionally, as all children, children with brain dysfunction are at risk for depressive symptoms when there is discord in the family. With respect to their depressive reaction to adverse family environments, children with brain dysfunction are similar to the general population of children.

These data suggest that certain aspects of family life of disabled children might be important targets for social and therapeutic intervention. In families of disabled children, those with and without brain dysfunction, the enhancement of cohesion may protect children, who are, due to their chronic illness, at high risk for depression, from additional risks for depression and demoralization.

REFERENCES

Breslau, N. (1985). Psychiatric disorder in children with physical disabilities. *Journal of the American Academy of Child Psychiatry, 24*(1), 87–94.

Breslau, N. (1990). Does brain dysfunction increase children's vulnerability to environmental stress? *Archives of General Psychiatry, 47,* 15–20.

Breslau, N., & Marshall, I. A. (1985). Psychological disturbance in children with physical disabilities: continuity and change in a 5-year follow-up. *Journal of Abnormal Child Psychology, 13*(2), 199–216.

Cadman, D., Boyle, M., Offord, D., Szatmari, P., Rae-Grant, N. I., Crawford, J., & Boyles, J. (1986). Chronic illness and disability in Ontario children: Findings of the Ontario Child Health Study. *Canadian Medical Association Journal, 135,* 761–767.

Cadman, D., Boyle, M., Szatmari, P., & Offord, D. R. (1987). Chronic illness, disability and mental and social well-being: Findings of the Ontario Child Health Study. *Pediatrics, 79,* 805–810.

Costello, A. J., Edelbrock, C., Dulcan, M. K., Kalas, R., & Klaric, S. H. (1984). *Development and testing of the NIMH Diagnostic Interview for children in a clinic population.* Rockville, MD: Center for Epidemiologic Studies. National Institute of Mental Health.

Dunn, L. M., Dunn, L. M. (1981). *PPVT, Peabody Picture Vocabulary Test—Revised.* Minneapolis, MN: American Guidance Service.

Gortmaker, S. L., & Sappenfield, W. (1984). Chronic childhood disorders: prevalence and impact. *Pediatric Clinics of North America, 31*(1), 3–18.

Moos, R. H., & Moos, B. S. (1981). *Family environment manual.* Palo Alto, CA: Consulting Psychologists Press.

Offord, D. R., Boyle, M. H., Szatmari, P., Rae-Grant, N. I., Links, P. S., Cadman, D. T., Byles, J. A., Crawford, J. W., Blum, H. M., Byrne, C., Thomas, H., & Woodward, C. A. (1987). Ontario Child health study. II. Six-month prevalence of disorder and rates of service utilization. *Archives of General Psychiatry, 44,* 832–836.

Pless, I. B., & Roghmann, K. J. (1971). Chronic illness and its consequences:

Observations based on three epidemiologic surveys. *Journal of Pediatrics, 79*(3), 351–359.

Richman, N., Stevenson, J., & Graham, P. J. (1982). *Pre-school to school: A behavioral study*. London: Academic Press.

Rutter, M. (1977). Brain damage syndrome in childhood: Concepts and findings. *Journal of Child Psychology and Psychiatry and Allied Disciplines, 18,* 1–21.

Rutter, M., Tizard, J., & Whitmore, K. (1970). *Education, health and behavior.* London: Longmans Group Limited.

Shaffer, D. (1985). Brain damage. In M. Rutter & L. Hersov (Eds.), *Child and adolescent psychiatry, modern approaches* (2nd ed., pp. 129–151). Boston: Blackwell Scientific.

Seidel, U., Chadwick, O., & Rutter, M. (1975). Psychological disorders in crippled children. A comparative study of children with and without brain damage. *Developmental Medical Child Neurology, 17,* 563–573.

Sines, J. O. (1987). Influence of the home and family environment on childhood dysfunction. In B. Lahey & A. Kazdin (Eds.), *Advances in clinical child psychology* (Vol. 10, pp. 1–54). New York: Plenum.

Stevenson, J., & Richman, N. (1978). Behavior, language and development in three-year old children. *Journal of Autism and Childhood Schizophrenia, 8,* 299–313.

Stevenson, J., & Richman, N. (1985). Behavior problems and language abilities at three years and behavioral deviance at eight years. *Journal of Child Psychology and Psychiatry and Allied Disciplines, 26,* 215–230.

CHAPTER 4

The Mutual Influence of Child Externalizing Behavior and Family Functioning: The Impact of a Mild Congenital Risk Factor

Charles F. Halverson, Jr.
University of Georgia

Karen S. Wampler
Texas Tech University

Rather than emphasizing the unidirectional influence of parents on children or children on parents, child functioning is now more often being conceptualized in the context of the family as a system with both children and parents in a mutual influence network over time (Gunnar & Thelen, 1989; Hinde & Stevenson-Hinde, 1988; Martin, 1987). One of the difficulties in studying the mutual influence process is that child and family contributions to child outcome are confounded. Studies of the transition to parenthood as well as studies of adoption are typical ways to examine the mutual influence process unconfounded by genetic relatedness.

We use another strategy, proposing a model based on a classification of children on an index of congenital minor physical anomalies (MPAs). The incidence of these anomalies is not influenced by the family environment but rather seem to result from deviations in the prenatal environment (see discussion later in this chapter for speculations on the origins and meaning of MPAs). Minor physical anomalies have been consistently associated with difficult temperament in children (Waldrop, Bell, & Goering, 1976; Waldrop, Bell, McLaughlin, & Halverson, 1978; Waldrop & Halverson, 1971) and constitute a relatively mild risk factor. Such a mild risk factor, present in the general population, from birth allows us to study the mutual effects of difficult temperament and the family environment and to some extent unconfound the direction of effects.

Past research has shown a consistent main effect for MPAs. High MPA children tend to have behavior problems in interactions with others (parents, siblings, teachers) characterized by impulsivity, aggression, and a failure to comply with requests from others. We have, however, in our past research on MPAs, neglected the effects of the family in moderating or contributing to the MPA-behavior relation. Although we view MPAs as a useful indicator of a risk for difficult temperament, nothing is known about whether MPAs contribute to child outcomes directly or whether their effects are mediated through various family domain variables.[1]

Based on the notion of MPAs as a congenitally based risk factor, we propose, for expository purposes, a match–mismatch model (Thomas & Chess, 1977) between families and children in order to examine the relative importance of aspects of the family environment that moderate the direction of influence between the family and child in the developing socialization system. The match–mismatch model predicts that when difficult children (high MPA) are raised by problem families, both families and children will get worse over time, with the predominant direction of effects from the difficult child (high MPA) to the vulnerable family. This could be termed the *child-driven model.*

When difficult children are raised by competent, low problem families, however, children will, over time, become less problematic and the families will continue to be competent over time. The direction of effect in this instance would be largely from family to child (the *family-driven model*). Rather than exploring a simple direction of effect model, we focus on the question: Under what conditions is change predominately child-driven or family-driven?

In this chapter, we use data from the first 2 years of our study of young children and their families to provide a partial test of our transactional model of the influence of children on the family and the family on children. The models tested represent a "main effects" approach. First, we predict child outcomes (externalizing behavior) from both parent and child MPAs and different domains of parental, marital,

[1]One might be tempted to see MPAs as a model for other sorts of developmental problems or physical defects like schizophrenia or mild cerebral palsy, but nearly all of the studies of MPAs involve normal samples of children, not clinical samples or psychiatric populations. Evidence for such relations to serious disorders is sparse and contradictory. It is clear that MPAs mark behavior associated with mild behavior problems in unselected samples. The index has not fared well in predicting variation in clinical samples, even though minor anomalies frequently are associated with the occurrence of major congenital malformations like cleft palate and spina bifida.

and family functioning. Second, we predict family functioning from the same set of predictors. These main effect tests allow us to assess the extent to which both family and child outcomes are driven by family and congenitally based child variables. By using MPAs we can assess directly child effects on family and child outcomes in combination with variables representing the family environment, including the domains of parenting, marital quality, whole family functioning, and individual parent characteristics.

Although there is considerable research documenting that parenting, marital quality, and whole family functioning are related to child outcome, much of this research is ambiguous as to direction of effects issues. For example, several researchers have included a consideration of multiple aspects of the family environment in longitudinal studies as they jointly impact child outcome (cf. Belsky, 1984; Belsky, Rovine, & Fish, 1989; Elder, Caspi, & Downey, 1986; Lambert, 1988; Masten et al., 1988; Patterson & Bank, 1989; Powers, Hauser, & Kilner, 1989; Rutter, 1988; Sameroff, 1989). These studies provide evidence of the impact of parenting quality, marital quality, and parent personality on child outcome. The evidence of the impact of parent personality on parenting, marriage, and child outcome is particularly strong (Belsky et al., 1989; Caspi & Elder, 1988; Lahey et al., 1988; Matheny, 1986; Powers et al., 1989; Rutter, 1988; Sameroff, 1989). Not all of the studies, however, include measures of child temperament. Some include a measure of child temperament that is retrospective and/or based solely on parental (usually the mother) reports, thus confounding family and child factors (see Halverson, 1988; Wampler & Halverson, in press). Those studies in which the impact of child temperament is examined appropriately consistently find evidence for a child effect (Hetherington, Stanley-Hagan, & Anderson, 1989; Lambert, 1988; Powers et al., 1989). Elder made a convincing case for the impact of child temperament on later relationships, particularly marital and parent–child relationships (Caspi & Elder, 1988; Elder et al., 1986; Liker & Elder, 1983). Even research based on strong assumptions of a predominant direction of effect from the family to the child tend to produce evidence of a child effect. For example, in a series of research studies, Patterson (1982; Patterson & Bank, 1989; Patterson & Dishion, 1988) produced evidence of a strong relation between parenting practices and child outcome. Yet, he also found that parents are less adept at parenting the child with conduct problems than they are at parenting a sibling, thus suggesting a child effect. Patterson (1982) also found that decreasing child's antisocial behavior leads to decreases in mother's depression.

Our point is not simply to reiterate the importance of child effects. Rather, we believe that much research is still guided by an undirectional model, one that examines only how the family influences the child. When adequate measures of child and parent are included, however, evidence for child effects may often be more compelling than evidence for parent effects (Halverson & Wampler, in press). The need is for longitudinal research that includes well-accepted observational and self-report measures across the family subsystems including congenital or biological factors. These factors need to be simultaneously considered in complex models to depict how the family subsystems are related to both child and family outcomes and changes over time. We have little documentation on how these subsystems interact. By identifying the relative importance of congenital, parent–child, marital, parental, and whole family characteristics to child and family outcomes we can begin to disentangle the direction of effects between child characteristics and family context.

MODELS TO BE TESTED

Our major main effect model involved seven latent variables derived from the first two waves of our longitudinal data set (the Georgia Longitudinal Study). Six of the constructs were derived from our first wave and were formed into a model to predict first, child outcome in Year 2, and then in a second model, family functioning in Year 2.

We chose this strategy of alternating child and family outcome variables in our structural models because of the indeterminate and complex problem of testing recursive, two-way models with structural equations modeling procedures. These alternating outcome models do tell us about recursiveness, albeit indirectly. Such relations as we have found need further replication to assure confidence in the bidirectionality of some of our findings.

The Child Outcome Model

We hypothesized that child outcome in Year 2, operationalized as child externalizing behavior (active, impulsive, difficult conduct), would be predicted first by a direct path from child MPAs. This direct path prediction stems from our earlier work where MPAs have been consistently and positively related to aggressive, impulsive, highly active behavior (Waldrop et al., 1976, 1978; Waldrop & Halverson, 1971). Second, in addition to the direct path to child behavior, we predicted that MPAs would have indirect effects on child externalizing through its effects on both the constructs marital quality and competent parenting.

For the first time, we also employed *parental* MPAs in our model, predicting that parental MPAs would have direct effects on three family subsystems—marital quality, individual parent stress, and family cohesion. The effects of parent MPAs on child externalizing could be mediated by paths from marital quality to parenting to child outcome and by a path from parent stress to family cohesion to child outcome. We predicted these paths in the expectation that MPAs would be related in adults to parental personality, most likely some aspect of negative emotionality, anxiety, and the tendency to become angry or upset easily.

The Family Outcome Model

The second model employed the same latent variables, but the focus was now on family cohesion in Year 2 as outcome. We chose family cohesion to represent competent family functioning and our interest was, in this use, how difficult externalizing behavior would impact on family cohesion. We chose cohesion as a family outcome measure because it is an excellent summary variable of how much family members like and feel close to each other. As such, it represents a good index of overall family life satisfaction. There exists evidence that family cohesion is sensitive to changes in relationships among family members (e.g., Belsky et al., 1989; Olson, Sprenkel, & Russell, 1979) and therefore is our choice for the major indicator of family stability and change.[2]

We predicted that child MPAs would directly relate to externalizing behavior as before, and that parental MPAs would directly impact parent stress and marital quality, which would, in turn, relate positively to family cohesion.

These two models were the necessary descriptive initial steps to linking the child and family subsystems by predicting first, variability in child externalizing as a function of both congenital factors (MPAs) and family system variables, and second, variability in effective family functioning as a function of both these same sets of predictors.

In each of these models, we included age and gender of child to assess their impact on the models. It seems likely that externalizing should show developmental declines over time in this preschool population and that boys should show higher externalizing behavior than

[2]In our own work as well as others (e.g., Olson et al., 1979), cohesion is repeatedly the first principal component extracted from self-report of family functioning and typically accounts for the major portion of shared variance.

girls (Waldrop et al., 1978; Waldrop & Halverson, 1971). We used parent resources, as indicated by mothers' and fathers' level of education and level of ego development (Loevinger, 1985) as a latent variable in the model to control for the impact of parent resources on the relation between child and family functioning.

To evaluate our causal models about the predictors of child externalizing and family cohesion, we used a method of modeling called Latent Variable Path Analysis with Partial Least Squares (LVPLS; Falk & Miller, 1991; Lohmoeller, 1984, 1989). LVPLS is a component analysis where composites (latent variables) are created from measured variables in such a way that optimal linear correlations are created among them. This is done by extracting the first principle component from the measured variables in such a way that maximal correlations are obtained. In many respects this procedure is similar to LISREL, having a measurement model and a structural model with specified paths among latent variables. LVPLS does not, however, require measurement at an interval level and is not sensitive to departures from multivariate normality and small samples as is LISREL.

METHOD

Sample

The sample includes 94 intact families who participated in the Georgia Longitudinal Study, an ongoing study of the role of child temperament and family functioning in child outcome. Complete data are available from Years 1 and 2 of the study. Each family had both parents living at home and at least one child between the ages of 3 and 6 (the target child) during Year 1. Families were recruited from preschools, day-care centers, and radio and newspaper announcements. Families and teachers were paid for their participation.

The sample was predominantly White and middle class, with the mean education level for mothers a college degree and for fathers some graduate training. Number of children ranged from 1 to 5 with the majority having two children. Mean age of the target child was 4.4 years in Year 1 (range, 2.9 to 6.2) and 5.4 years in Year 2 (range, 3.9 to 7.2). The sample was about equally divided between boys ($n = 46$) and girls ($n = 48$).

Families came into the laboratory and completed videotaped interaction tasks involving the marital dyad, mother and child, father and child, and mother, father, and child together. The parents each completed the Block Childrearing Practices Report Q-Sort in the laboratory and were given a questionnaire packet to mail back. Teacher questionnaires were returned by mail.

Measures

Control Variables. Child's gender at Year 1 (boy = 1, girl = 2), child's age at Year 1, and parent resources at Year 1 were used as control variables. The construct of parent resources was indicated by fathers' and mothers' levels of education and ego development. Ego development is a measure of cognitive complexity assessed by Loevinger's revised Washington University Sentence Completion Test (Loevinger, 1985). Two trained coders scored all the protocols with a mean interrater correlation of .86, ranging from .66 to .96 across the 36 items.

Minor Physical Anomalies. To assess both child and parent MPAs we used the scale developed by Waldrop, Pederson, and Bell (1968) that was based on earlier work by Goldfarb and Botstein (1964). In our study, the weighted MPA score for children included measures of the head, hands, and feet. The score for parents was based on measures of only the head and hands because the adults (mostly the fathers) objected to removing their shoes. A scoring manual for measuring MPAs is available from the first author (Waldrop, Halverson, & Shetterley, 1989).

The MPA index consists of 18 minor congenital growth abnormalities of the head, hands, and feet. These 18 MPAs can be assessed at any age and represent the primary diagnostic physical criteria for Trisomy 21. The MPAs are present at birth and are minor developmental deviations most likely resulting from some event occurring in early embryogenesis. Although diagnostic of Trisomy 21, anomalies are present in the general population with an average of 2–4 anomalies per person (range 0–15). In a number of studies, the MPA index has been found to predict impulsive, aggressive behavior in 2- to 12-year-old boys (Waldrop et al., 1978; Waldrop & Halverson, 1971) and withdrawn low activity for girls (Waldrop et al., 1976). Longitudinal data have shown that these relations can be predicted in 3-year-old children from MPAs assessed at birth (Waldrop et al., 1976).

The MPAs measured are as follows: head circumference out of normal range, multiple hair whorls, fine electric hair, low set ears, malformed ears, soft and pliable ears, asymmetries of the ears and face, high steepled palate, epicanthus, hyperteliorism, single palmar creases, short or curved fifth finger, third toe longer than the second, big gap between the first and second toes and partial syndactyly of the second and third toes. There are a number of other MPAs that have been coded in the past but for technical reasons are not included in routine screenings. They include such things as sacral dimples, irregularities in dermatoglyphics (e.g., obtuse ATD angles[3], ulnar loops and whorls), hairy nevuses, auricular pits, palpebral fissures, and anomalies of dentition.

All of these minor anomalies are ectodermal, arising from the same germinal layer as the central nervous system during embryogenesis. Whatever agent or agents responsible for the occurrence of MPAs presumably also has detectable effects on the developing central nervous system such that we can readily assess the behavioral concomitants of multiple minor anomalies in children and adults (see Waldrop & Halverson, 1971, for details). The relation of MPAs to difficult behavior in children is not due to high MPA children looking strange and thus eliciting negative reactions from others. Several studies have reported no relation between the incidence of MPAs and ratings of attractiveness. Even high MPA children are within the normal range for attractiveness. Although MPA is a congenital variable, the anomalies may or may not have a genetic basis. The evidence to date shows low to insignificant correlations among siblings and parents on the MPA index (Halverson, 1992), implicating nongenetic modes of transmission (i.e., intrauterine, prenatal, first trimester).

Minor physical anomalies for each individual were assessed by from two to eight raters over four periods of data collection. Mean interrater correlations were .87 for mothers, .89 for fathers, and .88 for the target child. The weighted scores ranged from 0 to 9 for mothers ($M = 4.0$), 0 to 10 for fathers ($M = 4.1$), and 0 to 12 for the target children ($M = 5.2$).

Child Externalizing Behavior. Child's externalizing behavior was measured at Years 1 and 2 from four sources, the mother, the father, the teacher, and the observation of the child in the laboratory. The externalizing score from parents and teachers is a sum of the Impulsivity subscale of the Preschool Rating Scale (Victor, Halverson, & Montague, 1985), the Activity Level, Emotional Intensity, Distractibility, and Persistence (negatively scored) subscales from the Temperament Assessment Battery (Martin, 1988) and the Conduct Problem subscale from the preschool version of the Behavior Problem Checklist (Quay & Peterson, 1979).

[3]The term *ATD* refers to the designations of the tri-radii of friction skin formed at the base of each finger (labelled A through D, from index to little finger). The tri-radius of friction skin located in the palm has been called the T tri-radius. The angle formed by the A, T, and D tri-radii has been called the ATD angle.

The observational measure of externalizing behavior was the Georgia Child Behavior Q-Sort (GCBQ) adapted by Halverson from items in the Block California Q-Set (1978) and the Baumrind Preschool Q-Sort (1971). These items represent those that characterized competence in preschool children in analyses reported by Waters, Garber, Gornal, and Vaughn (1983). Observers watched videotapes of the children in interaction tasks with each parent and with both parents together and then described the child's behavior using the GCBQ. Interrater Pearson product-moment correlations were .68 for Year 1 and .73 for Year 2. The externalizing score from this observational measure was the sum of the Active-Energetic, Direct and Persistent (negatively scored), Manageable (negatively scored), and Impetuous clusters from the GCBQ.

Parent Stress. Symptoms of stress were assessed using the Global Severity Index of the revised Symptom Checklist 90 (SCL-90; Derogatis, 1977). Even though the SCL-90 has subscales, it is considered best used as a measure of general psychological distress (Cyr, McKenna-Foley, & Peacock, 1985). The husband and wife scores, based on separate male and female norms for nonpatient samples, were used as indicators of the parent stress construct.

Marital Quality. The quality of the marital relationship was assessed by the separate husband and wife total scores from the Dyadic Adjustment Scale (Sharpley & Cross, 1982; Spanier, 1976), the separate husband and wife total scores from the Regard and Empathy subscales of the Relationship Inventory (Barrett-Lennard, 1978; Wampler & Powell, 1982), and a sum of the Positive Affect, Respect, and Negative Affect (negatively scored) clusters from the Marriage Q-Sort (Wampler & Halverson, 1990). Coders observed the couple discussing a disagreement over child rearing and then used the Q-Sort to describe the couple's interaction. Interrater agreement based on Pearson correlations for profiles was .78 in Year 1.

Parenting. Six variables were used as indicators of positive parenting. The 21 clusters identified by Susman, Trickett, Ionotti, Hollenbeck, and Zahn-Waxler (1985) of the Block Childrearing Practices Report Q-Sort (Block, 1980) were factor analyzed. Two of the resulting 7 clusters were summed to form a positive parenting attitudes score for husband and wife (Positive parenting minus Authoritarian control). Quality of parenting behavior was assessed by observing videotapes of each parent with the target child and then coding the observation using the 38-item Q-sort developed by Block (1980) (see also Buss, 1981, from the Block

Childrearing Practices Q-Sort; Block, 1980). The mean of the interrater profile correlations was .75. The items were formed into clusters based on factor analyses. The Love and Control (negatively scored) clusters were summed as a measure of positive parenting behavior for husband and wife. Similarity in parenting attitudes as assessed by the intraclass correlation of the husband and wife scores on the Block Childrearing Practices Report and similarity in parenting behavior as measured by the intraclass correlation of the parent scores on the observational Q-sort were used as the final two indicators of parenting quality. Similarity in parenting values and behavior has been identified as an important indicator of the quality of parenting (Deal, Halverson, & Wampler, 1989).

Family Cohesion. Family cohesion was indicated by the sum of the adaptability and cohesion subscales from FACES II (Olson et al., 1982) for husband and wife and the sum of the three cohesion scales from the Family Environment Scale (FES; Moos & Moos, 1986) for husband and wife. The cohesion scales on the FES are Cohesion, Expressiveness, and Conflict (negatively scored). Three clusters of the Georgia Family Q-Sort (Wampler, Halverson, Moore, & Walters, 1989) were summed as an observational indicator of family cohesion. These clusters were Positive affect, Reserved (negatively scored), and Negative affect (negatively scored). Coders observed a videotape of the family together building a house out of Lincoln Logs (Year 1) and building a model out of a set of plastic building blocks (Year 2) and used the Q-sort to describe the family interaction. Interrater profile agreement based on intraclass correlation was .56 for Year 1 and .77 for Year 2.

RESULTS

Measurement Model. In developing the measures of each construct, our strategy was to use variables from as many sources as possible. The variables used as indicators for each construct are listed in Table 4.1. The same constructs were included in all the models. The measurement model indicates excellent loadings for all the manifest variables on the latent variables with the exception of the observational measures of family cohesion in Year 2 (Table 4.1). In essence, the construct of family cohesion is a combination of self-report and observational measures in Year 1. When family cohesion is used as an outcome variable, it is more of a measure of husband and wife perceptions of family cohesion.

Child as Outcome. In the first set of models we used the child risk indicator (MPAs) and the family context measures in Year 1 as predictors

TABLE 4.1
Family–Child Externalizing Measurement Model

		Loading	
Construct	*Variable*	*Year 1*	*Year 2*
Child gender			
Child age			
Child anomaly			
Parent anomaly	Husband anomalies	73	
	Wife anomalies	73	
Parent resources	Husband education	83	
	Husband ego development	42	
	Wife education	72	
	Wife ego development	56	
Child externalizing	Husband externalizing	72	68
	Wife externalizing	79	77
	Teacher externalizing	67	63
	Q-externalizing	66	64
Parent stress	H-general symptom index	79	
	W-general symptom index	79	
Marital quality	H-dyadic adjustment scale	79	
	H-relationship inventory	70	
	W-dyadic adjustment scale	72	
	W-relationship inventory	68	
	Q-marriage positive affect	52	
	Q-marriage negative affect	−79	
	Q-marriage respect	74	
Parenting	Husband child-rearing practices	76	
	Husband Q-parent behavior	32	
	Wife child-rearing practices	72	
	Wife Q-parent behavior	58	
	Child-rearing similarity	81	
	Parent behavior similarity	61	
Family cohesion	Husband-FACES-II	51	77
	Husband-FES cohesion	60	76
	Wife-FACES-II	73	80
	Wife-FES cohesion	69	83
	Q-family positive affect	58	25
	Q-family reserved	−46	−23
	Q-family negative affect	−50	−04

of child externalizing in Year 2. In each case, child's age and parent resources were allowed to predict all of the other constructs except parent and child MPAs. Child's gender was also used as a predictor of all other constructs in the model for the total sample. The modified model indicating all paths greater than .20 is presented in Fig. 4.1. As can be seen, the only predictor of child externalizing behavior (other than age and gender) was child MPAs. The relations among the other

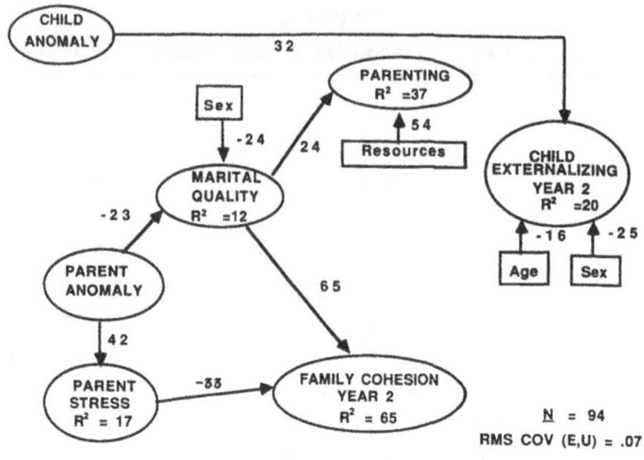

FIG. 4.1 Family factors in Year 1 predicting child externalizing in Year 2.

variables were as expected except that none of the family context constructs was related to the outcome of child externalizing in Year 2. Child's gender and age were related to child externalizing in a direction indicating that boys and younger children exhibited more externalizing behavior according to mothers, fathers, teachers, and observers in the laboratory. Child's gender was also related to marital quality, indicating that parents of boys exhibited lower levels of marital quality. The construct of parent resources was related only to parenting quality. The fit of the model was very good.

The same model was tested for boys and girls separately with different results. In the boys' model (Fig. 4.2), child MPAs and parent stress both predicted child externalizing. The amount of boys' externalizing behavior was not related to age. For girls (Fig. 4.3), child MPAs

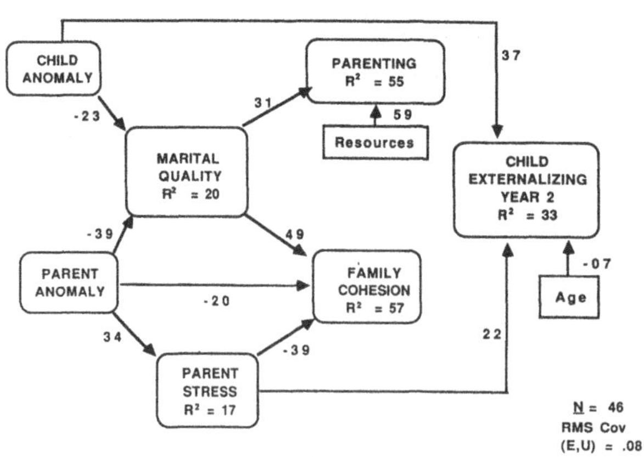

FIG. 4.2 Boys' family-to-child model.

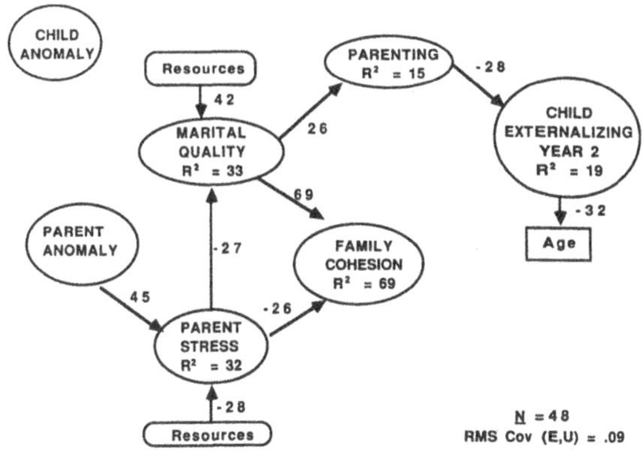

FIG. 4.3 Girls' family-to-child model.

were not related to child outcome. Both parenting quality and child's age were moderately related to girls' externalizing behavior in the expected direction. More of the variance in child externalizing was explained in the boys' model (.33) than in the girls' model (.19). Differences between the boys' and girls' models were also indicated by the different pattern of correlations among the latent variables in the model (Table 4.2).

Family as Outcome. In order to examine the impact of the child on the family, the model was reversed, *predicting family cohesion in Year 2 as outcome.* For the total sample, only a marginal impact of child externalizing on the family was apparent (Fig. 4.4). The strongest predictors of family cohesion in Year 2 were marital quality and parent stress. Again, parenting quality did not relate to family cohesion. The models were

TABLE 4.2
Correlations Among Latent Variables for Boy and Girl Families

Variable	*1*	*2*	*3*	*4*	*5*	*6*	*7*	*8*	*9*
1. Child age	X	−15	−21	−16	−14	−05	−07	−29*	−10
2. Child MPA	−09	X	33*	−03	53**	40**	−32*	−17	−29*
3. Parent MPA	−20	08	X	04	30*	45**	−39**	−11	−35*
4. Parent resources	−04	−04	−12	X	05	−04	16	65**	−10
5. Child externalizing	−25	22	28*	−12	X	46**	−37**	02	−48**
6. Parent stress	−09	−11	45**	−33*	19	X	−20	−09	−47**
7. Marital quality	00	11	−15	44**	−18	−43**	X	42**	62**
8. Parenting competence	−08	−15	−36**	41**	−34*	−31*	25	X	17
9. Family cohesion	−05	−02	−17	33*	−27	−47**	72**	32*	X

Note: Decimals omitted. Boys ($N = 46$) above the diagonal, Girls ($N = 48$) below.
*$p < .05$, two-tailed. **$p < .01$, two-tailed.

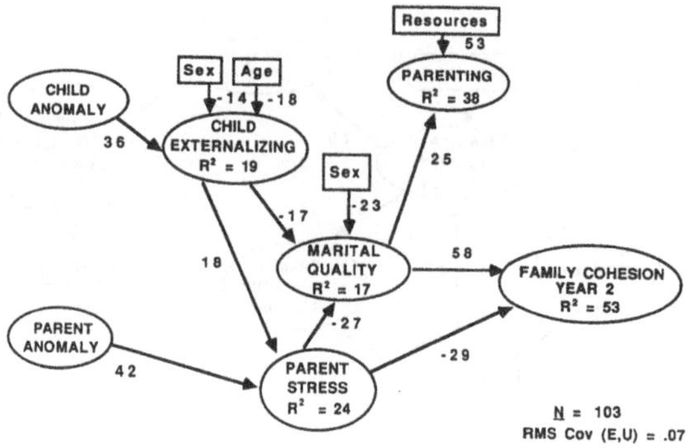

FIG. 4.4 Child externalizing in Year 1 predicting family cohesion in Year 2.

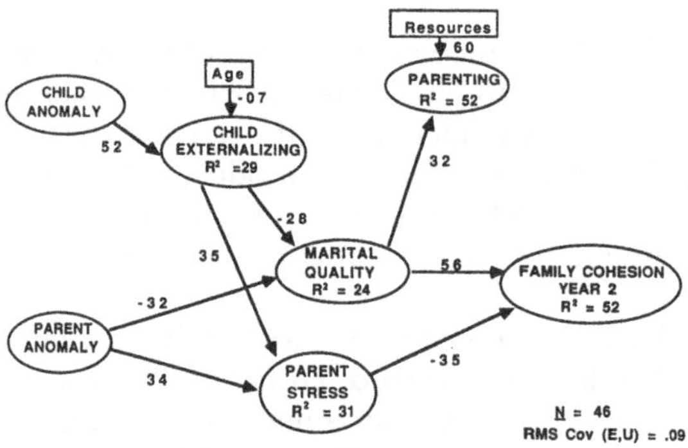

FIG. 4.5 Boys' child-to-family model.

quite different for boys and girls, however. For boys, there was a moderate impact of child externalizing on both marital quality and parent stress (Fig. 4.5). For girls, there was no impact of child externalizing on family cohesion, marital quality, or parent stress although girls' externalizing does relate to parenting quality (Fig. 4.6). A higher level of girls' externalizing was related to lower parenting quality in Year 1. Approximately the same amount of variance in family cohesion was explained in both the boys' and girls' models.

DISCUSSION

In the first series of contemporaneous models, we presented convincing evidence for a congenitally based contributor to preschool children's highly active, difficult, externalizing behavior. For the total sample, we

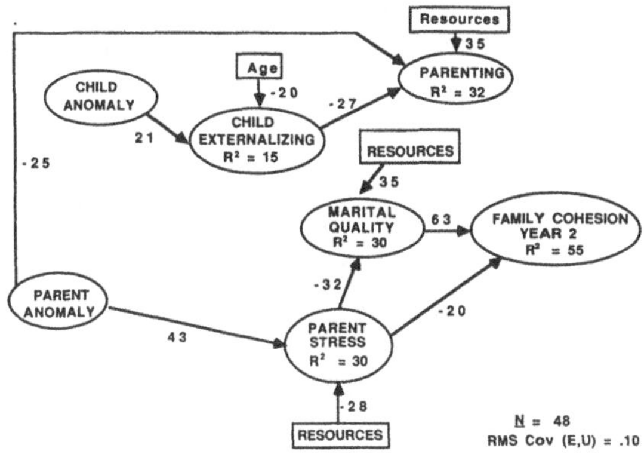

FIG. 4.6 Girls' child-to-family model.

were able to model both congenital and family systems contributors to child outcome with the overall result that the primary causal variable was within the child. In fact, for the model based on the combined sample of boys and girls, none of the family systems measures predicted child outcome in Year 2; only the child risk factor of MPAs was related to child externalizing behavior. When we analyzed the model separately for boys and girls, we found a replication of our model in boys. Parenting, marital quality, and family cohesion did not predict externalizing for boys. In contrast, girls congenital status was not related to difficult, externalizing behavior, whereas both parenting and marital quality made significant contributions to girls' externalizing. Also, girls' MPAs did not relate to family functioning. Clearly, externalizing has a strong congenital basis in boys and a strong family basis in girls.

Externalizing behavior was also higher in boys. Also, from the second series of models, we found that boys' externalizing behavior had more impact on the family than girls' externalizing. Girls' externalizing behavior had little impact on family functioning. In these results we have an interesting situation. Recall in our original model we were interested in when change was predominantly due to the child (the child-driven model) and when change was predominantly due to the family (the family-driven model). We made no predictions by child gender. The results, however, at least for a main effect model, clearly tell us that for boys we have a child-driven model. The variability in externalizing is related closely only to our congenital predictor and has considerable impact on all of the family functioning areas we measured.

For girls, we have a family-driven model. Their externalizing was related to how well the family was functioning but did not have the impact of boys' externalizing behavior. For these models, the answer to the question of when the child is influencing the family and when the family is influencing the child clearly involves knowing whether we are dealing with boys or girls.

Boys' externalizing behavior had an impact on parental and family functioning *because* it was difficult and negative by nature. Like many other studies (e.g., Halverson, 1992; Halverson, Victor, & Deal, 1990) we found that boys' high magnitude behavior was hard for parents to overlook. The boys were generally more difficult to socialize than the girls because the boys tend to be aggressive, impulsive, and noncompliant. Other data also confirm that negative behavior has an impact on parents (e.g., Lee & Bates, 1985; Rutter, 1988). This externalizing cluster has been found to be robust and coherent for boys. Boys' externalizing has this impact even in our sample, where the level of externalizing was relatively low compared to clinical samples. In other studies as well as our own, this cluster shows considerable generality and stability into middle childhood (e.g., Halverson et al., 1990; Radke-Yarrow, Richters, & Wilson, 1988).

In contrast, girls' externalizing seemed to be of a different nature. It did not show a relation to our congenital variable; it was significantly lower in overall magnitude than boys' externalizing and it also appeared to be produced by or influenced by family factors. Most significantly, the variable in girls had no impact on family functioning. It could be that variability in moderate levels of our externalizing cluster in girls was more akin to assertiveness or positively interpreted by parents as competence and/or sociability. If such were the case, variability in externalizing in girls, being smaller in magnitude and being more socially acceptable, probably indexes nonproblem behavior or behavior that falls below some threshold for disruptiveness in the family.

That externalizing was related to MPAs in boys is strongly supported in our earlier work (Waldrop et al., 1976; Waldrop & Halverson, 1971). In fact, in our current study, MPAs continue to relate to our externalizing cluster. When we model the relations between boys' MPAs and externalizing in Years 1 and 2, we find path coefficients of .56 (Year 1) and .38 (Year 2). The Year 2 path coefficient was substantial, even when Year 1 externalizing was controlled in the model (the autocorrelation was .48). Such a model suggests that MPAs in boys not only predict Year 1 externalizing but also predict the *increase* in externalizing in Year 2. The externalizing construct was strongly related over time to a congenital factor for boys. Because this is a congenital factor, present at birth, measurable during infancy, and predictive of externalizing, we have a firm basis for a generalization about child-driven effects for boys. It remains to be seen whether this externalizing is amenable to control or whether it may lessen in impact as these boys develop into middle childhood. It might be recalled that in our models, child age (from 3 to 6 years) was not correlated with externalizing for boys, but was substantially negatively related to age for girls (path coefficient = −.32). At least in the 2-year models we present here, there was no evidence for a lessening of externalizing for boys, whereas girls' externalizing not only was generally lower but was decreasing with age. In subsequent analyses we examine whether and when externalizing in boys can be reduced in this "normal" nonclinical group of boys. We suspect that those parents who are effective and competent, and who are mutually supportive of each other (cohesive) may, in time, have positive effects on this type of behavior in boys. We also suspect that even at the preschool ages studied here, parents of girls already are having a marked impact in reducing such behavior to low-level "nonproblem" levels.[4]

We included parental MPAs in our models to assess whether they too played an important role in family functioning. There are very limited data on adult MPAs and behavior (see Paulhus & Martin, 1986). What data there are, suggest that MPAs in adults may predict high energy, impulsive, impatient, negative, and irritable behaviors. In our data there were surprising relations between a latent variable consisting of both husband and wife MPA scores and individual and family functioning. In all models, these relations replicated for both parents of boys and girls: Parent MPAs were predictive of parent stress as operationalized by the general symptom index of the SCL-90. As MPAs increased, so did self-reported symptoms of depression, anxiety, and hostility in parents of boys ($r = .45$, $p < .01$) and girls ($r = .45$, $p < .01$). Further, stress symptoms were linked to family cohesion negatively in both samples and negatively to marital quality in the boy sample. In the girl sample, parental MPAs had an indirect effect on marital quality, mediated by parent stress.

These data show, for the first time, a congenital contributor to negative family functioning in parents of both boys and girls. Apparently, as the parental risk index increased, so did the negative parent personality that had direct and indirect effects on every family system in our model. These relations can also be fairly directly parsed as to direction of effects, even in contemporaneous and two-wave panels. There is an aspect of parent personality that is analogous to the early childhood externalizing that is related to diminished family functioning.

[4]Beginning in Year 3 (not included in this analysis) we have extensive sibling data. We intend in subsequent analyses to analyze the combined and interacting effects of sibling personality as well. It may be that gender effects in boy sibling pairs may be magnified over mixed-sex sibling pairs (e.g., older boy–younger girl).

Recall also that this was a nonclinical sample. We were not conceptualizing this parental behavior as an antisocial personality cluster (the behavior is not that extreme), but the parallels to the theorizing about the role of the antisocial parent personality in severe behavior problems (Lahey et al., 1988; Patterson & Dishion, 1988) are apparent. The data also are congruent with data that show that negative affective states (e.g., Tellegan, 1982) influence parenting (see Belsky & Pensky, 1988, for a review) and other family systems (e.g., McCrae & Costa, 1984). They also fit nicely with Belsky and Pensky's (1988) supposition that such links between parent personality and family domains may reflect genetic biological concordance. Whatever the case, we have direct and important effects of parent personality on the family systems of marriage, parenting, and family cohesion that are partly based in a congenital construct in the parents. It remains to be seen whether these irritable, negative parents will continue to contribute to child outcomes in girls and will take on increasing importance in boys' externalizing behavior as the children enter middle childhood.

One final gender effect in our data bears mentioning. In Fig. 4.4, where we depict the test of child characteristics as predictors of family outcome, we found the child's gender to be related to marital quality. Parents of boys indicated lower marital quality, even after the effects of child externalizing and parent stress were removed. This surprising result indicates that having boys, even when controlling for their externalizing difficult behavior, has an additional negative impact on marital quality. Obviously, we have not yet explained characteristics of male offspring that are affecting the parents in our study. Possibly, boys require more attention in general or fathers may be more involved with boys and less involved in the marriage leading to decrements in quality. At this time, we have no firm basis to speculate why male offspring have an impact on parents over and above their difficult behavior. There surely are patterns of behaviors, of which externalizing is only a part, that parents respond to in boys. These gender-linked associations are likely to be complex and not easily isolated in our somewhat global measurement system. They do warrant closer attention to see if we can identify what child characteristics, in addition to externalizing behavior, have a problematic impact on the parents of young boys.

Implications

Clearly, an understanding of the effects that families and children have on each other over time is crucial to the determination of the strategies that we need to employ in helping families and difficult children adapt to each other. That there are likely biologically based contributors to the temperament of boys points to the need to cast a wide net in search of these factors, including biologically based temperament constructs as well as those pertaining to parents as individuals, to dyadic family functioning, and to whole family functioning.

It is also apparent that even mild congenital inputs have noticeable consequences in normal families. The data we report here deal with development well within the normal range of families. It is also likely that there are other aspects of child behavior that influence, and are influenced by, families that may be predicted by either congenital MPAs or temperament in both boys and girls. One likely candidate is shy, withdrawn, internalizing behavior that has been found repeatedly in analyses of children's problem behavior. Although it may be that the impact of low-level behavior is muted in nonclinical families, analyses of the sort presented in this chapter assist us in discovering the family context supporting the maintenance or change of these behaviors as well. We do need this information to plan when and where our best intervention efforts should be directed. We need to know when children are the major influence on disharmonious family functioning and when individual parents are the sources of that influence, or when relationships within families are the major influences on family change and stability.

ACKNOWLEDGMENT

Authorship is equally shared. We thank D. Reiss for his comments on earlier drafts of this chapter. This research was supported by grant MH39899 from the National Institute of Mental Health.

REFERENCES

Barrett-Lennard, G. (1978). The relationship inventory. *JSAS Catalog of Selected Documents in Psychology, 8,* (Ms. No. 1732).

Baumrind, D. (1971). Current patterns of parental authority. *Developmental Psychology Monographs, 4,* (1, part 2).

Belsky, J. (1984). The determinants of parenting: A process approach. *Child Development, 55,* 83–96.

Belsky, J., & Pensky, E. (1988). Developmental history, personality, and family relationships: Toward an emergent family system. In R. A. Hinde & J. Stevenson-Hinde (Eds.), *Relationships within families: Mutual influences* (pp. 193-217). Oxford, England: Clarendon Press.

Belsky, J., Rovine, M., & Fish, M. (1989). The developing family system. In M. R. Gunnar & E. Thelen (Eds.), *Systems and development: The Minnesota Symposium on Child Psychology* (Vol. 22, pp. 119–166). Hillsdale, NJ: Lawrence Erlbaum Associates.

Block, J. (1978). *The Q-sort method in personality assessment and psychiatric research.* Palo Alto, CA: Consulting Psychologists Press.

Block, J. (1980). *The Child-Rearing Practices Report (CRPR): A set of Q items for the description of parental socialization attitudes and values.* Berkeley, CA: Institute of Human Development, University of California.

Buss, D. (1981). Predicting parent–child interactions from children's activity level. *Developmental Psychology, 17,* 59–65.

Caspi, A., & Elder, G. H., Jr. (1988). Emergent family patterns: The intergenerational construction of problem behaviour and relationships. In R. A. Hinde & J. Stevenson-Hinde (Eds.), *Relationships within families: Mutual influences* (pp. 218–240). Oxford: Clarendon Press.

Cyr, J. J., McKenna-Foley, J. M., & Peacock, E. (1985). Factor structure of the SCL-90-R: Is there one? *Journal of Personality Assessment, 49,* 571–578.

Deal, J. E., Halverson, C. F., & Wampler, K. S. (1989). Parental agreement on child-rearing orientations: Relations to parental, marital, family, and child characteristics. *Child Development, 60,* 1025–1034.

Derogatis, L. Q. (1977). *The SCL-90 Manual I: Scoring, administration and procedures for the SCL-90.* Baltimore, MD: Johns Hopkins University.

Elder, G. H., Jr., Caspi, A., & Downey, G. (1986). Problem behavior and family relationships: Life course and intergenerational themes. In A. B. Sorensen, F. E. Weinert, & L. R. Sherrod (Eds.), *Human development and the life course: Multidisciplinary perspectives* (pp. 293–340). Hillsdale, NJ: Lawrence Erlbaum Associates.

Falk, R. F., & Miller, N. B. (1991). A soft models approach to transitions. In P. A. Cowen & E. M. Hetherington (Eds.), *Family transitions* (pp. 273–301). Hillsdale, NJ: Lawrence Erlbaum Associates.

Goldfarb, W., & Botstein, A. (1964). *Physical stigmata in schizophrenic children.* Unpublished manuscript, Henry Ittelson Center for Child Research, Brooklyn, NY.

Gunnar, M. R., & Thelen, E. (Eds.). (1989). *Systems and development: The Minnesota Symposia on Child Psychology* (Vol. 22). Hillsdale, NJ: Lawrence Erlbaum Associates.

Halverson, C. F. (1988). Remembering your parents: Reflections on the retrospective method. *Journal of Personality, 56,* 435–444.

Halverson, C. F. (1992). *Minor physical anomalies and behavior: A review.* Unpublished manuscript, University of Georgia, Athens.

Halverson, C. F., Victor, J. B., & Deal, J. E. (1990, March). *Structure and stability of behavior problems in normal young children.* Paper presented at Conference on Human Development, Richmond, VA.

Halverson, C. F., & Wampler, K. S. (in press). Family influences on personality development. In S. Briggs, R. Hogan, & W. Jones (Eds.), *Handbook of personality psychology.* San Diego: Academic Press.

Hetherington, E. M., Stanley-Hagan, M., & Anderson, E. R. (1989). Marital transitions: A child's perspective. *American Psychologist, 44,* 303–312.

Hinde, R. A., & Stevenson-Hinde, J. (Eds.). (1988). *Relationships within families: Mutual influences.* Oxford, England: Clarendon Press.

Lahey, B. B., Hartdagen, S. E., Frick, P. J., McBurnett, K., Connor, R., & Hynd, G. W. (1988). Conduct disorder: Parsing the confounded relation to parental divorce and antisocial personality. *Journal of Abnormal Psychology, 97,* 334–337.

Lambert, N. M. (1988). Adolescent outcomes for hyperactive children. *American Psychologist, 43,* 786–799.

Lee, C., & Bates, J. (1985). Mother-child interaction at age two years and perceived difficult temperament. *Child Development, 56,* 1314–1325.

Liker, J. K., & Elder, G. H., Jr. (1983). Economic hardship and marital relations in the 1930s. *American Sociological Review, 48,* 343–359.

Loevinger, J. (1985). Revision of the sentence completion test for ego development. *Journal of Personality and Social Psychology, 48,* 420–427.

Lohmoeller, J. B. (1984). *LVLPS 1.6 Program Manual: Latent variable path analysis with partial least-squares estimation.* Cologne: Universitaet zu Koehn, Zentralarchiv fuer Empirische Sozialforschung.

Lohmoeller, J. B. (1989). *Latent variable path modeling with partial least squares.* New York: Springer-Verlag.

Martin, B. (1987). Developmental perspectives on family theory and psychopathology. In T. Jacob (Ed.), *Family interaction and psychopathology: Theory, methods and findings* (pp. 162–202). New York: Plenum Press.

Martin, R. P. (1988). *The Temperament Assessment Battery for Children.* Brandon: Clinical Psychology Publishing.

Masten, A. S., Garmezy, N., Tellegen, A., Pellegrini, D. S., Larkin, K., & Larsen, A. (1988). Competence and stress in school children: The moderating effects of individual and family qualities. *Journal of Child Psychology and Psychiatry, 29,* 745–764.

Matheny, A. P. (1986). Stability and change of infant temperament: Contributions from the infant, mother, and family environment. In G. Kohnstamm (Ed.), *Temperament discussed* (pp. 81–87). Berwyn, PA: Swets North America.

McCrae, R., & Costa, P. (1984). *Emerging lives, enduring disposition: Personality in adulthood.* Boston: Little, Brown.

Moos, R. H., & Moos, B. S. (1986). *Family environment scale manual* (2nd ed.). Palo Alto, CA: Consulting Psychologists Press.

Olson, D. H., Sprenkel, D. H., & Russell, C. S. (1979). Circumplex model of marital and family systems I: Cohesion and adaptability dimensions, family types and clinical applications. *Family Process, 18,* 3–28.

Olson, D., McCubbin, H., Barnes, H., Larsen, A., Muxen, M., & Wilson, M. (1982). *Family inventories.* St. Paul, MN: Family Social Science.

Patterson, G. R. (1982). *A social learning approach to family intervention: III. Coercive family process.* Eugene, OR: Castalia.

Patterson, G. R., & Bank, L. (1989). Some amplifying mechanisms for pathologic processes in families. In M. R. Gunnar & E. Thelen (Eds.), *Systems and development: The Minnesota Symposia on Child Psychology* (Vol. 22, pp.

167–209). Hillsdale, NJ: Lawrence Erlbaum Associates.

Patterson, G. R., & Dishion, T. J. (1988). Multilevel family process models: Traits, interactions, and relationships. In R. A. Hinde & J. Stevenson-Hinde (Eds.), *Relationships within families: Mutual influences* (pp. 283–310). Oxford, England: Clarendon Press.

Paulhus D. L., & Martin, C. L. (1986). Predicting adult temperament from minor physical anomalies. *Journal of Personality and Social Psychology, 50,* 1235–1239.

Powers, S. I., Hauser, S. T., & Kilner, L. A. (1989). Adolescent mental health. *American Psychologist, 44,* 200–208.

Quay, H. C., & Peterson, D. R. (1979). *Behavior problem checklist for children 2 to 5.* Unpublished manuscript, University of Miami, Coral Gables, FL.

Radke-Yarrow, M., Richters, J., & Wilson, W. E. (1988). Child development in a network of relationships. In R. A. Hinde & J. Stevenson-Hinde (Eds.), *Relationships within families: Mutual influences* (pp. 48–67). Oxford, England: Clarendon Press.

Rutter, M. (1988). Functions and consequences of relationships: Some psychopathological considerations. In R. A. Hinde & J. Stevenson-Hinde (Eds.), *Relationships within families: Mutual influences* (pp. 332–353). Oxford, England: Clarendon Press.

Sameroff, A. J. (1989). Commentary: General systems and the regulation of development. In M. R. Gunnar & E. Thelen (Eds.), *Systems and development: The Minnesota Symposium on Child Psychology* (Vol. 22, pp. 219–235). Hillsdale, NJ: Lawrence Erlbaum Associates.

Sharpley, C., & Cross, D. (1982). A psychometric evaluation of the Spanier Dyadic Adjustment Scale. *Journal of Marriage and the Family, 44,* 739–742.

Spanier, G. B. (1976). Measuring dyadic adjustment. *Journal of Marriage and the Family, 38,* 15–28.

Susman, E. J., Trickett, P. K., Ionotti, R. J., Hollenbeck, B. E., & Zahn-Waxler, C. (1985). Child-rearing patterns in depressed, abusive and normal mothers. *American Journal of Orthopsychiatry, 55,* 237–251.

Tellegan, A. (1982). *A Manual of the Multidimensional Personality Questionnaire.* Minneapolis, MN: University of Minnesota Press.

Thomas, A., & Chess, S. (1977). *Temperament and development.* New York: Brunner-Mazel.

Victor, J. B., Halverson, C. F., & Montague, R. B. (1985). Relations between reflection-impulsivity and behavioral impulsivity in preschool children. *Developmental Psychology, 21,* 141–148.

Waldrop, M., Bell, R., & Goering, J. (1976). Minor physical anomalies and inhibited behavior in elementary school girls. *Journal of Child Psychology and Psychiatry, 17,* 113–122.

Waldrop, M., Bell, R., McLaughlin, B., & Halverson, C. (1978). Newborn minor physical anomalies predict short attention span, peer aggression and impulsivity at age 3. *Science, 199,* 563–564.

Waldrop, M., & Halverson, C. (1971). Minor physical anomalies and hyperactive behavior in young children. In J. Hellmuth (Ed.), *The exceptional infant* (Vol. 2, pp. 343–380). New York: Brunner/Mazel.

Waldrop, M. F., Halverson, C. F., & Shetterley, K. (1989). *Manual for assessing minor physical anomalies.* Unpublished manuscript, University of Georgia, Athens.

Waldrop, M. F., Pederson, F. A., & Bell, R. Q. (1968). Minor physical anomalies and behavior in preschool children. *Child Development, 39,* 391–400.

Wampler, K. S., & Halverson, C. F., Jr. (1990). The Georgia Marriage Q-Sort: An observational measure of marital functioning. *American Journal of Family Therapy, 18,* 156–178.

Wampler, K. S. & Halverson, C. F. (in press). Quantitative measurement in family research. In P. G. Boss, W. Doherty, R. Larossa, W. Schumm & S. Steinmetz (Eds.), *Sourcebook of family theories and methods: A contextual approach.* New York: The Free Press.

Wampler, K. S., Halverson, C. F., Jr., Moore, J. J., & Walters, L. H. (1989). The Georgia Family Q-Sort: An observational measure of family functioning. *Family Process, 28,* 223–238.

Wampler, K. S., & Powell, G. (1982). The Barrett-Lennard Relationship Inventory as a measure of marital satisfaction. *Family Relations, 31,* 139–145.

Waters, E., Garber, J., Gornal, M., & Vaughn, B. (1983). Q-sort correlates of visual regard among preschool peers: Validation of a behavioral index of social competence. *Developmental Psychology, 19,* 550–560.

CHAPTER 5

Family Process and School Achievement: A Comparison of Children With and Without Communication Handicaps

Irving E. Sigel
Elizabeth T. Stinson
Jan Flaugher
Educational Testing Service

The research reported here is derived from an integration of the developmental concepts of Piaget (1962), Werner and Kaplan (1963), Polanyi (1958), and Kelly (1955), as well as from our own view that cognition emerges within a social matrix. The basic proposition of this research effort is that the family unit, however structured, provides the primal source of influence on the child's cognitive development as the only social unit wherein biogenetic and social factors merge. The family, in turn, is embedded in a larger, complex social network comprised of many significant individuals who provide an array of experiences that influence the child as the child influences others (Feiring & Lewis, 1987; Patterson, 1982).

DEVELOPMENTAL TRANSFORMATIONS

The developmental transformations that guide our work concern the changing nature of the child's ability to transform experience into some symbolic mode (e.g., knowing that an object in its three-dimensional form is equivalent to its representation in the form of a word, picture, or drawing). A child's knowledge of the concept of symbolic representation is acquired through social experiences and reflects an understanding of the rule that an event of any kind can be transformed into some other form. We view this cognitive shift as evidence of the child's understanding of the representational rule, a concept basic to intellectual development. Imagine what it would be like if we did not understand the idea that one instance can stand for or represent another? For example, knowing that a number can represent a value is the critical requisite for understanding mathematics.

Representational competence is an overarching term that encompasses three aspects: reconstruction of the past, anticipation or planning, and transcending the ongoing present. These competencies are hypothesized as requisites for cognitive functioning and evolve in the social context of the family. The family environment can influence the course of development of these competencies that are biologically based but socially triggered.

Socialization of Cognition. If cognition evolves in the course of social engagement, and the term *social* is broadly conceived to include the object and nonobject environment, then the argument follows that cognition is a product of environment and individual interaction, a bidirectional process that includes social exchanges among individuals.

This chapter examines the role the family plays as a provider of a social environment influencing cognitive development. Our particular focus is on parents' teaching behaviors that are expressions of their beliefs as to how children come to achieve representational competence. Such competence provides the foundation for subsequent academic proficiency in reading and mathematics.

As socialization agents, parents guide children's engagements with the environment by providing opportunities, materials, and support for the child's explorations. Alternately, children can also engage the world on their own, exploring through play and other types of social interactions with peers, with pets, with a host of stimuli. Overall, the child is experiencing an environmental milieu from which his or her sense of social reality is constructed.

Parents' Behaviors. As the primary caregivers, parents provide both physical and psychological resources as they engage with their children, and it is within this context that parenting actions influence the children's developmental course. We know, for example, that verbal social exchanges take myriad forms (e.g., sharing information, asking for clarification, making decisions, exchanging stories, asking questions, etc.).

Generally speaking, verbal exchanges between parents and children may be categorized into two broad areas: discipline/management events, and teaching situations in which the parent instructs, responds to the child's questions, or perhaps, reads stories. In either instance, the parent functions as a socializer. In the former case, parents deal with what to do and not do, what's right and what's wrong, as they help the child learn what the social requirements are for functioning in that particular environment. In the latter case, the parents' aim is to help the child learn about the world he or she lives in, the world of objects, of people, and of events.

Parents' Beliefs. Parents' actions are assumed to be related to their worldview, a view of self as a person and as a parent. Ultimately, this worldview intersects with the parents' knowledge of children, in general, and their own child in particular. These parental beliefs about the nature of children and how they learn have been found to relate significantly to children's cognitive and social development (Sigel, 1985). Moreover, children's own perceptions of their intellectual and social abilities have been shown to correspond to parents' beliefs about them (Parsons, Adler, & Kaczala, 1982; Phillips, 1987), suggesting the systemic nature of the familial cognitive set.[1]

In summary, we acknowledge that parents function on at least two levels: the action level (what is done) and the covert level (what is believed). Because actions do not emerge *de novo* but as expressions of a parental belief system, actions and beliefs are inextricably linked.

LINKAGES BETWEEN BELIEFS AND BEHAVIOR

Beliefs guide actions and determine the choice of events to which one reacts (Sigel, 1986). Moreover, beliefs are tied to actions in some context, that is, "apparent inconsistencies in manifestations of belief are reconciled when we acknowledge the extent to which situation and belief are tied to each other" (Schiebe, 1970, p. 35). To predict, then, to the situation, it is necessary to know the individual's beliefs in conjunction with contextual factors. Based on this perspective, we opted to explore parental beliefs in four knowledge domains within which parent–child interactions typically occur: physical, social, moral, and intrapersonal (emotions). The parental behaviors that are of interest here are those that parents employ as instructional strategies. This class of teaching behaviors has been categorized as distancing strategies (Sigel & Cocking, 1977).

[1]Additional theoretical and empirical analyses of family beliefs may be found in chapter 9.

Distancing Theory

The term *distancing* is used as a metaphorical construct denoting psychological separation of the person from the immediate, ongoing present. The distancing metaphor suggests that individuals can cognitively project themselves into the past or into the future, transcending the immediate present. This process of distancing is conceptualized as critical in the development of representational thinking because it serves to activate the child's cognitive processes in the direction of various representational schema (Sigel, 1982).

Distancing behaviors usually have a built-in demand quality, a demand to respond. Most typically, they are in the form of a question that may be direct (e.g., "Why do you think the spoon didn't float?") or indirect (e.g., "Tell me why the spoon didn't float"). They can vary in level from high to low; from abstract to concrete. High-level distancing strategies are typically open-ended and place cognitive demands on the child to infer causality, draw inferences, and generate alternatives. Low-level distancing strategies are closed-ended type questions that ask the child to name or describe objects and events.

Distancing strategies are assumed to generate discrepancies between what is experienced and what is expected, creating disequilibrium in the listener. Disequilibrium promotes tension that by its discomforting nature demands resolution. It is the resolution of the discrepancy that impels the individual to reconsider prior knowledge, reexamine assumptions or try out alternatives, and in so doing, restructure the ongoing cognitive schema.

This restructuring process involves representational thinking and presumably transforms the response. It is the parent's distancing strategy that sets the chain of events in motion. For example, if the child is working on a problem and the parent becomes aware that the child is having difficulty, the parent may ask the child to generate some alternative strategies (e.g., "How else might you tackle this task?"). Such a request, especially phrased as an inquiry, creates disequilibrium and the child now is in a position to refocus or restructure her or his approach.

The argument follows that such experiences for the child build his or her awareness of alternatives and enhance representational thinking. The test for representational capability is in the child's competence to engage in academic areas requiring representational thought, for example, reading, mathematics, or in more global activities that transcend the ongoing present (e.g., reconstruction of past events, anticipation, or prediction of future events). The growing competence of the child to formulate increasingly more complex responses to such cognitive demands presumably provides feedback to the parents who may then alter beliefs and behaviors, accordingly. Due to their interactive character, distancing strategies may thus appropriately be viewed as social events.

THE HISTORY OF THE PROJECT

Given our premise that the child's cognitive development and comprehension of the representational rule evolve in the family context, our 10-year research program has asked the following questions: (a) What parent variables in this context impinge on and influence the course of representational competence? (b) What are the determinants of such parent belief/behaviors? and (c) What effect do these parent actions have on the child's use of the representational rule, generally, and on school achievement, specifically?

The initial set of studies examined these questions in the context of the family with particular focus on parents as teachers of their children. In our initial study we discovered that birth order and spacing are familial structural factors that result in differential parent interactions and consequences for children. For example, one-child families were found to differ from three-child families in terms of parents' beliefs about how children learn, that is, the former favored adult instruction and guidance more than the latter who expressed more beliefs in the self-regulatory capabilities of the child (Sigel, McGillicuddy-DeLisi, & Johnson, 1980). Spacing of children had little effect on parenting beliefs, but level of education was highly related to how parents thought children learn.

Families of Communication Handicapped Children

The next phase of our efforts focused on examining parent behaviors with atypical populations. We elected to work with families in which the target child was communication handicapped. The rationale for such a choice was that parents' teach their children predominantly through verbal strategies. Due to their language impairment, however, communication handicapped (CH) children might be limited in their opportunities to interact verbally within the family environment. Paradoxically, this is the group that might be most likely to benefit cognitively and socially from distancing experiences. Comparing children with a diagnosed language impairment with nonhandicapped children would thus provide a natural experiment, enabling us to evaluate the effects of parent-teaching techniques. Moreover, CH children comprise a unique group in that deficient language development is identifiable (and potentially remediable) earlier than other learning disabilities. Language disorders are also among the more common, albeit most varied developmental abnormalities, encompassing a wide range of expressive and/or receptive linguistic problems. The prevalence of communication disorders among students classified as having special educational needs has been estimated at 28% (Case & Leavitt, 1986) to 90.5% of the learning disabled (LD) population as a whole (Gibbs & Cooper, 1989). Moreover, when educators were asked their views regarding the impact of communication disorders on academic performance, 66% noted their adverse effects on achievement (Bennett & Runyan, 1982).

The Nature of the Sample

For this next phase of our ongoing research effort, 240 families were recruited from the Princeton, New Jersey area through schools, speech clinics, and child study teams. Of this number, 120 had a CH child between the ages of 3½ and 7½ and 120 were control families matched on age, gender, and birth order of target child and family structural variables such as parent education, income, and occupational status. Children included in the CH category were those who demonstrated various degrees of developmental language disorders with no evidence of nonlinguistic functioning deficits or auditory impairment. Intellectual functioning of all children was determined to be within normal limits.[2]

What We Found at Time 1

Using observational data derived from videotaped interactions of parents and children in two contextually varied tasks (e.g., storytelling and paper-folding), we found that parent's low-level distancing strategies that were closed-ended and didactic, offering the child few options or alternatives, tended to relate negatively to children's cognitive functioning, particularly reconstructive memory. Conversely, parents' use of high-level distancing strategies that require the child to infer, compare, or abstract, were positively associated with children's memory for sentences and anticipatory imagery on a Piagetian task (Sigel, McGillicuddy-DeLisi, Flaugher, & Rock, 1983).

We were interested to find that obtained relationships between

[2]Screening procedures included the WWPSI, the PPVT, Ravens colored Progressive Matrices, and the Creighton Vocabulary test.

parental teaching strategies and child outcomes were clearly dependent on the task involved. Even more intriguing was the related finding that the child's competence on the paper-folding task varied with the gender of the parent working with her or him, indicating that mothers' and fathers' teaching strategies differentially influence children's spontaneous problem-solving capabilities (Sigel et al., 1983).

Current Study. At present we are analyzing data obtained on a subsample of families who participated 5 years earlier. We are specifically interested in the school performance of the CH children given the literature on the academic consequences of language impairment (McKinney, 1989). Seventy-eight, two-parent middle-class families (38 with a communication handicapped child and 40 nonhandicapped [NCH] controls) returned to Educational Testing Service (ETS) to participate in our follow-up study. As before, CH and NCH target children in the sample were matched on age, grade, gender of child and family socioeconomic status (SES).

Data Collection

Parent Interview. As in Time 1, we used a structured parent interview comprised of 12 vignettes covering everyday situations parents typically encounter with children in this age group. Vignettes were designed to tap similar content areas to those presented at Time 1, although situations were altered to make them more age-appropriate. Based on our earlier findings regarding the salience of context in parent–child interactions, we purposefully categorized interview items into knowledge domains to see if mothers' and fathers' self-reported beliefs and behaviors varied accordingly.

The following is an example of a vignette from the Moral/Social domain:

"You see (Child's name) copying someone else's homework and you establish that he or she plans to turn it in tomorrow as her or his own. You want to help (child) learn not to cheat."

First, to elicit parental teaching strategies, the parent is asked what he or she would do to help the child learn not to cheat. Then, to tap parental beliefs, the parent is asked how he or she thinks the reported strategy will help the child learn not to cheat. Coding definitions for parents' reported strategies and beliefs appear at the end of this chapter in Appendices A and B, respectively. Mothers and fathers were interviewed separately, and responses were coded simultaneously by the interviewer.

We had originally designed our 12 interview situations to reflect issues pertinent to four different learning domains. Confirmatory factor analyses, however, revealed the presence of three distinct content areas tapping how the child learns about the physical world, about emotions, and about moral/social behavior. Subsequently, these three domains were labeled *Physical Knowledge, Intrapersonal,* and *Moral/Social.*

Coding reliability was assessed by interrater agreement between two independent coders working from an audiotape of the interview. Mean interrater agreement across 20% of the 158 interviews (40 NCH mother–father pairs, 38 CH mother–father pairs) was 94%.

Child Measures

While parents were interviewed, children were administered a series of subtests from the Woodcock–Johnson Psycho-Educational Battery (WJPB) to measure their broad cognitive ability and achievement in mathematics and reading. As a standardized assessment instrument, the WJPB has been widely commended for its technical excellence and exceptional reliability and concurrent validity (Kaufman, 1985).

WHAT DID WE FIND AT TIME 2?

This section is presented in the following sequence: hypotheses of the current investigation are reviewed, findings are presented and discussed, and implications for applicability of results are considered.

On the basis of our theoretical premises and findings from earlier studies with younger children, we expected to find positive linkages between parents' reported use of distancing strategies and their beliefs that children learn through active participation in the learning process. Conversely, it was expected that parents who favored authoritative teaching strategies such as telling the child what to do, with or without explanations, would most likely believe that children learn best through direct instruction. It was further hypothesized that beliefs about how children acquire knowledge would differ among parents of CH and NCH children because of the differential nature of their child-rearing experiences. We know from the literature that parents of language-impaired children tend to hold different views of their teaching and socialization roles and manage their children differently than parents of nonhandicapped children (Freeman, 1971; Laskey & Klopp, 1982; Sigel et al., 1983). Parents of CH children, for example, are significantly more likely to believe their children acquire knowledge passively (e.g., through instruction and negative feedback) as opposed to actively (e.g., through their own experimentation and intellectual exploration) (Sigel et al., 1983). Moreover, studies of maternal communication patterns, for instance, have found that mothers tend to comment, expand upon, or otherwise acknowledge what their language disordered children say significantly less than controls (Schodorf & Edwards, 1983).

According to distancing theory, representational thinking is stimulated by the degree of cognitive demand parents place on their children to reason, reflect, and generate their own solutions. Presumably, these parental efforts encouraging the child's intrinsic capacity for self-directed as opposed to other-directed learning are guided by beliefs in cognitive processes. Academic subjects such as math and reading that require abstraction and transformation of information should thus be positively associated with beliefs mediated by strategies that further the development of representational thought.

Mindful of these expectations, we focus on the following findings: (a) the nature of parents' beliefs and their distribution across knowledge domains, (b) comparisons of CH and NCH parents' self-reported beliefs relative to their own child-rearing strategies, (c) relationships between parents' beliefs and children's math and reading achievement for the total group and separately for girls and boys, (d) connections between parents' self-reported beliefs and their teaching behaviors, and (e) within-group comparisons of achievement among handicapped children who are still receiving therapy versus those who have been remediated.

The Nature of Parents' Beliefs

Based on prior investigations using a similar version of the structured Parent Interview (Sigel et al., 1983), we theorized that parents hold a variety of beliefs regarding how their children learn and become socialized. We also anticipated that the situational context of the parent–child interaction would be important to the types of beliefs expressed. Table 5.1 illustrates how these beliefs distribute themselves within each knowledge domain. From the table it is apparent that the beliefs parents report as rationales for their teaching efforts tend to vary among groups (CH and NCH) and within groups (mothers vs. fathers). For the most part, however, parents in all groups endorse beliefs in cognitive processes most frequently in the Intrapersonal and Moral/Social domains but not in the Physical Knowledge domain where beliefs in direct instruction prevail. On the other hand, beliefs coded activity (e.g., learning by doing) are rarely alluded to outside of the physical

TABLE 5.1
Interview Belief Response Percentages by Domain

	Physical Knowledge								*Intrapersonal*								*Moral/Social*							
Beliefs	DI	EXS	ACC	CP	PF	NF	ME	ACT	DI	EXS	ACC	CP	PF	NF	ME	ACT	DI	EXS	ACC	CP	PF	NF	ME	ACT
	% of 114 possible responses								% of 114								% of 190							
CH Mothers N = 38	.45	.03	.01	.23	.06	.01	.08	.14	.24	.03	.01	.35 *	.32	.01	.04	.01	.23	.00	.00	.38 *	.04	.29	.07	.00
	% of 120 possible responses								% of 120								% of 200							
NCH Mothers N=40	.37 *	.02	.01	.34	.04	.00	.04	.18	.15	.04	.00	.50 *	.27	.00	.03	.01	.21	.00	.01	.51 *	.03	.20	.04	.01
	% of 114 possible responses								% of 114								% of 190							
CH Fathers N = 38	.56 *	.04	.00	.26	.05	.00	.01	.07	.19	.02	.01	.42 *	.29	.00	.05	.00	.30	.00	.02	.29	.04	.31 *	.02	.01
	% of 120 possible responses								% of 120								% of 200							
NCH Fathers N = 40	.48 *	.01	.00	.26	.09	.00	.04	.12	.19	.05	.00	.43 *	.29	.00	.03	.00	.19	.01	.00	.49 *	.03	.24	.04	.01

DI = Direct Instruction
EXS = Exposure
ACC = Accumulation

CP = Cognitive Processes
PF = Positive Feedback
NF = Negative Feedback

ME = Manipulation of Environment
ACT = Activity (learning by doing)

*Highest frequency percentages

knowledge sphere, whereas positive and negative feedback beliefs are most frequently expressed in relation to socialization concerns.

As anticipated, the content of the learning domain clearly has an impact on the types of beliefs elicited. However, we find that four major categories apparently account for 87% of all stated beliefs: cognitive processes, direct instruction, and positive and negative feedback. These beliefs encompass the primary learning perspectives of parents as reported in the interview and basically represent two dichotomous views of how individuals acquire knowledge (i.e., internally vs. externally). Of these two perspectives, the former reflects a freedom dimension (i.e., cognitive processes) where children are encouraged to think and solve problems through their own reasoning and initiative, whereas the latter reflects an authoritative dimension characterized by directives, reinforcement, and control by the parent or adult authorities (i.e., direct instruction, positive and negative feedback). Subsequent analyses were based on these four representative beliefs, while the remainder were dropped or incorporated into another category.[3]

Comparisons of CH and NCH Parents' Beliefs

To determine whether CH and NCH parents' beliefs differed significantly from each other, *t* tests were done on the mean proportions of responses of mothers and fathers within each domain. The results presented in Table 5.2 show that differences between the groups are more pronounced in the Moral/Social domain than in any other area. As a group, parents of NCH children expressed significantly more beliefs in their children's ability to think/reason on their own in the Moral/Social domain than CH parents did. CH fathers, in particular, were substantially ($p < .03$) more likely to think that children learn best by being told what to do than NCH fathers who were much more likely to encourage their children to draw their own conclusions ($p < .001$).

This tendency to view the child as capable of inferential thinking and autonomous problem solving was also significantly more characteristic of NCH mothers than their CH counterparts in the Intrapersonal domain ($p < .05$) of feelings, but less apparent in the realm of Physical Knowledge ($p < .09$).

In summary, it is apparent from Table 5.2 that parents are significantly more likely to express different views about how children learn if they are rearing a handicapped child. Specifically, mothers and fathers

[3]Beliefs in self-regulation and experimentation were included under the theoretically similar category of cognitive processes.

TABLE 5.2
Group (CH/NCH) Comparisons of Parents' of CH and NCH Children Interview Beliefs by Domain

	Parents of CH Group (N = 38)		*Parents of NCH Group (N = 40)*			
Belief	*M*	*(SD)*	*M*	*(SD)*	T	*p*
	Mothers					
Cognitive processes (PK)	.228	(.281)	.338	(.284)	1.71	.09
Cognitive processes (IP)	.351	(.337)	.500	(.311)	2.03	.05
Cognitive processes (M/S)	.379	(.242)	.509	(.282)	2.18	.03
Negative feedback (M/S)	.288	(.241)	.200	(.203)	1.75	.08
	Fathers					
Cognitive processes (M/S)	.295	(.230)	.489	(.285)	3.30	.001
Direct instruction (M/S)	.299	(.220)	.186	(.224)	2.23	.03

Domains: PK = Physical Knowledge
IP = Intrapersonal Knowledge
M/S = Moral/Social Knowledge

of CH children appear to perceive them as needing higher levels of direction and control than parents of NCH children, a finding that is consistent with our own data of 5 years ago as well as with the literature on families with problem children (Grolnick & Ryan, 1987; Mash, 1984).

Child Achievement in Relation to Parents' Beliefs and Teaching Strategies

Table 5.3 illustrates relationships between parents' self-reported beliefs and teaching strategies and CH and NCH children's math and reading achievement. To assess parents' overall inclination toward a particular belief orientation or teaching strategy, high-frequency responses were first summed across all situations and then divided by the total number of responses to derive mean proportions. These mean percentages of reported beliefs and teaching strategies were then correlated with the child's standardized achievement scores from the WJPB. As Table 5.3 demonstrates, different patterns of associations emerge for each group, suggesting that the handicap status of the child and the gender of parent each influence observed outcomes.

Turning first to the CH group, we find that fathers' preferences for particular teaching strategies, specifically distancing and negative reinforcement, are more highly associated with children's achievement than mothers' are. Additionally, fathers' orientation toward beliefs in cogni-

TABLE 5.3
Pearson Correlations Between Interview Strategies, Beliefs, and Achievement

	Child Achievement			
	(CH Group)		*(NCH Group)*	
Parent Variables	*Math*	*Reading*	*Math*	*Reading*
Strategies (Mothers)				
Distancing	−.13	−.15	.05	−.28†
Rational Authoritative	−.06	−.00	−.12	.13
Direct Authoritative	.23	.15	.07	.18
Negative Reinforcement	−.03	−.07	−.01	.06
Positive Reinforcement	−.19	−.10	.16	.08
Beliefs (Mothers)				
Cognitive Processes	−.13	−.17	.03	−.12
Direct Instruction	.17	.20	−.09	.30†
Negative Feedback	−.08	−.10	.03	−.01
Positive Feedback	−.01	.00	.04	−.19
Strategies (Fathers)				
Distancing	.22	.41*	−.16	.11
Rational Authoritative	.15	.23	.03	−.21
Direct Authoritative	.06	−.10	.17	.08
Negative Reinforcement	−.26	−.33*	.26	.08
Positive Reinforcement	−.20	−.05	−.07	−.09
Beliefs (Fathers)				
Cognitive Processes	.23	.39*	−.01	.10
Direct Instruction	−.03	−.01	−.17	−.34*
Negative Feedback	−.22	−.25	.22	.08
Positive Feedback	−.16	−.30†	−.10	.01

*$p < .05$. †$p < .10$.

tive processes are positively related to reading achievement among communication handicapped children ($r = .39$, $p < .05$). This finding is noteworthy because it suggests the positive link between a father's commitment to helping the handicapped child think through everyday problems and the child' performance in an area requiring representational skills. Mathematics achievement among CH children, however, was not significantly associated with parents' overall belief orientation or their self-reported actions.

Conversely, in the NCH group, we find that fathers' preferred teaching strategies appear unrelated to child achievement, whereas mothers' reported use of distancing is marginally ($p < .10$) but negatively related to reading. Table 5.3 also reveals oppositional relationships between children's reading achievement and mothers' and fathers' endorsement of direct instruction beliefs. The more fathers believe in telling children what to do and how to do it, the lower their children's reading achievement scores are ($r = -.34$, $p < .05$). Mothers' same belief statements, however, do not reach statistical significance for reading achievement ($r = .30$, $p < .10$). It may well be that gender differential patterns of parental behaviors relative to the same beliefs account for these oppositional correlations, or the nonhandicapped child may just respond more positively to directiveness from mothers than from fathers.

For the most part, however, these global bivariate results were somewhat perplexing in terms of their magnitude and limited findings of significance. Thus, further analyses were undertaken to address the following questions: (a) Do the behavioral mechanisms by which beliefs are transmitted to the child vary according to domain and parent gender?; (b) Are the relationships between parents' beliefs and children's achievement what we would expect given the literature on the differential socialization of boys and girls (Antill, 1987; Block, 1983)?; (c) Does CH children's therapy status (e.g., still in therapy vs. remediated) affect achievement outcomes?

Belief–Behavior Response Patterns

Based on inspection of frequency data in which parents' beliefs were paired with their reported behaviors (teaching strategies) it became clear that there is considerable variability in the behavioral expression of those beliefs. Tables 5.4 and 5.5 illustrate belief–behavior response patterns of parents in the CH group where it can be seen that the same beliefs activate different teaching strategies depending on parent gender and knowledge domain. Parents apparently hold a few core beliefs that guide their interactions with children, but the operationalization of those beliefs is complex and highly variable.

Parental Beliefs in Relation to Girls' and Boys' Achievement. Correlational findings presented in Tables 5.6 and 5.7 show relationships between parents' core beliefs within each domain and child performance on the WJPB for the total sample as well as for boys and girls. Consistent with earlier results, we find different patterns of associations for the CH and NCH groups, as well as mothers and fathers. Moreover, when the sample is divided by gender, correlations do indicate that parents' beliefs are differentially associated with girls' and boys' achievement. In Table 5.6, for example, correlations of parents' beliefs and CH children's achievement are largely nonsignificant until child gender is taken into account. Then, significant linkages emerge that were previously obscured (see Table 5.6). Paternal beliefs that are significantly related to girls' achievement have little or no relation to boy's achievement.

When we look at the correlational findings in the NCH group,

TABLE 5.4
Interview Belief to Behavior Response Patterns

Mothers of CH Children

Domain	Belief	Strategies	Belief	Strategies	Belief	Strategies
Physical Knowledge	CP (23%)	DS 73%; DA 15%; Other 12%	DI (45%)	DA 37%; RA 33%; JP 14%; Other 16%	ACT (14%)	DA 44%; JP 38%; Other 18%
Intrapersonal	CP (34%)	DS 64%; PR 21%; Other 15%	DI (24%)	DA 67%; RA 19%; Other 14%	PF (32%)	PR 89%; Other 11%
Moral/Social	CP (37%)	DS 62%; NR 17%; RA 14%; Other 7%	DI (22 %)	RA 45%; DA 40%; Other 15%	NF (28%)	NR 81%; DS 8%; RA 8%; Other 3%

Beliefs	*Strategies*
CP = Cognitive Processes	DS = Distancing
DI = Direct Instruction	JP = Joint Participation
ACT = Activity	PR = Positive Reinforcement
PF = Positive Feedback	ME = Manipulation of Environment
NF = Negative Feedback	DA = Direct Authoritative
	RA = Rational Authoritative
	NR = Negative Reinforcement

similar gender differential patterns of relationships emerge but they are not the same as those observed for the CH group. As presented in Table 5.7, mothers' cognitive process beliefs in the Physical Knowledge domain relate positively to girls' overall achievement, whereas fathers' beliefs in direct instruction relate negatively to girls' reading achievement in two out of three domains. These results are largely consistent with our theoretical expectations. However, the positive correlation between paternal negative feedback beliefs and girls' achievement is surprising given the literature that generally reports negative linkages between parental control and intellectual outcomes (Deci & Ryan, 1987). There may be a cross-gender effect that alters how girls' perceive their fathers' limit-setting stance in moral/social areas. Perhaps preadolescent

TABLE 5.5
Interview Belief to Behavior Response Patterns

Fathers of CH Children

Physical Knowledge

Belief	Strategies
CP (26%)	DS 77%, JP 10%, Other 13%
DI (54%)	RA 48%, DA 29%, JP 21%, Other 2%
ACT (7%)	JP 63%, ME 13%, DA 13%, RA 10%

Intrapersonal

Belief	Strategies
CP (39%)	DS 39%, PR 30%, DA 18%, Other 13%
DI (19%)	DA 55%, PR 23%, RA 18%, Other 4%
PF (29%)	PR 85%, DA 9%, Other 6%

Moral/Social

Belief	Strategies
CP (29%)	DS 65%, RA 15%, ME 9%, Other 11%
DI (29 %)	RA 61%, DA 30%, Other 9%
NF (30%)	NR 79%, DA 7%, RA 5%, Other 8%

Beliefs
CP = Cognitive Processes
DI = Direct Instruction
ACT = Activity
PF = Positive Feedback
NF = Negative Feedback

Strategies
DS = Distancing
JP = Joint Participation
PR = Positive Reinforcement
ME = Manipulation of Environment
DA = Direct Authoritative
RA = Rational Authoritative
NR = Negative Reinforcement

females view paternal restrictiveness in the Moral/Social domain as indicative of caring and involvement in their welfare rather than punitiveness.

Finally, as was the case in the CH group, the achievement of nonhandicapped male children minimally related to parents' beliefs beyond chance. We can only speculate on the possible reasons why boys and girls show such different patterns of correlations between their achievement and parents' beliefs given the nature of our data. It may well be that girls are socialized to be more dependent on what others think of them than boys are. We know from the literature (Block, 1983;

TABLE 5.6
Correlations Between CH Parents' Interview Beliefs and Child Achievement

	Math Achievement			*Reading Achievement*		
Parental Beliefs	*Girls* (n = *13)*	*Boys* (n = *25)*	*Total* (n = *38)*	*Girls* (n = *13)*	*Boys* (n = *25)*	*Total* (n = *38)*
			Mothers (n = *38)*			
Cognitive processes (PK)	.07	.00	−.02	−.03	−.06	−.13
Direct instruction (PK)	−.16	−.08	−.10	−.02	−.01	−.00
Cognitive processes (IP)	.17	−.04	−.01	.14	−.01	−.00
Direct instruction (IP)	−.05	.25	.18	.16	.22	.18
Positive feedback (IP)	−.17	−.33†	−.26	−.34	−.23	−.21
Cognitive processes (M/S)	−.22	−.19	−.21	−.15	−.19	−.22
Direct instruction (M/S)	−.10	.31	.18	−.16	.28	−.17
Negative feedback (M/S)	.23	−.18	−.07	.17	−.23	−.13
			Fathers (n = *38)*			
Cognitive processes (PK)	−.07	.18	.13	.09	.24	.25
Direct instruction (PK)	.17	−.25	−.18	.15	−.20	−.21
Cognitive processes (IP)	−.17	.23	.14	.00	.24	.19
Direct instruction (IP)	.31	.00	.05	.24	.05	.06
Positive feedback (IP)	−.07	−.25	−.21	−.03	−.29	−.24
Cognitive processes (M/S)	.51†	.10	.17	−.64*	.29	.32*
Direct instruction (M/S)	.12	.01	.04	−.06	.07	.05
Negative feedback (M/S)	−.58*	−.08	−.21	−.54†	−.18	−.23

*$p < .05$. †$p < .10$.
PK = Physical Knowledge; IP = Intrapersonal; M/S = Moral/Social

Huston, 1983) for example, that sons are encouraged to be autonomous in their play and learning experiences, whereas daughters are rewarded for being empathetic and sensitive to others. Whatever the explanation, these gender differential correlations are clearly indicative of the need to study outcomes in terms of gender of child.

Within-CH Group Achievement Differences

Our CH group consisted of children diagnosed as communication handicapped when enrolled in Study 1. Noting greater variability in test performance among CH children in our sample, we decided to take a closer look at this group, particularly at their therapy status. Initially, all of these children were receiving some type of remedial help (i.e., speech or language therapy). However, from our updated family histories, we found that many of the children earlier diagnosed as language impaired were now mainstreamed or no longer in therapy of any kind. We subsequently divided the sample into two groups: those who were still

TABLE 5.7
Correlations Between NCH Parents' Interview Beliefs and Child Achievement

Parent Beliefs	*Math Achievement* Girls (n = 14)	Boys (n = 26)	Total (n = 40)	*Reading Achievement* Girls (n = 14)	Boys (n = 26)	Total (n = 40)
			Mothers (n = 40)			
Cognitive processes (PK)	.66**	.13	.27†	.59*	−.13	.04
Direct instruction (PK)	−.08	−.01	−.07	.10	.26	.21
Cognitive processes (IP)	.20	−.27	−.14	−.01	−.23	−.15
Direct instruction (IP)	.24	.13	.16	.39	.34†	.36*
Positive feedback (IP)	−.38	.14	−.02	−.26	−.00	−.09
Cognitive processes (M/S)	.12	−.06	−.01	.17	−.30	−.13
Direct instruction (M/S)	.10	−.26	−.18	.38	.03	.15
Negative feedback (M/S)	−.21	.07	.03	−.36	.15	−.01
			Fathers (n = 40)			
Cognitive processes (PK)	−.22	.11	.00	−.03	.09	.04
Direct instruction (PK)	−.10	−.32	−.28†	−.46†	−.17	−.23
Cognitive processes (IP)	.15	.36†	.29†	.06	.14	.11
Direct instruction (IP)	−.34	−.12	−.17	−.56*	−.01	−.21
Positive feedback (IP)	.13	−.32	−.19	.35	−.17	.01
Cognitive processes (M/S)	−.38	−.10	−.20	−.18	.17	.07
Direct instruction (M/S)	.02	.07	.05	−.22	−.25	−.24
Negative feedback (M/S)	.47†	.08	.22	.49†	−.10	.08

$^{*}p < .05$. $^{**}p < .01$. $^{\dagger}p < .10$.
PK = Physical Knowledge; IP = Intrapersonal; M/S = Moral/Social

receiving language therapy ($n = 16$) and those whose handicap condition had been remediated ($n = 22$).

One-way ANOVAs comparing the mean standard scores on the WJPB Mathematics and Reading achievement subtests of children in the therapy CH group, the remediated CH group, and the NCH group were computed. On both WJPB tests of achievement, differences between groups were highly significant ($p < .000$). Post hoc analyses using Scheffe's tests indicated differences at the .05 level between achievement means of the CH therapy group and both other groups, suggesting that the CH remediated group has largely attained achievement parity with their nonhandicapped classmates. These results would strongly suggest that CH children who remain in therapy beyond the third grade are at greater risk for academic failure than children whose therapy is of shorter duration.

FAMILY BELIEF ORIENTATIONS

It seemed worthwhile, at this point, to address whether the ideological environment of the home (i.e., parents' combined beliefs about how children learn) differed as a function of the therapy status of the child. We had anticipated finding differences in parents' ideas regarding the course of children's intellectual development in the presence of a learning disability. When one-way ANOVAs were performed on mean proportions of reported parental ($N = 78$) beliefs, we found significant between group differences ($p < .006$) on endorsement of cognitive processes and near significant ($p < .06$) differences on endorsement of direct instruction. Post hoc analyses indicated that the family belief systems of both CH subgroups (therapy and remediated) were more similar than not, and both groups were significantly different from families with nonhandicapped children. These results are provocative on several accounts. We would have expected the developmental beliefs of parents of the remediated group to more closely approximate those of the NCH group now that their children's achievement levels are equivalent. With a standardized mean of 115, both groups' academic performance falls in the high average range. Yet, parents of children in the remediated group tend to endorse higher levels of beliefs in direct instruction than either of the other two groups which is surprising given their children's demonstrated ability to transcend earlier learning deficits. Perhaps there is an enduring parental belief that these children are still communication handicapped despite academic evidence to the contrary. Such a view might be maintained because people tend to hold on to beliefs that are confirmed by their own experiences. An alternative explanation is that parents of children who were diagnosed as communication handicapped but now have remediated believe their directive orientation facilitated the process of "catching up" for their children. Conversely, it is conceivable that the directive orientation expressed by these parents characterizes their paramount beliefs about how children generally acquire knowledge, irrespective of handicap condition. This latter speculation, however, would need to be verified through data on parents' interactions with the CH child's siblings.

DISCUSSION

In the course of reviewing these results it became evident that three convergent phenomena were accounting for our findings: (a) mothers and fathers differ in the behavioral expression of their stated beliefs, (b) boys' and girls' achievement is differentially related to the parenting beliefs and strategies of their parents, and (c) CH children who have remediated deficits and those still in therapy differ significantly in achievement levels and family orientation.

On the first point, our data indicate that the teaching strategies parents say they employ as they act upon their beliefs tend to vary by learning domain and gender of parent (see Tables 5.4 and 5.5). Depending on the situational context, mothers and fathers report similar levels of core beliefs but differ in their manner of behaviorally expressing them. In essence, the patterns that emerge in Tables 5.4 and 5.5 reflect the complex reality of the socialization task faced by parents as each knowledge domain has its own demand quality. The process of helping a child learn to solve a mathematics problem, for instance, requires a different approach than that used to help the child cope with emotional distress or fear of failure. Moreover, fathers and mothers tend to take a different tack with their child even when their reported rationales (e.g., to get the child to think) are the same. Thus, although we find that parental beliefs and behaviors individually relate to academic outcomes of children, their relationship to each other tends to vary according to gender and domain. It is the case that the belief–behavior connection cannot be accurately described as a linear phenomenon.

Relative to the second point concerning the relation of parents' beliefs to their children's performance, our correlational results demonstrate how important it is to view parent–child relationships through a gender-sensitive lens. Our own bivariate analyses indicate that preadolescent girls' and boys' achievement in the CH sample is differentially related to how their mothers and fathers think they learn, lending credence to the argument that socialization experiences of female and male children (handicapped or not) are dissimilar (Block, 1983).

Although a large body of literature has begun to accumulate on the gender-differentiated socialization emphases of parents (see review by Block, 1983), few researchers of learning-impaired children have attended to gender differences, often grouping boys and girls together as if their common handicap status overrode all other concerns.

Admittedly, the well-documented disproportionate number of males (4:1) compared to females in the LD population has made gender-balanced sampling difficult. Nevertheless, there is evidence that girls in need of special education are, in fact, more intellectually handicapped than boys (Owen, 1980). Moreover, it appears that patterns of dysfunctional classroom behavior among LD adolescents differ for girls and boys, much as they do among NCH students (Ritter, 1989). Our data serve as further evidence of the methodological fallacy of minimizing or even ignoring gender differences when investigating performance levels among LD children. However, the specific family socialization processes set in motion by parental beliefs about handicapped sons and daughters remain elusive until we have the opportunity to observe parent and child interact in a variety of contexts.

We know from the literature, for example, that the socialization goals of mothers and fathers differ (e.g., fathers tend to be concerned with the child's acquisition of instrumental, cognitive skills, whereas mothers have been shown to assume responsibility for moral/social learning; Block, 1983). Yet, how do these differentiated socialization roles play themselves out when the child is handicapped? How are the traditional gender-typed socialization patterns, such as emphasizing independence for male but not female children, altered in the presence of a language handicap? These are just a few of the questions raised by our findings that point up the importance of incorporating both child gender and handicap status into future research efforts.

The third and final point concerns our within-CH group differences stemming from the therapy status of the child. The persistent problem of sample heterogeneity has often frustrated research efforts seeking to build a generalizable fund of knowledge about learning impairments (Speece, McKinney, & Appelbaum, 1985). Thus, our discovery of a more severely disabled subsample of children within our CH group is consistent with findings of other longitudinal studies focusing on characteristics of LD students. For many of these children, a learning disability represents a *chronic*, seriously handicapping condition that results in persistent academic underachievement if unremediated via special education in the primary grades (McKinney, 1989). Moreover, the disparity in achievement between children who require special educational services beyond third grade and their nonhandicapped peers has been reported to increase developmentally (McKinney, 1989). This pattern of achievement disparity was clearly evident within our subsamples of remediated and nonremediated CH children who were both diagnosed as language impaired 5 years ago.

SUMMARY AND CONCLUSIONS

Longitudinal research on children with learning disabilities is rare and subsequently there has been a lack of understanding of how individual differences in cognitive functioning develop and change through the elementary school years or how they contribute to academic failure (Kavale, 1988). Our efforts have sought to provide such longitudinal information on how school achievement of children with early-diagnosed communication handicaps relates to the learning orientations of their parents. Further, our intent has been to broaden the base of knowledge about CH children to include the family context as the primary socialization influence. In the course of our longitudinal effort, we interviewed the same families with and without a language-impaired child twice, at two developmentally sensitive points of transition (i.e., prior to school entry and at preadolescence). We found that as a group, parents of handicapped children were consistent in maintaining their perceptions of the child as a passive learner, whereas parents of nonhandicapped preadolescents were more likely to view their child as capable of drawing her or his own conclusions. Highly significant CH/NCH group differences in parental beliefs concerning how the child acquires moral/social concepts, indicate that parents of communication handicapped children are more likely to give advice and tell their children what to do in interpersonal situations than parents of the NCH group. Given the age of these children and the fact that over half (22) of the CH group are no longer in therapy of any kind, it is surprising that there does not appear to be a shift toward beliefs supporting the child's autonomy (e.g., encouraging the child's own decision-making capabilities) as has been observed among parents of nonhandicapped preadolescents (Power & Shanks, 1989). It may well be that despite academic remediation, parents continue to perceive their children as handicapped in social interactions and there socialization efforts may reflect this concern.

A diagnosis of communication disorder has been called "practically synonymous" with a learning disability (Gibbs & Cooper, 1989). Although the majority of the CH children in our sample overcame initial deficits in receptive and expressive language and "caught up" to the achievement levels of their peers, over one third did not. Why is this so? One explanation lies in the diffuse nature of diagnoses of speech and language disorders. There are a variety of syndromes involving impairment in communication that vary widely in terms of severity and duration (Speece, McKinney, & Appelbaum, 1985). However, it may well be that opportunities for effective intervention reside within the context of the family, specifically in terms of parent' learning orientations and how they act upon them.

Since the advent of P.L. 94–142 (Education for all Handicapped Children Act), parents have increasingly been included in the special education process and the salience of their roles as teachers and language facilitators recognized (Sigel et al., 1983). Our data indicate that intervention agents working with families of CH children would do well to check out parents' belief systems regarding the handicapped child's learning capabilities. Parents of CH children in our sample maintained their directive orientation despite changes in their children's age and handicap status. Yet, there is accumulating evidence in the LD field that impaired learners may require more rather than less encouragement to be independent thinkers and problem solvers (Martin & Henderson, 1989). Our own findings relative to distancing theory have clearly shown that parents whose socialization practices enhance the child's opportunities to think, anticipate, imagine, and actively engage in the learning experience positively influence their children's representational competence and academic achievement.

APPENDIX A: TYPES OF DISTANCING STRATEGIES CATEGORIZED BY LEVELS

High-Level Distancing	*Medium-Level Distancing*	*Low-Level Distancing*
evaluate consequence	sequence	label
evaluate competence	reproduce	produce information
evaluate affect	describe similarities	describe, define
evaluate effort and/or performance	describe differences	describe–interpretation
evaluate necessary and/or sufficient	infer similarities	demonstrate
infer cause-effect	infer differences	observe
infer affect	symmetrical classifying	
generalize	asymmetrical classifying	
transform	enumerating	
plan	synthesizing within classifying	
confirmation of a plan		
conclude		
propose alternatives		
resolve conflict		

APPENDIX B: DEFINITIONS OF PARENTAL BELIEFS

Parental Belief	*Definitions*
Accumulation (ACC)	the child learns through practice and additive experiences.
Activity (ACT)	the child learns by doing, through hands-on experience.
Cognitive Processes (CP)	the child learns through thinking and reasoning, considering options, drawing inferences and weighing of consequences.
Direct Instruction (DI)	the child learns from being told what to do, from explanations or advice.
Experimentation (EXM)	the child learns by trying out alternate solutions in problem solving, trial and error.
Exposure (EXP)	the child learns through imitation and modeling.
Manipulation of the environment (ME)	the child learns through adult structuring of activities and learning tasks.
Negative Feedback (NF)	the child learns through being punished or criticized for behavior.
Positive Feedback (PF)	the child learns through experiencing success, approval and support.
Self-Regulation (SR)	the child learns through figuring out own solutions.

ACKNOWLEDGMENT

Part of the research reported in this chapter was supported by the National Institute of Child Health and Human Development Grant No. R01-HD10686 to Educational Testing Service, National Institute of Mental Health Grant No. R01-MH32301 to Educational Testing Service, and Bureau of Education of the Handicapped Grant No. G007902000 to Educational Testing Service.

REFERENCES

Antill, J. (1987). Parents' beliefs and values about sex roles, sex differences, and sexuality. In P. Shaver & C. Hendrick (Eds.), *Sex and gender* (pp. 294–328). Beverly Hills, CA: Sage.

Bennett, C. W., & Runyan, C. M. (1982). Educators' perceptions of the effects of communication disorders upon educational performance. *Language, Speech and Hearing Services in Schools, 13,* 260–263.

Block, J. H. (1983). Differential premises arising from differential socialization of the sexes: Some conjectures. *Child Development, 54,* 1335–1354.

Case, E. J., & Leavitt, A. (1986). *Mental Health Project, P. L. 94–142: 1985–86 Evaluation Report.* Albuquerque, NM: Albuquerque Public Schools.

Deci, E. L., & Ryan, R. (1987). The support of autonomy and the control of behavior. *Journal of Personality and Social Psychology, 53,* 1024–1037.

Feiring, C., & Lewis, M. (1987). The child's social network: Sex differences from three to six years. *Sex Roles: A Journal of Research, 17,* 621–636.

Freeman, M. A. (1971). A comparative analysis of patterns of attitudes among mothers of children with learning disabilities, and mothers of children who are achieving normally. *Dissertation Abstracts International, 31,* 5125.

Gibbs, D. P., & Cooper, E. B. (1989). Prevalence of communication disorders in students with learning disabilities. *Journal of Learning Disabilities, 22,* 60–63.

Grolnick, W. S., & Ryan, R. M. (1987). Autonomy in children's learning: An experimental and individual difference investigation. *Journal of Personality and Social Psychology, 52,* 890–898.

Huston, A. (1983). Sex-typing. In P. H. Mussen (Series Ed.) & E. M. Hetherington (Vol. Ed.), *Handbook of child psychology: Vol. 4. Socialization, personality, and social development* (4th ed., pp. 387–467). New York: Wiley.

Kaufman, A. (1985). Review of the Woodcock-Johnson Psychoeducational Battery. In J. V. Mitchell (Ed.), *Ninth mental measurement yearbook* (Vol. 2, pp. 1762–1765). Lincoln, NE: University of Nebraska Press.

Kavale, K. A. (1988). The long-term consequences of learning disabilities. In M. C. Wang, H. J. Wallberg, & M. C. Reynolds (Eds.), *The handbook of special education: Research and practice* (pp. 303–344). Oxford, England: Pergamon Press.

Kelly, G. A. (1955). *The psychology of personal constructs* (2 vols.). New York: Norton.

Laskey, E., & Klopp, K. (1982). Parent-child interactions in normal and language disordered children. *Journal of Speech and Hearing Disorders, 47,* 7–18.
Martin, C. E., & Henderson, B. B. (1989). Adult support and the exploratory behavior of children with learning disabilities. *Journal of Learning Disabilities, 22,* 67–68.
Mash, E. J. (1984). Families with problem children. In A. Doyle, D. Gold, & D. S. Moskowitz (Eds.), *Children in families under stress. New Directions for Child Development* (No. 24). San Francisco: Jossey-Bass.
McKinney, J. D. (1989). Longitudinal research on the behavioral characteristics of children with learning disabilities. *Journal of Learning Disabilities, 22,* 141–150.
Owen, F. W. (1980). Dyslexia—Genetic aspects. In A. L. Benton & D. Pearl (Eds.), *Dyslexia: An appraisal of current knowledge.* New York: Oxford University Press.
Parsons, J. E., Adler, T. F., & Kaczala, C. M. (1982). Socialization of achievement attitudes and beliefs: Parental influences. *Child Development, 53,* 310–321.
Patterson, G. R. (1982). *Coercive family process.* Eugene, OR: Castalia Publishing.
Piaget, J. (1962). *Play, dreams and imitation in childhood.* New York: Norton.
Phillips, D. A. (1987). Socialization of perceived academic competence among highly competent children. *Child Development, 58,* 1308–1320.
Polanyi, M. (1958). *Personal knowledge.* Chicago: The University of Chicago Press.
Power, T. G., & Shanks, J. A. (1989). Parents as socializers: Maternal and paternal views. *Journal of Youth and Adolescence, 18,* 203–220.
Ritter, D. R. (1989). Social competence and problem behavior of adolescent girls with learning disabilities. *Journal of Learning Disabilities, 22,* 460–461.
Schiebe, K. S. (1970). *Beliefs and values.* New York: Holt, Rinehart & Winston.
Schodorf, J., & Edwards, H. (1983). Comparative analysis of parent-child interactions with language-disordered and linguistically normal children. *Journal of Communication Disorders, 16,* 71–83.
Sigel, I. E. (1982). The relationship between parental distancing strategies and the child's cognitive behavior. In L. M. Laosa & I. E. Sigel (Eds.), *Families as learning environments for children* (pp. 47–86). New York: Plenum.
Sigel, I. E. (1985). A conceptual analysis of beliefs. In I. E. Sigel (Ed.), *Parental belief systems: The psychological consequences for children* (pp. 347–371). Hillsdale, NJ: Lawrence Erlbaum Associates.
Sigel, I. E. (1986). Reflections on the belief-behavior connection: Lessons learned from a research program on parental belief systems and teaching strategies. In R. D. Ashmore & D. M. Brodzinsky (Eds.), *Thinking about the family: Views of parents and children* (pp. 35–65). Hillsdale, NJ: Lawrence Erlbaum Associates.
Sigel, I. E., & Cocking, R. R. (1977). Cognition and communication: A dialectic paradigm for development. In M. Lewis & L. A. Rosenblum (Eds.), *The origins of behavior: Vol. 5. Interaction, conversation, and the development of language* (pp. 207–226). New York: Wiley.
Sigel, I. E., McGillicuddy-DeLisi, A. V., Flaugher, J., & Rock, D. A. (1983). *Parents as teachers of their own learning disabled children* (ETS RR 83-21). Princeton, NJ: Educational Testing Service.

Sigel, I. E., McGillicuddy-DeLisi, A. V., & Johnson, J. E. (1980). *Parental distancing, beliefs and children's representational competence within the family context* (ETS RR 80-21). Princeton, NJ: Educational Testing Service.

Speece, D. L., McKinney, J. D., & Appelbaum, M. I. (1985). Classification and validation of behavioral subtypes of learning disabled children. *Journal of Educational Psychology, 77,* 67-77.

Werner, H., & Kaplan, B. (1963). *Symbol formation: An organismic developmental approach to language and the expression of thought.* New York: Wiley.

CHAPTER 6

Parent Child-Rearing Values, Parent Behaviors, and Child Achievement Among Communication Handicapped and Noncommunication Handicapped Children

Jane L. Pearson
Elizabeth T. Stinson
Irving E. Sigel
Educational Testing Service
Princeton, NJ

As part of a broader effort to better understand family processes among atypical children, this chapter addresses parents' behaviors and their underlying values that may be particularly salient to the communication handicapped (CH) child's academic achievement. Communication handicap reflects a number of communication problems, both receptive and productive, found in children within a normal range of intelligence and a normal range of hearing and vision. As outlined in the *DSM-III-R* (American Psychiatric Association [APA], 1987), developmental language and speech disorder diagnoses include a variety of communication problems: misarticulation, expressive language limitations, and receptive language impairments. Communication handicaps are also one of the most frequent childhood disorders, with prevalence estimates for children below age 8 being approximately 10% (APA, 1987).

Although a number of communication handicaps can be remedied by therapy, we consider developmental language or speech disorders as handicaps that could decrease the fulfillment of a "normal" role for an individual–in this case a child's experience in the family and his or her academic achievement in school. Indeed, there is considerable evidence that children with communication handicaps are at risk for failure in a school environment that requires adequate language competence (Baker & Cantwell, 1987; Silva, Williams, & McGee, 1987; Weiss & Duffy, 1979). Because the family is the child's primary socialization milieu, it is critical to understand how the family adapts its efforts in the presence of the disability, and how various adaptation attempts help or hinder academic achievement.

The family subsystems we focus on here include the father-child and mother-child dyads. Based on two earlier Educational Testing Service (ETS) studies of this population (McGillicuddy-DeLisi & Sigel, 1982; Sigel, McGillicuddy-DeLisi, Flaugher, & Rock, 1983), we anticipated that parents of school-aged CH children would continue to differ in their child-rearing goals and teaching strategies from parents of noncommunication handicapped (NCH) children. Moreover, parenting differences would also be expected from the extant literature describing altered family processes in the presence of childhood chronic illness. Of particular concern to us was the degree to which these differing family processes may affect child academic achievement outcomes.

Parent Behavior With Atypical Children

A number of researchers examining family interactions across a diversity of child disorders report that parents of atypical children exhibit high levels of control in their child-rearing behaviors. These include parents of children who have hearing impairments (Brinich, 1980; Henggeler, Watson, & Cooper, 1984), learning disabilities (Humphries & Bauman, 1980), mental retardation (Cummings, 1976; Schneider & Gearhart, 1988), spina bifida (Varni & Wallander, 1988), and diabetes (Anderson, Miller, Auslander, & Santiago, 1981; Minuchin, Rosman, & Baker, 1978). Although parents' protective and controlling stance may be viewed as an adaptive strategy when dealing with an atypical child, when carried to excess, these efforts may result in the child becoming overly dependent on the parents. This dependency can hinder rehabilitative efforts, particularly those aimed at enhancing the child's independent problem solving (Drotar, Crawford, & Bush, 1984).

Siblings and Peers of Atypical Children

Other socialization agents besides parents–namely peers and siblings–have also been found to adjust their interactions to the atypical child.

These younger socialization agents have also been reported to take on protective and controlling roles with handicapped children. From an earlier investigation of family interaction patterns drawn from the same sample from which this chapter is based (McGillicuddy-DeLisi, DeLisi, Flaugher, & Sigel, 1987), younger siblings of CH children were observed to assume leadership roles and initiate and control play interactions, as if the older CH child were less competent than the younger siblings. During play with peers, CH children have also been described as being subject to the commands and interruptions of nonhandicapped playmates (Siegel & Cunningham, 1984). Thus, it would appear that family and peer environments experienced by the CH child are often characterized by external direction and control.

Although the aforementioned studies suggest that increased control by family members of atypical children may decrease the handicapped child's ability to independently problem solve, there are few studies that have examined, systematically, the effect of parent beliefs or behaviors on atypical child achievement outcomes. Because of the dearth of information on variability in parent child-rearing values as the result of a child's disability, we review here briefly the literature on "normal" parent child-rearing values, behaviors, and child achievement outcomes, and how it may pertain to families with atypical children.

Parent Values and Behaviors

There is a growing literature that describes the linkages between parents' behaviors and the behaviors they value in their children (Goodnow, 1988; Miller, 1988; Sigel, 1985). A child-rearing value reflecting a directive parenting style is conformity (Kohn, 1977). As theorized by Kohn, parents who value conformity want their children to be neat, polite, and obediant to authority figures. Accordingly, they tend to enforce stricter discipline and impose greater constraints upon their children's behavior. In point of fact, Luster, Rhoades, and Hass (1989) recently demonstrated that mothers with higher conformity values are more likely to restrict their infants' actions and discourage self-initiated behaviors, compared to mothers with lower conformity scores. Whether a similar relationship exists between parents' conformity values and controlling behaviors when their children reach school age remains to be seen. We do know that parents of preschool-aged CH children believe their children learn best through directive teaching strategies and critical feedback (Sigel et al., 1983). However, the degree to which parents' conforming values or their attendant behaviors relate to academic performance among school-aged disabled children is not known.

Parent Conformity, Control, and Child Achievement

There is significant evidence indicating that parental conforming values and parental controlling behaviors, separately, are associated with child academic achievement. Schaefer and Edgerton (1985) examined the association between parent values and child achievement. On the language and math scales of the Test of Basic Experience, they found that school entry-aged children of mothers who valued conformity scored lower than children whose mothers valued self-direction (Kohn's conceptual opposite of conformity). Similarly, Hilliard and Roth (1969) described how parental attitudes of protectiveness and restrictiveness negatively affected child achievement and verbal development.

In regard to the effects of parenting behavior on child academic achievement among nonhandicapped children, Hess and his associates have consistently demonstrated the detrimental effect of maternal control on children's cognitive performance (Hess, Holloway, Dickson, & Price, 1984; Hess, Shipman, Brophy, & Baer, 1968). These same controlling behaviors, which frequently appear among parents of handicapped children, would presumably have similar negative effects on disabled children's achievement.

Indeed, McGillicuddy-DeLisi and Sigel (1982) have questioned whether parents' tendencies to attempt to "match" their teaching strategies to their CH child's assumed lower ability level may serve to maintain rather than ameliorate deficits. In contrast, maternal display of positive affect and support has been positively related to child achievement (Estrada, Arsenio, Hess, & Holloway, 1987). At present, no investigation has attempted to link parent conformity values, controlling or supportive behaviors, and child academic achievement concurrently within a handicapped population.

Hypotheses

Given that parents of CH children maintain that their children benefit from directiveness, that parents of children who are cognitively or physically disabled act more controlling, and that excessive parental controlling behaviors have negative effects on child academic achievement outcomes, we derived four related hypotheses. First, parents of CH children would value conformity more and behave in a more controlling manner than parents of NCH children. Second, parental conformity values and controlling behaviors would be positively correlated for both CH and NCH populations. Conversely, accepting or supporting behavior should be negatively related to conforming values. Third, child academic achievement would be negatively related to both parental conformity and controlling behaviors, and positively related to parental acceptance. Finally, the potential negative academic consequences of parental conforming values and controlling behaviors would be compounded for CH children given their existing performance deficits, and as such may be evidenced by stronger associations (e.g., greater variance accounted for in a multiple regression model).

METHODS

Sample

The 78 families described here were a subset of 240 families first reported by Sigel et al. (1983). Assessments of child academic achievement and parent values and behaviors were obtained at the follow-up phase of the original study. Our subsample included 38 CH children and their parents (CH families) and 40 NCH children and their parents (NCH families). Child communication handicap status was defined as a diagnosis or classification given to the child by a service agency (e.g., a public school child study team, speech and hearing clinic, or private speech therapist). Children were considered eligible for the study if they were not hearing impaired and their full-scale IQ fell within the normal range. This criteria for mild impairment ensured that the children would be capable of performing the tasks in the study and would allow for more stringent tests of our hypotheses.

NCH families were matched with the CH families as closely as possible on target child age, gender, number and spacing of children in the family, as well as parent education. The children's ages ranged from 8 to 14 at this follow-up period, with an average age of 11 years. The majority were boys, consisting of 25 CH and 26 NCH boys ($N = 51$), and 13 CH and 14 NCH girls ($N = 27$). This predominance of boys diagnosed with a language disorder is consistent with previous reports (Baker & Cantwell, 1987). Parents in all families had been married to each other for a minimum of 10 years. To control for the broader effects of socioeconomic status (SES) on family functioning, only families of primarily middle- to upper middle-class were sampled. Their occupational prestige on the Hollingshead index averaged 7; their average family income was $55,600; their average education level was postsecondary.

Parent Measures

Conforming Values. Conforming child-rearing values were measured with Schaefer and Edgerton's (1985) revision of Kohn's scale of parental values. This measure is comprised of 15 items–6 indicating conforming values, 6 reflecting self-direction values, and 3 designated as social values. The items are presented to the parent in three sets of five items where each scale is proportionately represented. The parent is instructed to rank items in each set from 1 (least valued) to 5 (most valued). This study focuses on the six items of the conformity scale indicating whether the parent values his or her child's: (a) keeping him or herself and his or her clothes clean, (b) being polite to adults, (c) obeying parents and teachers, (d) keeping things neat and in order, (e) being a good student, and (f) having good manners. The total possible score ranged from 6 to 30. Test–retest reliability over a 6-month period for the conformity scale has been reported to be $r = .79$ (Schaefer & Edgerton, 1985). Internal consistency as measured by Cronbach's alpha for the conformity scale in this sample was .63 for mothers, and .55 for fathers.

Parent Behaviors. The parent behaviors we examined were based on separate observations of mothers and fathers in a teaching task with the target child. Each parent was videotaped with the target child in a 10-minute session during which four different knots were displayed. The parent was asked to help the child learn how to tie each knot with ropes provided. In total, the child experienced two different series of knots that were similar in degree of difficulty (one with each parent). The videotapes were coded by two independent raters using the Parent–Child Social Interaction (PCSI) rating scales developed by Sigel, Flaugher, LaValva, and Dahn (1986). The PCSI is an instrument designed to capture the affective, cognitive, and social demand aspects of parent–child interactions. A 6-point scale is used to rate the frequency of occurrence and the intensity of each dimension, with 1 being the lowest frequency of occurrence/intensity, and 6 being the highest.

From the PCSI, two categories of rated behaviors were selected on the basis of their hypothesized relationship to conformity and achievement. "Control" represents a parental behavior congruent with conformity, and "accepts solution" represents a behavior incongruent with conformity and control. Control is defined as the degree to which the parent attempts to dominate and direct the task. It is evidenced by the use of many imperatives and directive statements and was generally associated with lack of attentiveness to the child's actions or statements. Accepts solution refers to the parents' agreement with the idea or solution offered by the child. Interrater agreement by two raters on 36 (23%) ratings (18 mother and father pairs) of both codes, after dichotomizing (low = 1, 2, 3 and high = 4, 5, 6), was 86% for accepts solution, and 69% for controlling behavior.

Child Measures

Reading and Math Achievement. Child academic achievement was indicated by standard scores obtained from the Woodcock-Johnson reading and mathematics clusters (Woodcock & Johnson, 1977). The reading cluster consists of three reading skills—letter-word identification, word attack, and passage comprehension. The mathematics cluster consists of two subtests—calculation and applied problems. The median reliabilities reported for each of these clusters are .96 for reading, and .85 for math (Woodcock, 1978). Concurrent validity of the reading cluster with other similar assessment instruments (Peabody Individual Achievement Test [PIAT], Wide Range Achievement Test [WRAT]) range from .75 to .92 (Woodcock, 1978). Concurrent validity of the math cluster with other measures of math achievement (Iowa Tests of Basic Skills—Total Mathematics, Keymath Diagnostic Arithmetic Test, math subtests of the PIAT and the WRAT) range from .46 to .85 (Hessler, 1984).

RESULTS

We first assessed the degree to which CH and NCH families differed by group levels of parent and child variables. The means and standard deviations of these variables for the two family groups are presented in Table 6.1. Contrary to our hypothesis, parents' conformity values did not differ between groups (CH vs. NCH mothers: t (76) = .27, n.s.; CH vs. NCH fathers t (76) = 1.01, n.s., one-tailed tests), nor did ratings of the parental behaviors, t (76) $\leq$ .98 for mothers' and fathers' controlling and accepts solution behaviors. As might be expected, comparisons of academic achievement among CH and NCH children revealed that CH children had lower achievement scores (see Table 6.1).

Consistent with previous reports pertaining to task-oriented behavior in father-child interactions (e.g., Mazur, 1980), fathers (mean

TABLE 6.1
Means and Standard Deviations for Parent and Child Variables for Families of CH and NCH Children

	CH N = 38		NCH N = 40	
Variables	*Mean*	*(SD)*	*Mean*	*(SD)*
Parent values				
Mother conformity	12.47	(3.1)	12.70	(4.2)
Father conformity	13.16	(3.4)	13.98	(3.7)
Parent behaviors				
Mother controlling	3.37	(1.2)	3.30	(1.5)
Father controlling	3.74	(1.3)	3.70	(1.4)
Mother accepts solution	4.50	(.98)	4.48	(1.0)
Father accepts solution	4.10	(1.1)	4.33	(.92)
Child achievement				
Reading	99.18	(18)	112.80	(13)
Math	105.21	(24)	115.23	(14)

Note: None of the parent variables significantly differed; differences in child achievement, for Reading: t (76) = 3.80, $p < .001$; for Math: t (76) = 2.22, $p < .03$.

score = 3.72) were more controlling than mothers (mean score = 3.33); t (77) = 2.05, $p < .05$. Differences in mean scores for accepting behavior indicated that mothers (mean score = 4.49) tended to exhibit this behavior more frequently than fathers (mean score = 4.22) as well; t (77) = 1.86, $p = .06$. Mothers and fathers did not differ on their conforming values.

We next examined the intercorrelations among parent values and behaviors and child achievement within child status groups, despite no significant differences between CH and NCH groups on the parent variables. This analysis strategy was employed because mean level comparisons do not necessarily reflect possible differences in correlations among variables. Examination of correlation patterns allowed us to further explore possible group differences in family processes, particularly involving parent variables hypothesized to relate to child academic achievement.[1] The correlations of interest are described in three sections: (a) parental values and behaviors, (b) parental values and child achievement, and (c) parental behaviors and child achievement.

[1]For these sample sizes, a significant difference between correlations, using Fisher's Z transformation (Glass & Stanley, 1970), would have to exceed the value of .43 at the $p < .05$ level, on the average. Given the exploratory nature of these analyses, however, we have proceeded to display all coefficients so that magnitude of relations can be explored.

Parental Values and Behaviors

Table 6.2 shows the zero-order correlations among parental values and behaviors. Mothers' conformity values were positively related to their controlling behaviors for both CH and NCH families as expected. However, this relationship did not appear for fathers. There were negative relationships between parents' conformity values and accepts solution behaviors as expected.

Parental Values and Child Achievement

In general, conformity was negatively related to child academic achievement as expected (see Table 6.2). However, the magnitude of the relationships varied by child handicap status. For both fathers and mothers, the relationships indicating higher conformity and lower achievement were greatest between NCH parents and their children. Thus, the expected relations among parental values and child achieve-

TABLE 6.2
Pearson Correlations Among Fathers' and Mothers' Values, Behaviors, and Child Achievement for Families of CH (N = 38) and NCH (N = 40) Children

	Mothers				
Fathers	*Conformity Values*	*Control Behavior*	*Accepts Sol. Behavior*	*Reading*	*Math*
Conformity					
CH		.27*	−.18	−.13	−.17
NCH		.39**	−.04	−.30*	−.39**
Control Beh.					
CH	.16		−.30*	−.09	−.25
NCH	.06		−.37**	−.09	−.40**
Accepts Sol.					
CH	−.23	−.22		.45**	.43**
NCH	−.07	−.52***		.30*	.23
Reading					
CH	−.08	.27*	−.05		
NCH	−.22	−.12	.27*		
Math					
CH	−.12	.14	−.02		
NCH	−.24	−.22	.12		

Note: Mothers' correlations are in the upper right triangle of the matrix, and fathers' correlations are in the lower left triangle. *$p < .05$. **$p < .01$. ***$p < .001$, one-tailed tests.

ment were less consistently found among CH families. This lack of relationship may have been in part due to less consistency in the conformity construct itself for CH parents. Cronbach's alphas for the conformity scale were relatively lower for CH parents (.41) compared to NCH parents (.66).

Parental Behavior and Child Achievement

As shown in Table 6.2, mothers' controlling behavior was negatively related to child math achievement, and it was not related to reading achievement for either CH or NCH children. Mother's accepting behaviors were substantially and positively related to both indicators of achievement for all children. Similar to mothers, fathers' controlling behavior was associated with lower reading achievement among NCH children. However, fathers' controlling behaviors were positively related to reading among CH families. Fathers' accepting solution behavior had little association with child achievement, with the exception of higher reading scores among NCH children. In summary, these patterns of relations suggest that, unlike parents of "typical" children, the fathers in CH families appeared to have a unique interactive role with their children that is associated with child achievement. That is, parental controlling behaviors typically associated with poorer achievement among nonhandicapped children, may in fact be related to better achievement in CH children when exhibited by fathers.

Relative Contributions of Parent Variables to Child Achievement

In order to explore the relative contributions of parental values and behaviors to child achievement among CH and NCH children, four hierarchical multiple regressions were conducted (2 handicap status × 2 achievement). Based on the simple correlations among parental variables and child achievement, both maternal and paternal conforming values were entered as a first step, and the behavioral observations of maternal acceptance and paternal control were entered as a second step. By entering maternal acceptance and paternal control together, we also explored the potential additive effects of these behaviors as representing an authoritative parenting style, which has been found beneficial for child cognitive development (Baumrind, 1973). One equation resulted in significant ($p \leq .05$) variance accounted for in achievement, and two approached significance.

Despite these modest effects, the patterns were consistent across equations (see Table 6.3). First, when considering the effects of parental behaviors beyond parental values by group, the behaviors of parents of CH children account for about twice the amount of variance in achievement scores, compared to NCH parents. Second, when mothers and fathers' relative contributions are compared, mothers' values account for greater variance among NCH children's achievement, and mothers' accepting behaviors account for greater variance among CH children, in expected ways. Although paternal conforming values and control behaviors appear to have relatively minimal contributions to achievement when considered in consort with maternal variables, the differential

TABLE 6.3
Multiple Regressions of Parent Variables Predicting Child Achievement

Step	*Variables*	*Raw Beta*	*Standardized Beta*	*Cumulative* R^2	*Significance*
			CH Reading (N = 38)		
1.	Mother Conformity	−.479	−.081		.614
	Father Conformity	.067	.012	.024	.943
2.	Mother Accept Sol.	7.29	.389		.039
	Father Control Beh.	2.23	.156	.227	.374
Total Equation					.068
			NCH Reading (N = 40)		
1.	Mother Conformity	−.807	−.269		.097
	Father Conformity	−.389	−.115	.113	.470
2.	Mother Accept Sol.	3.29	.265		.094
	Father Control Beh.	−.818	−.089	.197	.569
Total Equation					.095
			CH Math (N = 38)		
1.	Mother Conformity	−.804	−.104		.528
	Father Conformity	−.017	-2.38^{E-03}	.044	.989
2.	Mother Accept Sol.	9.84	.400		.038
	Father Control Beh.	.455	.024	.193	.891
Total Equation					.123
			NCH Math (N = 40)		
1.	Mother Conformity	−1.265	−.372		.019
	Father Conformity	−.418	−.109	.174	.475
2.	Mother Accept Sol.	2.45	.174		.247
	Father Control Beh.	−2.26	−.215	.261	.154
Total Equation					.028

pattern for paternal control by handicap group still appeared. That is, paternal control had positive beta weights on achievement scores for CH children, and negative beta weights for NCH children.

STUDY CONCLUSIONS

The purpose of this study was to consider family process variables that influence academic achievement outcomes among communication handicapped children. We first summarize our expectations, results, and interpretations specific to the study presented, and then take the opportunity to speculate about the implications for understanding family adaptations to the presence of an atypical child.

Based on the extant literature, we hypothesized that parents of CH children would have more conforming beliefs, and exhibit more controlling behaviors, compared to parents of NCH children, with possible adverse effects on CH children's academic achievement. Contrary to our hypothesis, we did not find significant differences in mean levels of parents' conformity values, nor in observed parent controlling and accepting behaviors. The lack of mean differences in parent variables found here is consistent with Kazak's (1989) conclusion that well-matched studies of families of atypical and "normal" children rarely reveal mean differences.

Also consistent with Kazak's recommendations, however, we did find the examination of processes within family types, as indicated by correlations and regressions within group, to be a useful approach to understanding how families with handicapped and nonhandicapped children may differ in their adaptive processes. First, with regard to similarities between groups, mothers' acceptance of the child's solution was positively related to academic achievement for both CH and NCH children with or without the consideration of paternal variables. These effects are consistent with previous reports that maternal display of positive affect enhances child cognitive functioning (Estrada et al., 1987).

With regard to differences between handicap status groups, the behaviors of parents of CH children shared more variance with child outcomes, relative to parents of NCH children, after the effects of parental values were controlled for. This may reflect CH parents' ongoing educative rehabilitation efforts, as well as perceived child needs and demands. A second, and more specific family process variation between groups was found among the relations between fathers' controlling behaviors and child academic achievement. Among CH children, paternal control had a positive association with achievement, whereas among NCH children, paternal control had a negative association. The findings pertaining to decreased achievement and paternal control among NCH children is similar to previous research on maternal control among nonhandicapped children (Hess et al., 1968, 1984; Jennings & Connors, 1989). The positive relationship between paternal control and achievement among CH children is consistent with reports of family functioning among parent–child interactions among chronically ill children (e.g., Henggeler et al., 1984). Thus, it would appear that in the context of the father–CH child teaching interaction, paternal controlling involvement can be an adaptive, rather than a deficit maintaining process, when child achievement outcomes are considered.

In addition to parental control, several other associations among parent values, behaviors, and child academic achievement differed by parent gender. Consistent with Luster et al.'s (1989) findings with mothers of infants, maternal conformity values were positively related to maternal controlling behaviors. The lack of association between fathers' conformity values and behaviors in this study may have occurred for a number of reasons. In comparison to mothers, fathers may have less opportunity to consider their values and/or to interpret their interactions with their children, due to less parenting involvement in general. Some support for this hypothesis lies in the lower reliability estimate for conformity for fathers, compared to mothers. Obtaining estimates of fathers' daily child-rearing involvement, particularly teaching-related activities, would be a better test of this explanation.

The results of our study also extend reports of relations among parental values and child achievement. The negative correlations between parental conformity values and NCH child academic achievement extend Schaefer and Edgerton's (1985) findings to an older group of "normal" children, and also indicate that in addition to maternal conformity, paternal conformity is also negatively related to child achievement. The lack of association between parent values and achievement among CH families, however, deserves further exploration. It may be that the particular conformity item, "being a good student," may have been rated by some CH parents as low due to their assumption that their child would continue to lag in achievement. In contrast, other CH parents may have given this item a high rating because of their achievement remediation expectations for their children.

It is not clear to us as to why controlling behaviors by mothers were negatively related to math achievement, and were not related to reading achievement. Because there are no studies with this age group that have reported similar differences for reading and math achievement per se, it is difficult to say whether this finding is spurious or not. However, there are studies with younger children indicating a similar pattern of results. Maternal directiveness and restrictiveness have been found to relate more strongly to number conservation than vocabulary (Hatano, Miyake, & Tajima, 1980) and nonverbal compared to verbal aspects of intelligence (Jennings & Connors, 1989; Olson, Bates, & Bayles, 1984). In addition, the rope-tying task used here may have elicited more nonverbal or perceptual-organizational teaching strategies on the part of the parents, which may have been most relevant to parent–child interactions around math-related tasks and math achievement.

Limitations, Speculations, and Implications

Because communication handicap can be considered a less severe disability in day-to-day living and mortality risk than, for example, cystic fibrosis or diabetes, we clearly are hesitant to extend these findings to all chronic illness conditions. However, because communication handicap is less debilitating than many other childhood disabilities, it gives us an opportunity to make a bridge between family process studies of "normal" children, and those describing the adaptation of families with children who are atypical. It can also be seen as a more stringent test of possible changes in family process in the presence of an atypical child. After discussing other strengths and limitations of the study, we proceed with some discussion of possible implications for future research.

In terms of limitations, the cross-sectional, correlational nature of this study does not permit an interpretation of the causal links in parent values, parent–child interactions, and child achievement outcomes. However, the extant literature relating parent values, parent–child interaction, and child achievement outcomes among "normal" families is rather compelling in terms of causal links. Longitudinal studies examining many of these links have found parent values and parent–child interaction frequently predicting later child achievement above and beyond initial achievement and parent IQ scores (e.g., Hess et al., 1984; Schaefer & Edgerton, 1985). Furthermore, authoritarian child-rearing values are quite stable (Iannotti, Cummings, Pierrehumbert, Milano, & Zahn-Waxler, 1989), and may serve to maintain of these patterns.

Although parental values and behavior appear to preceed later child outcomes in these studies, remediation of, or increased disability in the child's condition, could certainly be considered a causal influence in studies of families with atypical children. Unfortunately, we do not know of any studies that have examined family processes of atypical children longitudinally in terms of parent values, behaviors, and child achievement outcomes. Such a study would be particularly illuminating if changes in the child's condition (improvements, decrements) were monitored along with periodic assessments of parent values and behaviors. For instance, in families where the child's communication handicap has remitted, we speculate that beliefs and behaviors could become either more or less conforming and controlling. That is, some parents may cope by becoming less controlling in their parenting style as the disability remits, whereas other parents may increase control, because their past controlling behavior appeared to pay off. Along with reassessing parents' child-rearing values, an interview designed to capture parental perceptions and attributions of changes of their children's disabilities would be useful.

Another way to view potential family process changes as a disabled child's condition changes, is from both the child and the family's developmental phase or stage. Thinking of the atypical child in terms of developmental stage, rather than chronological age per se, may be particularly useful when considering disorders where children continually lag in skills in comparison to their age peers (Bishop & Edmundson, 1987). For example, among "normal" children, parental control has been found to be more effective among preadolescents, than adolescents (Amato, 1989). Thus, among normal children the enhancing effects of paternal control fade at a certain developmental level or age. However, for children who are lagging in developmental stage for age due to a disability, the salutary effects of parental control may be effective for longer period of time.

From the viewpoint of the family as a unit, altered perceptions of the atypical child and daily demands brought on by special needs most likely slow the family's development as well. As our understanding of family development increases (e.g., Cowan et al., 1985), we may be better equipped to assess family developmental phases or stages in families with atypical children. The developmental course of a family with an atypical child may have a slowed or varied trajectory due to changes in several family subsystems. For example, the marital subsystem is less likely to regroup and recommit to its own growth after childbearing if the needs of a special child are taking the "more than usual" energies, leaving the marriage lacking and stressed. Similarly, normal siblings of the disabled child may receive less attention from their parents with regard to their own developmental needs, as parents are focusing more of their attention on the disabled child. Siblings may also be preoccupied by their felt responsibility to assist in caregiving of the disabled sibling (Powell & Ogle, 1985). Moreover, these subsystems can of course affect each other, with individual family members' beliefs about chronic illness driving these subsystems. For example, the degree to which siblings' normal development is affected is likely to be related the individual parents' adjustment and attitudes toward the chronically ill child (Graliker, Fishler, & Koch, 1962; Tew & Laurence, 1973). Variation in family structure may also affect individual and subsystem functioning, as sibling constellation and gender have also be found to affect sibling outcomes (Breslau, 1982; Breslau, Weitzman, & Messenger, 1981).

Indeed, there are many family process factors likely to affect child achievement outcomes in disabled children that we did not assess in our study. One family subsystem process that we feel is particularly worthy of further consideration is the level of parental agreement in child-rearing values, and the degree to which both parents consistently act upon these ideas. In this study, for example, parent pairs could be considered in terms of their congruency and complementarity, according to their level of agreement on values and behaviors. This would go beyond entering mother and father variables simultaneously in a regression equation (as we did here), by categorizing subgroups of parents based on their agreement. Questions arising from this type of parental categorization include: What are the effects on child achievement if both parents have highly conforming values and highly controlling behaviors? Do children whose parents are low on conformity, low on control, and high on accepting behavior have the best achievement outcomes? Or, is the most optimal parent combination for a handicapped child a complementary parent pair, with one parent more accepting, and the other more directive and controlling? Based on our study, we suggest that parent values and behaviors should be considered separate attributes with potentially separate effects on child achievement.

In summary, our findings not only add to the growing literature on how family processes vary with the presence of a handicapped child (e.g., Kazak, 1989), but also to other areas of the family process literature: These include the family's effect on child behavior at school (e.g., MacDonald & Parke, 1984), how fathers' influences on child development may differ from mothers' (e.g., Lamb, 1981), paternal influences on child achievement in particular (e.g., Forehand, Long, Brody, & Fauber, 1986), and how parents' values affect parent behavior and child achievement (e.g., Sigel, 1985). Future studies on atypical children and their family processes will no doubt continue to contribute to our understanding by gathering additional information on children's interactions with other important socialization agents, such as siblings (see Lobato, Faust, & Spirito, 1988), peers and teachers, and by assessing their values and the day-to-day quality of interactions with the target child (as opposed to laboratory measures, see Schneider & Gearhart, 1988). Examination of developmental stage of both the child and family, as well as consistency within the parental dyad, seem to be fruitful areas for the development of family adaptation models. These models, in turn, should be the basis of interventions designed to reduce the risk of poor achievement outcomes among disabled children.

ACKNOWLEDGMENTS

This investigation was supported by grants from the National Institute of Child Health and Human Development, no. R01-HD10686, the National Institute of Mental Health, no. R01-MH32301, and the Bureau of Education of the Handicapped, no. G007902000. Data analyses and preparation of this report was supported by the National Institute of Mental Health Postdoctoral Training Grant to the Consortium on Family Process and Psychopathology.

REFERENCES

Amato, P. R. (1989). Family processes and the competence of adolescents and primary school children. *Journal of Youth and Adolescence, 18,* 39–53.

American Psychiatric Association. (1987). *Diagnostic and statistical manual of mental disorders* (3rd ed., rev.). Washington, DC: Author.

Anderson, B., Miller, J., Auslander, W., & Santiago, J. (1981). Family characteristics of diabetes adolescents: Relationship to metabolic control. *Diabetes Care, 4,* 586–594.

Baker, L., & Cantwell, D. P. (1987). Factors associated with the development of psychiatric illness in children with early speech/language problems. *Journal of Autism and Developmental Disorders, 17,* 499–510.

Baumrind, D. (1973). The development of instrumental competence through socialization. In A. D. Pick (Ed.), *Minnesota symposium on child psychology* (Vol. 7, pp. 3–46). Minneapolis: University of Minnesota Press.

Bishop, D. V. M., & Edmundson, A. (1987). Specific language impairment as a maturational lag: Evidence from longitudinal data on language and motor development. *Developmental Medicine and Child Neurology, 29,* 442–459.

Breslau, N. (1982). Siblings of disabled children: Birth order and age-spacing effects. *Journal of Abnormal Child Psychology, 10,* 85–96.

Breslau, N., Weitzman, M., & Messenger, K. (1981). Psychological functioning of siblings of disabled children. *Pediatrics, 67,* 344–353.

Brinich, P. M. (1980). Childhood deafness and maternal control. *Volta Review, 13,* 75–81.

Cowan, C. P., Cowan, P. A., Heming, G., Garrett, E., Coysh, W. S., Curtis-Boles, H., Boles, A. J. III. (1985). Transitions to parenthood: His, hers, and theirs. *Journal of Family Issues, 6,* 451–481.

Cummings, S. T. (1976). The impact of the child's deficiency on the father: A study of fathers of mentally retarded and of chronically ill children. *Journal of Orthopsychiatry, 46,* 246–255.

Drotar, D., Crawford, P., & Bush, M. (1984). The family context of childhood chronic illness: Implications for psychosocial intervention. In M. G. Eisenberg, L. C. Sutkin, & M. S. Jansen (Eds.), *Chronic illness and disability throughout the life span: Effects on self and family* (pp. 103–129). New York: Springer.

Estrada, P., Arsenio, W., Hess, R., & Holloway, S. (1987). Affective quality of the mother-child relationship: Longitudinal consequences for children's school relevant cognitive functioning. *Developmental Psychology, 23,* 210–215.

Forehand, R., Long, N., Brody, G. H., & Fauber, R. (1986). Home predictors of young adolescents' school behavior and academic performance. *Child Development, 57,* 1528–1533.

Glass, G., & Stanley, J. (1970). *Statistical methods in education and psychology.* Englewood Cliffs, NJ: Prentice-Hall.

Goodnow, J. J. (1988). Parents' ideas, actions, and feelings: Models and methods from developmental and social psychology. *Child Development, 59,* 286–320.

Graliker, B. V., Fishler, K., & Koch, R. (1962). Teenage reactions to a mentally retarded sibling. *American Journal of Mental Deficiency, 66,* 838–843.

Hatano, G., Miyake, K., & Tajima, N. (1980). Mother behavior in an unstructured situation and child's acquisition of number conservation. *Child Development, 51,* 379–385.

Henggeler, S. W., Watson, S. M., & Cooper, P. F. (1984). Verbal and nonverbal maternal controls in hearing mother–deaf child interaction. *Journal of Applied Developmental Psychology, 5,* 319–329.

Hess, R. D., Holloway, S. D., Dickson, W. P., & Price, G. G. (1984). Maternal variables as predictors of children's school readiness and later achievement in vocabulary and mathematics in sixth grade. *Child Development, 55,* 1902–1912.

Hess, R. D., Shipman, V. C., Brophy, J., & Baer, D. (1968). *The cognitive environment of urban preschool children.* Chicago: Graduate School of Education, University of Chicago.

Hessler, G. L. (1984). *Use and interpretation of the Woodcock-Johnson Psychoeducational Battery.* Allen, TX: DLM Teaching Resources.

Hilliard, T., & Roth, R. (1969). Maternal attitudes and the non-achievement syndrome. *Personnel and Guidance Journal, 47,* 424–428.

Humphries, T., & Bauman, E. (1980). Maternal child rearing attitudes associated with learning disabilities. *Journal of Learning Disabilities, 13,* 459–462.

Iannotti, R. J., Cummings, E. M., Pierrehumbert, B., Milano, M. J., & Zahn-Waxler, C. (1989, April). *Parental influences on prosocial behavior and empathy in early childhood.* Paper presented at the biennial meetings of the Society for Research on Child Development, Kansas City, MO.

Jennings, K. D., & Connors, R. E. (1989). Mothers' interactional style and children's competence at 3 years. *International Journal of Behavioral Development, 12,* 155–175.

Kazak, A. E. (1989). Families of chronically ill children: A systems and

social-ecological model of adaptation and challenge. *Journal of Consulting and Clinical Psychology, 57,* 25–30.
Kohn, M. L. (1977). *Class and conformity: A study of values* (2nd ed.). Chicago: University Press of Chicago.
Lamb, M. E. (1981). *The role of the father in child development* (2nd ed.). New York: Wiley.
Lobato, D., Faust, D., & Spirito, A. (1988). Examining the effects of chronic disease and disability on children's sibling relationships. *Journal of Pediatric Psychology, 13,* 389–407.
Luster, T., Rhoades, K., & Hass, B. (1989). The relationship between parental values and parenting behavior: A test of the Kohn Hypothesis. *Journal of Marriage and the Family, 51,* 139–147.
MacDonald, K., & Parke, R. (1984). Bridging the gap: Parent-child play interaction and peer interactive competence. *Child Development, 55,* 1265–1277.
Mazur, E. (1980). Parent-child interaction and the acquisition of lexical information during play. *Developmental Psychology, 16,* 404–409.
McGillicuddy-DeLisi, A., DeLisi, R., Flaugher, J., & Sigel, I. E. (1987). Familial influences on planning. In S. L. Friedman, E. K. Scholnick, & R. R. Cocking (Eds.), *Blueprints for thinking: The role of planning in cognitive development* (pp. 395–427). New York: Cambridge University Press.
McGillicuddy-DeLisi, A., & Sigel, I. E. (1982). Effects of the atypical child on the family. In L. A. Bond & J. M. Joffe (Eds.), *Facilitating infant and early childhood development* (pp. 197–233). Hanover: University Press of New England.
Miller, S. A. (1988). Parents' beliefs about children's cognitive development. *Child Development, 59,* 259–285.
Minuchin, S., Rosman, B. L., & Baker, L. (1978). *Psychosomatic families.* Cambridge, MA: Harvard University Press.
Olson, S. L., Bates, J. E., & Bayles, K. (1984). Mother-infant interactions and the development of individual differences in children's cognitive competence. *Developmental Psychology, 20,* 166–179.
Powell, T. H., & Ogle, P. A. (1985). *Brothers and sisters—A special part of exceptional families.* Baltimore: Paul H. Brookes.
Schaefer, E. S., & Edgerton, M. (1985). Parent and child correlates of parental modernity. In I. E. Sigel (Ed.), *Parent belief systems: The psychological consequences for children* (pp. 287–318). Hillsdale, NJ: Lawrence Erlbaum Associates.
Schneider, P., & Gearhart, M. (1988). The ecocultural niche of families with mentally retarded children: Evidence from mother-child interaction studies. *Journal of Applied Developmental Psychology, 9,* 85–106.
Siegel, L. S., & Cunningham, C. E. (1984). Social interactions: A transactional approach with illustrations from children with developmental problems. In A. Doyle, D. Gold, & D. S. Moskowitz (Eds.), *Children in families under stress. New Directions for Child Development* (Vol. 24, pp. 85–98). San Francisco: Jossey-Bass.
Sigel, I. E. (1985). Introduction. In I. E. Sigel (Ed.), *Parental belief systems: The psychological consequences for children* (pp. 1–5). Hillsdale, NJ: Lawrence Erlbaum Associates.

Sigel, I. E., Flaugher, J., LaValva, R., & Dahn, A. (1986). *Manual for parent-child and family social interaction ratings scales.* Copyrighted manuscript, Educational Testing Service, Princeton, NJ.

Sigel, I. E., McGillicuddy-DeLisi, A. V., Flaugher, J., & Rock, D. A. (1983). *Parents as teachers of their own learning disabled children* (ETS RR 83-21). Princeton, NJ: Educational Testing Service.

Silva, P. A., Williams, S., & McGee, R. (1987). A longitudinal study of children with developmental language delay at age three: Later intelligence, reading and behaviour problems. *Developmental Medicine and Child Neurology, 29,* 630-640.

Tew, B., & Laurence, K. M. (1973). Mothers, brothers, and sisters of patients with spina bifida. *Developmental Medicine and Child Neurology, 15,* 69-76.

Varni, J. W., & Wallander, J. L. (1988). Pediatric chronic disabilities: Hemophilia and spina bifida as examples. In D. K. Routh (Ed.), *Handbook of pediatric psychology* (pp. 190-221). New York: Guilford Press.

Weiss, M. A., & Duffy, M. R. (1979). Oral language disorders in children: Identification and remediation. *Journal of Clinical Child Psychology, 8,* 206-211.

Woodcock, R. W. (1978). *Development and standardization of the Woodcock-Johnson psycho-educational battery.* Hingham, MA: Teaching Resources Corp.

Woodcock, R. W., & Johnson, M. B. (1977). *Woodcock-Johnson Psycho-educational Battery. Part two: Tests of achievement.* Allen, TX: DLM Teaching Resources.

CHAPTER 7

Expressed Emotion, Communication, and Problem Solving in the Families of Chronic Schizophrenic Young Adults

Robert E. Cole
Catherine F. Kane
Thomas Zastowny
University of Rochester

Wendy Grolnick
Clark University
Anthony Lehman
University of Maryland

Schizophrenia is a severe and disabling illness. Families working to maintain patients at home are faced with a complex and often unrelenting caregiving task (Grad & Sainsbury, 1963; Runions & Prudo, 1983). Unlike many other severe illnesses however, the extraordinary diversity and complexity of the symptoms make it difficult to provide clear guidelines for care (Hatfield, 1987). Family members often have difficulty even recognizing patient behaviors as symptomatic (Lefley, 1987). With no clear understanding of the illness and conflicting perspectives among the professionals with whom they might work (Holden & Lewine, 1982; McElroy, 1987), the development of an effective, consistent response is extremely difficult for the family.

To complicate matters further, the patient's behavior, the therapist's prognosis, and the family's reaction to the patient may change over time. Patients often have long premorbid periods during which they withdraw from social interaction. Personal hygiene and self-care may deteriorate and other unusual behaviors may become marked. Then, in what may seem to the family to be a very short time, the patient may become violent, striking out at family members or acting demonstrably "crazy," talking to the television or the radio, responding to voices or to bizarre delusions.

During the premorbid phase of the illness, in the absence of the classic diagnostic markers of schizophrenia, therapists frequently diagnose the early signs of the illness as an adolescent adjustment disorder or as a family overreaction to or overinvolvement in the normal difficulties of adolescence (Terkelsen, 1987a). Terkelsen (1987b) reported that therapy often undermines and confuses otherwise effective parents whose coping skills have been temporarily overwhelmed. Parents know something is seriously wrong and a diagnosis of adjustment disorder clearly communicates that the therapist does not agree. Parents are left confused, anxious, and defeated.

Once schizophrenia is diagnosed, therapists may still express some degree of optimism about the patient's prognosis, allowing family members to hope that their relative will be one of the lucky few who recover relatively quickly or who have a well-controlled intermittent course. Later, the therapist will most likely have to help the family accept a more disabling and chronic course of illness. Wynne (1983) described the clinical importance of working with families through the various phases of adjustment to the illness. Terkelsen (1987a) listed 10 stages of family adjustment to chronic schizophrenia. Two of these stages, "ignoring what is coming" and "the first shock of recognition" are typically completed even before a diagnosis is made. Terkelsen described in detail the complexities encountered by families working their way from ignorance regarding mental illness to understanding and acceptance. The process is prolonged due to the ambiguities of the illness itself and the conflicting professional perspectives on the cause and course of the illness. According to Terkelsen (1987a):

> The process is usually characterized by diversity and fluidity of attitudes within and between family members, by dramatic forward strides in understanding and equally dramatic reversals, and always by a wide array of disagreeable emotions. Families faced with unremitting, prolonged, or fluctuating levels of infirmity in an affected member eventually experience a collapse of therapeutic optimism and the sorrow of letting go of the dreams of unattainable futures. (p. 165)

Clearly, how a family responds to this stress depends to a great degree on the phase and specific manifestation of the illness. The family's response to schizophrenia is not static. It changes in response to the developmental course of the disorder, a changing prognosis, and an improving understanding. Any model of the relationship between family process and the course of schizophrenia must have a developmental perspective that accommodates these changes.

TWO KEY DIMENSIONS OF FAMILY INTERACTION

There is a large and substantive literature describing the relationships between various dimensions of family behavior and the presence and course of schizophrenia. Two general classes of interaction have been found to be related to either the presence or course of schizophrenia: (a) affective expression and (b) communication difficulties (see e.g., Doane, 1978; Goldstein, 1987; Jacob, 1975, for reviews). Until relatively recently, the failure to consistently replicate specific findings across research centers left only a limited and imprecise understanding of the relationship between patterns of family interaction, patient function, and outcome.

Communication Deviance

Communication deviance (CD) has been an important focus for both risk research and for the development of family therapy treatment strategies for almost three decades. Communication deviance is a measure of a speaker's inability to maintain a shared focus of attention with a listener. Communication deviances include speech fragments; unintelligible responses and comments; gross indefiniteness; contradictory information; and inconsistent references, disruptive behavior, peculiar language, and logic. Singer and Wynne (1963; Singer, 1967) conducted a number of studies that demonstrated specific communication problems among the parents of schizophrenics. Doane, West, Goldstein, Rodnick, and Jones (1981), Jones (1977), Jones et al. (1984), Goldstein (1987), and Wynne and Cole (1983) all found that CD measured in a variety of contexts with a number of methods was predictive of outcome among children and adolescents at risk for mental illness.

Several of the major family therapy interventions (Blechman, 1991; Falloon, Boyd, & McGill, 1984) emphasize teaching communication and problem-solving skills to the families of schizophrenics. Blechman and Delamater (chapter 1, this volume) write persuasively that these skills enable families to negotiate problems simply and effectively and to improve both the adaptive capacity of the family and the mood of its members. Communication skills not only are essential to effective problem solving but also help reduce the intrusiveness and coerciveness of interpersonal interaction within the family.

Expressed Emotion

Brown, Birley, and Wing (1972) and later Vaughn and Leff (1976; Leff & Vaughn, 1980), provided the first clear evidence that family behavior is predictably related to the course of schizophrenia, specifically the relapse of the positive symptoms. Their summary variable, expressed emotion (EE), is a two-factor index based on (a) the number of critical remarks (unambiguous statements of dislike, disapproval, or resentment) made by a family member about a patient during an interview at which the patient is not present, and (b) a rating assigned by the interviewer describing the degree to which the family member is emotionally overinvolved with the patient. The ratings are based on both the content of the respondent's remarks and his or her tone of voice. Following discharge from the hospital, patients returning to households in which one or more family members were high in expressed emotion were much more likely to relapse during the follow-up interval than patients returning to families with neither critical nor emotionally overinvolved relatives.

In this initial study the strength of the relationship between EE and relapse was striking. It accounted for a threefold increase in the frequency of relapse during a 9-month follow-up period even after controlling for the patient's degree of disability at discharge from the hospital (Brown et al., 1972). The relationship was strengthened after also controlling for the fidelity with which the patient adhered to a regime of antipsychotic medication and the amount of face-to-face contact the relatives had with the patient.

Vaughn and Leff (1976) replicated precisely the Brown et al. finding and subsequently Vaughn, Snyder, Jones, Freeman, and Falloon (1984) replicated these results again in Southern California—a notable achievement given the dramatic differences in the mental health systems of the two communities. The first two studies were conducted in England where patients had extended hospital stays, were stabilized on medications prior to discharge, and went home to live with parents or spouses for the full follow-up period. In California, the patients' hospital stays were brief, patients were often discharged before being stabilized, and frequently did not return to their parents or spouses. Shortly thereafter, several other replications were reported (Karno et al., 1987; Leff, Wig et al., 1990; Moline, Singh, Morris, & Meltzer, 1985; Nuechterlein et al., 1986).

These early studies used EE as a marker of what was presumed to be a stable pattern of family interaction, but provided no evidence that what a person says in an interview is related to his or her actual face-to-face interaction with the patient. Thus, it was unexplained why the interview measures predicted relapse. A series of studies at UCLA (Hahlweg et al., 1989; Miklowitz, Goldstein, Falloon, Doane, 1984; Strachan, Leff, Goldstein, Doane, & Burtt, 1986; Valone, Norton, Goldstein, & Doane, 1983) later confirmed that EE is related to the frequency of critical and intrusive remarks in direct family interactions. In addition, Miklowitz et al. (1983) found that high EE relatives were more likely to evidence communication deviance. Expressed emotion thus reflects conjoint family interaction.

Critical Summary of EE Research

Unfortunately the EE research has not afforded a systemic view of the family or its response to chronic illness. Expressed emotion is typically viewed as a stressor for the patient in a diathesis stress view of relapse, although Hooley (1985) suggested that EE may represent an affective response of relatives to particular symptoms or behavioral deficits of patients. Others (Doane, Falloon, Goldstein, & Mintz, 1985; Hahlweg et al., 1989; Strachan et al., 1986) view EE as a measure of attitudes held by relatives toward the patient.

Brown et al. (1972) defined EE as a "measure of the relative's propensity to react [with hostility, criticism or overinvolvement] . . . to that particular patient and represent(s) an enduring potential characteristic of the relative's behavior towards the patient" (p. 246). In our own interviews, critical comments are most often complaints about patient behavior.

Regarding EE as a response to specific patient behaviors rather than as a generalized emotional attitude allows for an examination of the complex interactions that occur within families and in which critical comments may occur. Unfortunately, EE has been used most often as a simple dichotomous classification variable independent of the nature of the family system. This classification greatly oversimplifies the differences among those families rated as high or low on EE, ignores the enormous variance within each of these two groups, and provides no insight into actual patient or family system characteristics that might lead a parent to respond critically or intrusively.

In addition, the research lacks a developmental perspective giving little attention to the phase of the patient's illness. There is an assumption that EE is fixed over time, responding only to innovative family therapy (Leff, 1976). In fact, several studies (Brown et al., 1972; Dulz & Hand, 1986; Hogarty et al., 1986; Leff, Berkowitz et al., 1989, 1990; Leff, Kuipers et al., 1982, 1984) suggest that EE is quite variable over time and that a high EE rating at one point is not necessarily predictive of high EE later.

Finally, recent studies have failed to replicate the original work (Kottgen, Sonnichsen, Mollenhauser, & Jurth, 1984a, 1984b; MacMillan, Gold, Crow, Johnson, & Johnstone, 1986; McReadie & Phillips, 1988;

Parker, Johnston, & Hayward, 1988) and because the work has not emerged from a comprehensive systemic model there has been no framework from which to understand these discrepancies. Kottgen et al. (1984b) actually found that high EE is related to a better outcome, which taking the diathesis/stress model at face value, is inexplicable. Further, although Hogarty et al. (1988) did report a negative relationship between EE and patient adjustment, they also reported a tendency toward more frequent free-time social activities among patients in high EE families. A better understanding of what EE represents and a more complex model of the familial response to schizophrenia may help resolve these discrepancies.

We now present a description of a longitudinal intervention with 30 families of young adult chronic schizophrenics. This study attempted to streamline methods for examining family interactions as well as to develop a more comprehensive model of family interaction and schizophrenia.

OBJECTIVES OF THE CURRENT STUDY

Among the original objectives of our research were to:

1. streamline the EE and CD methodologies so they could be incorporated into a larger number and wider variety of studies, especially those making repeated family assessments;
2. test the validity of these shortened measures of EE and CD by comparing them to related measures obtained during a conjoint family problem-solving task;
3. examine the relationships among the components of EE (i.e., critical remarks and emotional overinvolvement), CD, patient illness, and patient behavior in a sample of families of young adult chronic schizophrenics;
4. measure the impact of communication and problem-solving training on
   (a) the EE and CD of the parents of this sample of chronic schizophrenics,
   (b) the communication clarity and affective expression of the family members in a conjoint problem-solving task, and
   (c) the patient's symptoms and function.

METHODOLOGY

The study was conducted on a specialized unit of a local state psychiatric facility (Evaluation and Training Unit [ETU]) supervised and staffed by the faculty and residents of a University teaching hospital. The staff of the ETU reviewed the diagnoses and medications of all patients admitted to the unit. This often led to adjustments or changes in medication. In addition, the unit's high staff–patient ratio permitted more intensive and consistent individual therapy and made family interventions possible.

All families who participated in this study agreed to random assignment to one of two psychoeducational treatments. One protocol, behavioral family management (BFM; Falloon et al., 1984), explicitly taught, modeled, and reinforced several key communication and problem-solving techniques. It also provided information about schizophrenia and offered families advice and support. However, unlike the Falloon model, home visits were not conducted until the patient was discharged, and then only infrequently. The alternative, supportive family management (SFM; Bernheim, 1982; Bernheim & Lehman, 1985), offered education, support, and advice, but did not specifically teach communication or problem solving.

The Sample

Patients were eligible for the study if (a) they were between 18 and 35 years old, (b) were hospitalized at the ETU with a *DSM-III-R* diagnosis of schizophrenia, (c) their families were available and willing to participate in their care, and (d) their treatment plans included preparation for discharge from the hospital within 4 months.

Ninety-five consecutive admissions to the ETU over a period of 2 years were reviewed. There were 39 of these patients who did not meet our diagnostic criteria or had no current family contact. An additional 7 patients were discharged before we could discuss the program with them. Fifteen patients refused to participate. Thirty-four families agreed to participate, but 2 never started the program and 2 attended only two sessions and were considered refusals. In summary, we were able to enroll 30 (61%) of the eligible patients we were able to contact.

The mean age of the patients was 24, although they ranged in age from 18 to 35. Twenty-five were male and all but 3 were Caucasian. The remainder were Black. All but 10 had completed high school and 6 had some college. None of the patients was married. Despite their young age, the average patient had been ill for 4 years and had had 3.3 hospital admissions. Other intervention samples typically include older individuals with fewer hospitalizations (Leff, Berkowitz et al., 1989, 1990; Leff et al., 1982, 1985; Tarrier et al., 1988, 1989). In this study, 53% had been psychiatric inpatients for at least 6 months prior to the present admission. By comparison, only 6% of the patients in the Falloon et al. (1982, 1985) studies had been hospitalized for more than 6 months.

All of the families participating in the intervention were families of origin. The families were primarily middle class (81% Hollingshead classes I-III). In 21 families (70%), parents were married and living together. Nine were single-parent households, all but one headed by the patient's mother. All had maintained regular contact with the patients during their extensive hospitalizations and were willing to participate in this study, although many were skeptical about its value.

Assessment Schedule

The patients and families were assessed at four points: entry into the study, at the end of the weekly family sessions (at 16 weeks, about the time the patient was scheduled to be discharged), and again 6 and 12 months following the patient's originally scheduled discharge date. Data from the first, second, and fourth assessments are presented here. Data from the third assessment are not included because of more than usual missing data at that point.

Patient Measures

The patient assessments covered four domains: symptomatology, general functioning, social adjustment, and quality of life. The measures relevant to this report are discussed here.

The Brief Psychiatric Rating Scale (BPRS; Overall & Gorham, 1962). The BPRS, completed by the patient's primary therapist, includes 24 seven-point scales designed to capture a wide variety of symptoms including anxiety, depression, anergia, thought disturbance, activation, hostility, and suspiciousness.

The Global Assessment Scale (GAS; Endicott, Spitzer, Fleiss, & Cohen, 1976). The GAS, completed by experienced interviewer/raters, provides a measure of the patient's overall level of function in the recent past on a scale ranging from 1 (needs constant supervision) to 100 (superior independent functioning).

Scale for the Assessment of Negative Symptoms (SANS; Andreasen, 1982). The SANS, also completed by experienced interviewer/raters, includes five key negative schizophrenic symptoms: affective flattening, alogia, avolition, anhedonia, and attentional impairment. Each is rated on a 6-point scale based on information from multiple sources of information including patient interview, observation, and staff report. We anticipated that affective flattening and alogia would have the most variance in this sample and would be the most prominent of the negative symptoms displayed and therefore selected these subscales for assessment.

Family Measures

Although other family measures were employed during the course of the study, only the Camberwell Family Interview (CFI) and conjoint family interaction measures are described and reported on here.

Conjoint Family Problem-Solving Task. This task is a modification of the revealed differences task developed by Strodtbeck (1951) and is similar to the task developed by Goldstein, Judd, Rodnick, Alkire, and Gould (1968) and implemented by Miklowitz et al. (1984). In our version, the patient and his or her parent(s) were presented with an issue all of them had previously selected as an area of conflict from the 53 items on the Family Conflict Questionnaire (Liberman, Falloon, & Aitchison, 1984) that was administered prior to the session. The family was asked to discuss the problem and to try to reach agreement about a potential solution. The interaction was audio- and videotaped and a verbatim transcript of the interaction was prepared.

Each interaction unit, defined as a change in speaker or in communication code, was assigned 1 of 3 affect codes (positive, negative, or neutral) and 1 of 20 communication/problem-solving codes (Cole, Grolnick, & Perkins, 1986). The communication/problem-solving codes are listed in Table 7.1. The affect codes were designed to capture the same affects coded from the CFI. The negative affect codes reflect both criticism (invalidating or critical remarks) and emotional overinvolvement (dominating, directive, guilt-inducing statements). The positive affect codes reflect those affects included in the CFI rating of warmth: sympathy, concern, understanding, reassurance, enjoyment, and enthusiasm.

Percent agreement among all pairs of the three raters ranged from 75% to 80% with kappas from .60 to .66 for the communication and problem-solving codes, and from 88% to 90% with kappas of .60 to .64 for the affect codes. In the analyses that follow, the 20 communication and problem-solving codes have been collapsed into three broad categories: (a) constructive problem solving and targeted communication

TABLE 7.1
Communication and Problem-Solving Code Categories

1) Problem Solving	
	Problem definition statements
	Problem solution statements
	Summarizing and consensus statements
	Invitations to discuss
2) Targeted Communication	
	Constructive requests for behavior change
	Positive feedback for specific positive behaviors
	Constructive expression of negative feelings
3) On-Task, Facilitative	
	Paraphrasing, clarifying statements or questions
	Acknowledgment
	Relevant information statements
	Constructive disagreement
4) On-Task, Nonfacilitative	
	Minimal acknowledgment
	Refusal to participate in discussion
	Defensive responses
	Fragments
5) Off-Task, Unrelated	
	Clear statements unrelated to the ongoing discussion
6) Unclear	
	Unclear or self-contradictory statements
7) Unscorable	
	Statements too soft or too garbled to score

(Categories 1 and 2 in Table 7.1), (b) other on-task facilitative statements (Category 3), and (c) nonfacilitating/disruptive statements (Categories 4 through 7). Each of these code categories is expressed as a percent of the number of speeches made by the speaker.

Streamlining the EE Methodology

The original Camberwell Family Interview (CFI) required between 5 and 6 hours to complete. Vaughn and Leff (1976) developed an abbreviated form of the CFI that shortened the interview from 5 hours to under 2 hours. In our previous work, however, even the abbreviated format required an average of 90 minutes to complete. The length of the interview makes it difficult to incorporate into many studies and extremely difficult to use as a repeated measure.

Vaughn and Leff suggested that it may not be necessary to conduct even a 2-hour interview. They reported that the majority of the critical remarks made during an interview occurred within the first hour and stated that "if the sole purpose of the interview were to rank the relatives on the basis of criticism voiced, it would be unnecessary to prolong it [the interview] beyond one hour" (p. 163). Our analysis of 20 interviews made in Rochester during an earlier study suggested that the majority of the critical remarks occurred during the first two segments of the interview, the review of the patient's general psychiatric history and his or her irritability. By the end of the irritability segment, which on average took 38 minutes to complete, 66% of the total number of critical comments had been made (see Table 7.2).

More importantly, the correlation between the number of critical remarks made at this point and the total number made during the full interview was .93. Further, the rating of emotional overinvolvement (EOI) made by independent raters from information taken from these two sections were correlated .95 with the rating made from the full interview. These analyses indicate that a 40-minute interview would provide reliable estimates of the standard EE ratings. The average number of critical remarks made during the short interview was clearly less than the number made during the full interview, but there was sufficient variance in the counts and ratings to provide accurate estimates of the full interview measures.

Based on this preliminary work, a modified CFI interview was developed that took about 45 minutes to complete and covered history, irritability, and the respondent–patient relationship. Using this shortened interview format, the mean for critical comments (CC) per interview was 3.09, the standard deviation was 3.07, and the range was 0–13. Seventeen families were rated high EE, using the traditional criterion that at least one of the parents made six or more critical comments or scored 3 or greater for EOI. Twenty-five (55%) of the 45 parents were rated high EE, 16 (36%) were rated high EOI only, 4 were rated high CC only (9%), and 5 (11%) were rated both high CC and EOI. Because we

TABLE 7.2
Scoring of the Partial and Full Camberwell Family Interview (n = 20)

	Critical Comments		*Emotional Overinvolvement*	
Interview Segments Rated	*r*	*M*	*r*	*M*
1) History	.84	4.2	.86	1.48
2) History & Irritability	.93	6.6	.95	1.75
3) Household Tasks & (2)	.95	7.0	.94	1.90
4) Symptoms & (2)	.97	8.5	.99	1.85
5) Relationship & (2)	.96	7.4	.94	1.85
6) Full Interview	-	10.0	-	1.93

r – correlation between the rating based on these segments and the full interview.
M – the mean rating based on these segments.

shortened the interview, the traditional cutoffs for EE levels may not be appropriate. Therefore, our analyses include both EE scores based on the traditional classification as well as a classification based on a median split.

Streamlining the CD Methodology

Most of the existing methods for assessing communication are extremely labor intensive, lengthy, and expensive. The system we used to code the problem-solving task requires 20 minutes for each minute of observed family interaction (approximately 3 hours for 10 minutes, including transcription). Yet after listening to many CFI interviews, we felt that it was possible to extract a measure of communication skill from the CFI. While recognizing that we would lose useful information if we were to rely on a simplified system, especially one based on an interview and not directly observed family interaction, we were nevertheless encouraged by two sets of findings. First, there are several reports that communication deviance and communication clarity measured during the administration of an individual projective test are related to child and/or patient function. Singer and Wynne (1965; Singer 1967; Wynne, Singer, Bartko, & Toohey, 1977) found that CD measured during parents' individual Rorschachs differentiated normal, neurotic, and schizophrenic spectrum offspring. Doane et al. (1982) reported that mothers' CD, also measured during an individual Rorschach, is related to the school function of children at risk for mental illness, although not as highly as comparable measures taken during a conjoint family consensus task. Schuldberg, Singer, and Wynne (1990) reported that parental communication skill (competence enhancing) assessed during parents' individual Rorschachs is related to the school function of their children, independent of the CD measures. Finally, Jones, Rodnick, Goldstein, McPherson, and West (1977) reported that parental CD assessed during an individual Thematic Apperception Test (TAT) is related to the outcome of adolescents at risk for schizophrenic spectrum disorder. These studies offer support for the predictive validity of communication measures taken from individual (as compared to) interaction tasks.

In addition, Singer (1967) found that a single measure of the "visualizability" of the percepts offered during an individual Rorschach was a good indicator of the overall impact of communication deviance. Therefore it might not be necessary to score in detail a large number of communication parameters. A single measure of the overall impact of the speaker on the listener might be sufficient.

Based on the visualizability notion, Cole developed a 4-point scale measuring the comprehensibility of the opening passages of the CFI, rated in terms of CD (absent, mild, moderate, and severe). A comprehensible low CD passage (a rating of 0) contains clear, followable responses to all questions. The respondent spontaneously provides all relevant material and is able to orient the listener to the timing and sequence of events. A passage with mild CD (a rating of 1) is clearly followable, but requires some clarification by the listener. In a passage with moderately high CD (a rating of 2), understandable responses are obtained, but only as the result of an active dialogue between the interviewer and the respondent. Frequent probes or structuring statements are needed to clarify contradictory or ambiguous statements or to structure a respondent who frequently loses the main thread of his or her story. In a high CD response (a rating of 3), the respondent is unable to answer clearly even a direct question. Questions by the interviewer have no apparent effect on the respondents "stream of consciousness."

This scale was strictly exploratory, but a potentially useful exercise that if successful would, like a shortened CFI, make it possible to incorporate at least approximate measures of communication deviance into a wider range of studies, especially those with repeated family assessments. This scale has adequate interrater reliability (intraclass correlation of .75 between two raters on 20 interviews) and, as we summarize here, is related to family communication and problem-solving skill in the conjoint family problem-solving task.

Validation of the EE and CD Measures

To confirm that the EE and CD measures taken from our 45-minute interview were related to actual family interaction, we examined the correlations between these measures and our more detailed coding of the problem-solving task. It should be noted that the individuals who rated the problem-solving sessions did not conduct, rate, or hear the CFI.

Father's Interaction. It is clear from Table 7.3 that all three of the father's interview measures (the number of critical remarks, emotional overinvolvement and communication deviance) are strongly related to comparable behaviors in the problem-solving task. Father's CC during the interview is strongly related to the frequency of his negative affect statements in the conjoint task ($r = .64$, $p < .01$). Father's EOI, reflecting a dominating and intrusive demeanor, is positively related to nonfacilitating/disruptive remarks made during the problem-solving task ($r = .51$, $p < .05$). Father's CD is strongly and inversely related to the percentage of problem-solving statements during the problem-solving task ($r = -.73$, $p < .01$).

TABLE 7.3
Relationships Among the Problem-Solving and CFI Codes

	Problem-Solving Task			*Camberwell Family Interview*	
	SN	*NF*	*NA*	*CD*	*CC*
Fathers at Baseline (n = 17)					
Problem-solution statements (SN)					
Nonfacilitating statements (NF)	−0.11				
Negative affect (NA)	−0.48*	0.07			
Communication deviance (CD)	−0.73**	0.21	0.65**		
Critical comments (CC)	−0.44*	0.25	0.64**	0.38	
Emotional overinvolvement (EOI)	−0.13	0.51*	0.08	0.42*	−0.16
Fathers at 16 Weeks (n = 17)					
Problem-solution statements (SN)					
Nonfacilitating statements (NF)	−0.58**				
Negative affect (NA)	−0.24	0.39*			
Communication deviance (CD)	−0.47*	0.61**	0.53**		
Critical comments (CC)	−0.05	0.45*	0.61**	0.70**	
Emotional overinvolvement (EOI)	−0.31	0.24	0.32	0.39*	0.28

*$p < .05$. **$p < .01$

It also seems that communication, problem solving, and negative affect are not independent. Communication deviance is related to the frequency of father's negative affect ($r = .65$, $p < .01$). Fathers' CC is negatively related to the proportion of problem-solving statements made ($r = -.44$, $p < .10$) as is negative affect ($r = -.48$, $p < .05$). This is consistent with a study by Forgatch (1989) that describes the disruptive effect of negative affect on problem solving. Communication deviance is related to EOI ($r = .42$, $p < .05$) and marginally related to CC ($r = .38$, $p = .11$). From the second part of Table 7.3, it can be seen that these patterns remain relatively stable over time.

Mother's Interaction. Mother's interaction data also provides some support for the validity of the three interview measures (see Table 7.4). Mothers' CD is related to the percentage of nonfacilitating/disruptive speeches ($r = .33$, $p < .05$ at Time 1 and $r = .51$, $p < .01$ at Time 2). Mother's criticism is marginally related to the percentage of problem-solving statements ($r = -.30$, $p < .15$) at baseline and to negative affect ($r = .34$, $p < .05$) at 16 weeks. Finally, EOI is related to the frequency of negative affect during problem solving ($r = .35$, $p < .05$), although this relationship is not apparent at Time 2.

In summary, the measures of CC, EOI, and CD taken from the short version of the CFI are related to the respondent's behavior during face-to-face interaction with other family members. In addition, com-

TABLE 7.4
Relationships Among the Problem-Solving and CFI Codes

	Problem-Solving Task			*Camberwell Family Interview*	
	SN	*NF*	*NA*	*CD*	*CC*
Mothers at Baseline (n = 26)					
Problem-solution statements (SN)					
Nonfacilitating statements (NF)	−0.17				
Negative affect (NA)	−0.42*	−0.10			
Communication deviance (CD)	−0.21	0.33*	0.27		
Critical comments (CC)	−0.30	0.20	0.15	−0.16	
Emotional overinvolvement (EOI)	−0.20	0.16	0.35*	0.19	0.11
Mothers at 16 Weeks (n = 24)					
Problem-solution statements (SN)					
Nonfacilitating statements (NF)	−0.50**				
Negative affect (NA)	0.15	0.06			
Communication deviance (CD)	−0.08	0.51**	−0.06		
Critical comments (CC)	0.27	−0.08	0.34*	−0.13	
Emotional overinvolvement (EOI)	0.09	−0.04	0.11	−0.25	0.02

*$p < .05$. **$p < .01$

munication effectiveness and the expression of negative affect, although conceptually distinct, are themselves related, especially among the fathers. Although the direction of effects between measures is not evident in these analyses, one can speculate about the processes underlying these relationships. For example, difficulties in communication may lead to poor problem solving, misunderstandings, and frustrations that result in angry and critical remarks. Further, this anger may disrupt communication and problem solving. The goals of the problem-solving sessions shift from the creation of constructive solutions of long-standing difficulties to simply winning arguments and obtaining revenge for prior insults. It seems that poor communication and anger work to disrupt problem solving and to reinforce one another. Some exploratory sequential analyses support this interpretation. More systematic analyses are underway. Blechman and Delameter (chapter 1, this volume) make a similar point.

PARENT BEHAVIOR, PATIENT BEHAVIOR, AND PATIENT ILLNESS

Parents' communication, problem solving, and negative affect are related to the patients' illness, but not as we originally expected. In the original EE research (Brown et al., 1972), relatives' criticism and emotional overinvolvement were directly related to the severity of the patient's illness, the more severe the disability, the greater the criticism and emotional overinvolvement.

Given these patterns, we anticipated that communication deviance, problem-solving difficulties, criticism, and negative affect would all be related to higher levels of patient disability and longer histories of hospitalization. This is consistent with a diathesis/stress model in which poorly functioning patients may be seen as responding to higher levels of interpersonal stress.

There are several alternative considerations, however, that might predict different results. One perspective is that for chronically and persistently ill patients, family behavior is unrelated to patient illness. The patients might be too ill and the course of their illnesses too unrelenting to be affected by their families' emotional responses or problem-solving capabilities. From this perspective, the illness is essentially biologically driven.

Another perspective is that family behavior and patient illness are related, but in a more complex fashion than described by the diathesis/stress model. The relatively high functioning (communicative, able to manage activities of daily living), yet symptomatic patient poses a dilemma for his or her family. This patient often has unrealistic social and/or employment goals given the nature and severity of his or her illness. The family wants to support and encourage the patient but at the same time is concerned that the patient's unrealistic goals will subject both family members and the patient to repeated frustration and failure.

For the chronically mentally ill, family members' concerns for the patient and their attempts to set more stringent limits increase as the illness progresses through recurring phases of relapse and remission. In the early stages of the illness, the family is hopeful that the illness will be brief, or at least well controlled, and the patient will eventually resume more or less normal functioning. As the patient begins to improve, the family encourages him or her to make plans and to resume normal activities. In many cases these episodes end in disaster, as the patient relapses and returns to the hospital. Gradually, the family becomes more wary of these temporary improvements and less supportive of the patient's future plans and attempts to resume active social or work lives. The patient's hopeful statements are met with ambiguous responses, silence, or outright resistance as the family tries both to support and encourage the patient's recovery and to reduce his or her expectations, in an attempt to protect both the patient and itself. Among the chronically ill, improvements in patient functioning sometimes disrupt problem solving as the family tries to neither encourage nor discourage the patient. This ambiguity and tension may also lead to frustration and anger as the patient reacts to the family's surprising lack of encouragement.

For example, in one problem-solving session a father repeatedly reminded his son of how limited his son's actual work experience had been, and how these experiences almost always ended in disaster. "Do you remember the last time you worked in the store? . . . Do you remember what happened? . . . You only lasted 2 hours!" Another father exhausted himself trying to get his son to accept certain limits and lower his expectations by interrogating him about how he would implement his plan. "Do you know *when* the program meets? Do you know *where* it is? Do you know *which* bus to take to get there?"

For families of lower functioning patients, maintaining a balance between limit-setting and support is less problematic because these patients are too ill to even begin to carry out their often unrealistic plans. Unlike the situation for higher functioning patients, there is less need for limit-setting because the patients are consumed with simply managing the activities of daily living.

Another dimension of the family dilemma is the family's understanding of the degree to which the patient is responsible for his or her own behavior. The families of higher functioning patients may be more likely to hold patients accountable for their own behavior, and therefore to respond more critically to the patients' unrealistic plans and symptomatic behavior. Families of lower functioning patients may be less likely to hold patients accountable. Their behavior is much more likely to be attributed to the illness.

These perspectives are clearly speculative. We have no data regarding patient goals and expectations or the family's attributions of responsibility. However, the data that are available support this more complex view of the relationship between family interaction and patient functioning, and show a dependence on the phase or length of the patient's illness.

The contemporaneous measures of patient function and constructive family communication are inversely related (see Table 7.5). Overall patient function (GAS) is directly related to father's nonfacilitation ($r = .52$, $p < .01$) and negative affect ($r = .59$, $p < .01$) in the problem-solving task and to critical comments in the interview ($r = .61$, $p < .01$). The symptom rating from the BPRS is inversely related to communication deviance ($r = -.45$, $p < .05$). The more symptomatic the patient, the clearer the father's communication. Affective flattening, one of the two key negative symptoms assessed, is directly related to father's problem solving ($r = .46$, $p < .05$) and inversely related to negative affect ($r = -.45$, $p < .05$). Alogia was not related to any of the family measures and is not included in the table.

Mother's data follows a similar pattern. Patient symptoms as mea-

TABLE 7.5
Parent Problem Solving, Affect, and Patient Illness at Baseline

	Problem Solving Task			*Camberwell Family Interview*		
	SN	*NF*	*NA*	*CD*	*CC*	*EOI*
Fathers at Baseline (n = 17)						
Overall Patient Function (GAS)	0.07	0.52*	0.59**	0.38	0.61**	0.09
Overall Symptom Rating (BPRS)	−0.04	−0.07	0.00	−0.40*	0.04	−0.34
Affective Flattening (SANS)	0.46*	0.00	−0.45*	−0.31	−0.27	0.00
Mothers at Baseline (n = 26)						
Overall Patient Function (GAS)	0.05	−0.18	0.04	0.20	0.19	0.07
Overall Symptom Rating (BPRS)	0.18	−0.39*	0.01	−0.02	−0.15	−0.16
Affective Flattening (SANS)	0.38*	0.01	−0.25	−0.31	−0.21	−0.35*

*$p < .05$. **$p < .01$

sured by the BPRS are inversely related to the proportion of nonfacilitating statements made during problem solving ($r = -.39$, $p < .05$). Affective flattening is positively related to mother's problem solving ($r = .38$, $p < .05$) and negatively to emotional overinvolvement ($r = -.35$, $p < .05$). In summary, fathers are more critical of their better functioning children and both mothers and fathers perform less well during problem solving with higher functioning patients.

The somewhat oversimplified family systems model outlined here does not fully capture the role of the patient. It suggests only that positive moves toward recovery are sometimes met with frustrating attempts to set limits. It is possible, however, that the relatively higher functioning, but still chronically ill and frequently hospitalized patients, behave differently from their lower functioning counterparts during these problem-solving tasks and may be more disruptive of family communication. They may actually stimulate and reinforce critical and defensive responses from their parents. Table 7.6 summarizes the correlations between rated patient function and behavior in the problem-solving task. In fact, there is a direct relationship between patient function and both the percent of patient nonfacilitating remarks and the frequency of negative affect statements. The higher the overall function, the more disruptive and more negative the patient. The remaining correlations, although not statistically significant, support this general pattern. There is a strong tendency for the lower functioning patients to be less disruptive and less negative. Although these correlations are not large, the higher functioning patients do seem to behave differently than lower functioning patients. The parents may not only act in response to their expectations but also to the disruptive quality of the patient's

TABLE 7.6
Patient Function, Communication, and Problem Solving

	Problem-Solving Task		
	SN	*NF*	*NA*
Patients at Baseline (n = 25)			
Overall Patient Function (GAS)	−0.27	0.34*	0.37*
Overall Symptom Rating (BPRS)	0.29	−0.29	−0.22
Affective Flattening (SANS)	0.07	0.01	−0.26

*$p < .05$

behavior. That these differences in patient behavior affect the parents is illustrated in Table 7.7.

The patient's behavior clearly impacts the parents as we would expect. The more constructive the patient's contribution to problem solving, the less critical the father. Specifically, the higher the proportion of problem-solving statements made by the patient, the less critical are both father ($r = -0.48$, $p < .05$) and mother ($r = -0.50$, $p < .05$). The higher the proportion of nonfacilitating patient remarks, the higher the frequency of negative remarks by both mother and father. The more frequently the patient expresses negative affect, the more frequently the mother expresses negative affect ($r = 0.45$, $p < 0.05$) and the higher her EOI ($r = 0.40$, $p < 0.05$).

In summary, the correlations among the measures of patient symptomatology and patient and parent interaction are consistent with the family systems model and also with the hypothesis that higher func-

TABLE 7.7
Patient and Parent Communication and Problem Solving

	Problem-Solving Task			*Camberwell Family Interview*		
Patient Communication & Problem Solving	*SN*	*NF*	*NA*	*CD*	*CC*	*EOI*
	Fathers at Baseline (n = 17)					
Problem-solution statements (SN)	−0.04	−0.15	−0.27	−0.19	−0.48*	0.25
Nonfacilitating statements (NF)	0.04	−0.14	0.44*	0.18	0.34	0.26
Negative affect (NA)	−0.08	0.01	0.33	0.21	0.19	−0.17
	Mothers at Baseline (n = 26)					
Problem-solution statements (SN)	0.16	−0.28	−0.11	−0.08	−0.50**	0.03
Nonfacilitating statements (NF)	0.00	−0.08	0.34*	0.03	0.19	−0.14
Negative affect (NA)	−0.29	−0.04	0.45**	0.03	−0.09	0.40*

*$p < .05$. **$p < .01$

tioning chronically ill patients act differently than lower functioning chronically ill patients. The higher functioning patients are more negative, more disruptive during problem solving. This is related to less constructive problem solving and more negative affect by the parents. In addition, the anticipation of relapse as the patient prepares for discharge may unsettle the parents who try to balance encouragement with caution. This difficult balancing act also disrupts problem solving. In contrast, the lower functioning patients are less disruptive and also have lower expectations. The parents of these patients can be more consistently supportive.

Although all of the patients had been ill for some time, there was still considerable variance in the total length of the patients' illnesses. Given this variance and the potential for differences in the phases of the patient's illnesses, we looked for differences in the relationships between patient function and parent behavior conditioned upon total length of hospitalization. We expected that the parents of those patients with the longest hospitalizations would respond more strongly to the potential threat of the patient's impending discharge. We also wondered whether the relationship between patient function and behavior would change as a function of length of prior hospitalization; that is, would the inverse relationship between symptoms and function be stronger among the more chronically ill.

In fact the data support these speculations. The relationships between patient function and a number of parent behaviors (father's criticism, negative affect, and problem solution statements) are conditioned on the length of the patient's prior hospitalization. This is illustrated in Fig. 7.1 by the relationship between patient function (GAS) and father's criticism controlling for total weeks of lifetime hospitalization. Father's criticism is only related to patient function if the patients have had long histories of hospitalization. Clearly, the inverse relationship between the father's CC and patient function occurs only within the families of patients with the longest total hospitalization. This confirms the importance of a developmental perspective.

Figure 7.2 illustrates the relationship between patient symptoms and overall function for different lengths of prior hospitalization. Higher functioning patients exhibit more positive symptoms than do low-functioning chronic patients, but this is only true for those patients with long histories of hospitalizations. It seems there are two types of long-stay patients. One group consists of low-functioning patients with many negative but few positive symptoms. These patients draw parental support. The second group includes higher functioning patients with more positive symptoms who disrupt the families' stability and draw criticism.

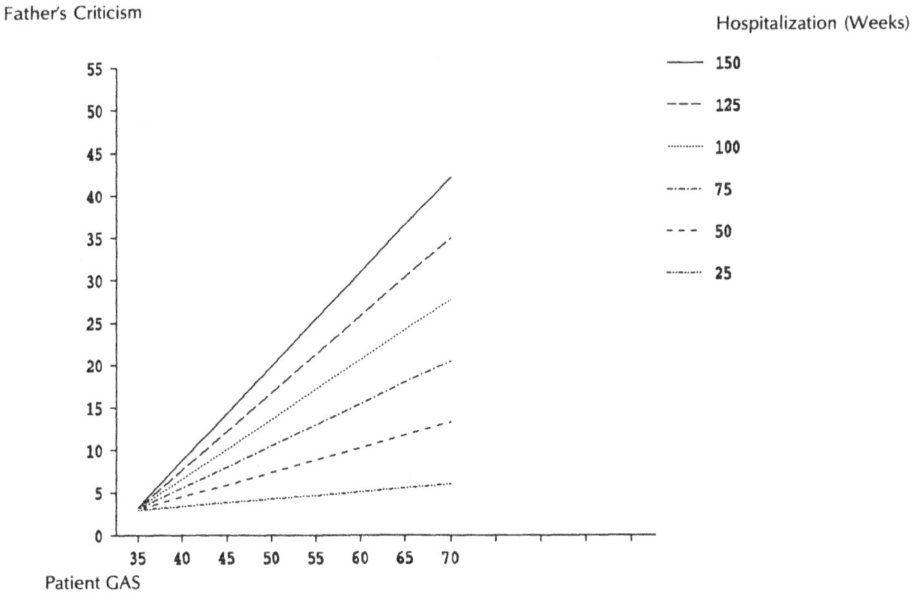

FIG. 7.1. Father's critical comments as a function of patient GAS, controlling for length of hospitalization.

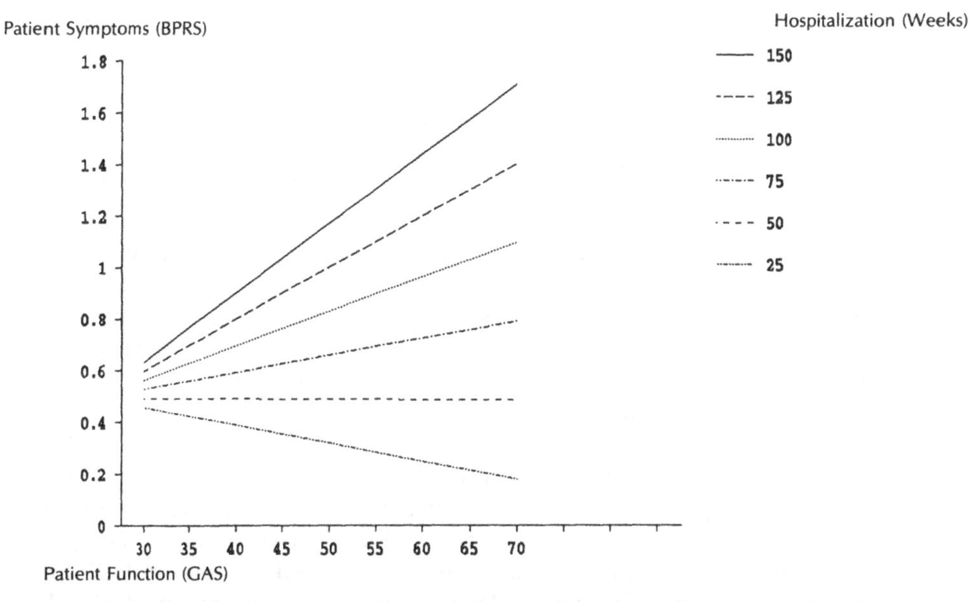

FIG. 7.2 Patient symptoms versus overall function, controlling for total length of hospitalization.

CHANGES IN PARENT BEHAVIOR

Recall that 20 mothers and 13 fathers completed a 16-week psychoeducational intervention. One intervention offered information, advice, and support; the other offered these plus direct instruction in communication and problem solving. Although the foci of this chapter are the cross-sectional relationships among the patients' symptomatology and behavior and parent communication, a review of the families' change over time seems warranted, given our emphasis on the changing responses of the families.

All of the analyses presented here have been corrected for changes in patient medication. As part of the hospital unit where the intervention took place, the medication of each patient was reviewed and changed if that seemed appropriate. In general, there was a significant increase over time in the chlorpromazine (cpz) equivalents of the medications taken by the patients. In order to avoid confounding changes in patient and family behavior due to the family intervention with change attributable entirely to the effect of medications, we controlled for chlorpromazine equivalents in all of these analyses. This may not have been necessary given that amount of medication prescribed was related to very few patient behaviors and the few significant relationships were inconsistent. Nevertheless, we adopted this conservative strategy of correcting for medication.

In general, both mothers' and fathers' communication and problem solving improved over time, although only the changes in communication deviance in the interview were statistically significant (see Tables 7.8 and 7.9). Positive changes in both mothers' and fathers' negative affect also occurred. Over time, fathers made fewer critical remarks during the interview and fewer negative affect statements during family problem solving although these changes were not statistically significant. Mothers, too, made fewer critical remarks and expressed less negative affect during problem solving over time. For mothers, only the change in critical remarks was statistically significant, although the reduction in negative affect by those mothers in the behavioral group was substantial, falling 59% from 7.0 to 2.9 statements.

There were also significant changes in both mothers' and fathers' ratings of emotional overinvolvement. Emotional overinvolvement is rated on a scale that ranges from 0 (not involved) through 2 (involved) to 5 (overinvolved). In the existing literature on expressed emotion, respondents are classified as either emotionally overinvolved (≥ 3) or not overinvolved (≤ 2). In this sense, then, reductions in EOI are desirable. It seems, however, that 2 (involved) is more desirable clinically than is 0, even though they have not heretofore been distin-

TABLE 7.8
Changes Over Time in Fathers' Expressed Emotion, Communication, and Problem Solving

	Baseline	*16 Weeks*	*16 Months*	*Group Effect*	*Time Effect*	*Time/Group Effect*
Problem-solution statements				$F(1,10)$	$F(2,21)$	$F(2,21)$
Supportive	0.22	0.29	0.23			
Behavioral	0.29	0.40	0.24	0.98	3.29	0.62
Nonfacilitating statements						
Supportive	0.19	0.14	0.19			
Behavioral	0.12	0.06	0.11	6.24*	1.08	0.02
Negative affect						
Supportive	7.10	3.00	4.50			
Behavioral	5.10	2.00	1.20	0.98	2.64	0.26
Communication deviance				$F(1,13)$	$F(2,27)$	$F(2,27)$
Supportive	0.93	0.46	0.49			
Behavioral	0.51	0.32	0.17	1.14	5.27*	0.74
Critical comments						
Supportive	2.00	2.10	1.50			
Behavioral	2.00	0.50	0.40	1.83	1.73	1.29
Emotional overinvolvement						
Supportive	2.00	1.80	1.60			
Behavioral	1.00	1.50	1.70	1.19	0.22	3.85*

*$p < .05$

guished. Fathers in the supportive group reduced their level of emotional overinvolvement from 2.0 to 1.6, whereas the fathers in the behavioral group increased their level of involvement from 1.0 to 1.7. The mothers reduced their levels of overinvolvement from 2.8 to 1.9 in the supportive group and from 2.3 to 2.0 in the behavioral group. These changes, movement toward acceptable involvement, accounts for the only statistically significant interaction in these analyses. In summary, both sets of parents moderated their levels of involvement to a degree the interviewers felt was more appropriate than it had been initially.

Although the numbers in both groups are small, the data are internally consistent and suggest that the parents are changing over time. Their communication and problem solving is improving, their feelings of anger and frustration with the patient are diminishing and, in most instances, they are distancing themselves from the patients while remaining actively involved. Because there was no true control group we cannot unequivocally attribute these changes to the intervention. It may be that both groups of parents would have changed without the intervention or it may be that both interventions were effective and led to greater change than would have occurred with no intervention. The literature strongly suggests that a wide range of interventions are helpful for family members (Kane, 1991), so it is not unreasonable to

TABLE 7.9
Changes Over Time in Mothers' Expressed Emotion, Communication, and Problem Solving

	Baseline	*16 Weeks*	*16 Months*	*Group Effect*	*Time Effect*	*Time/Group Effect*
Problem-solution statements				$F(1,17)$	$F(2,35)$	$F(2,35)$
Supportive	0.18	0.27	0.24			
Behavioral	0.19	0.30	0.24	0.17	3.07	0.07
Nonfacilitating statements						
Supportive	0.14	0.13	0.11			
Behavioral	0.15	0.14	0.14	0.10	0.60	0.18
Negative affect						
Supportive	3.50	3.10	4.30			
Behavioral	7.00	3.50	2.90	0.11	0.93	0.18
Communication deviance				$F(1,19)$	$F(2,39)$	$F(2,39)$
Supportive	0.91	0.51	0.46			
Behavioral	0.86	0.48	0.34	0.09	3.88*	0.05
Critical comments						
Supportive	3.60	2.10	1.80			
Behavioral	3.30	1.20	0.80	0.79	9.90**	0.44
Emotional overinvolvement						
Supportive	2.80	2.30	1.90			
Behavioral	2.30	1.80	2.00	1.54	3.33*	1.21

*$p < .05$. **$p < .01$

conclude that both groups were useful. Where differences emerged it seems that the behavioral intervention was somewhat more effective, although these differences only approached statistical significance.

CHANGES IN PATIENT BEHAVIOR

The patients also changed over time. The patients' overall level of function (GAS) improved and their negative symptoms attenuated, at least among those whose families were in the behavioral intervention. Overall symptomatology remained constant (see Table 7.10).

The patients' behavior during problem solving changed quite dramatically. The proportion of patients' solution statements increased and the proportion of nonfacilitating statements decreased. Patients in the behavioral group reduced the percentage of their nonfacilitating statements by nearly 75%, from .43 to .13. This difference between the supportive and behavioral groups produced a time by group interaction. This interaction was in part due to the very high initial levels of nonfacilitation by the patients in the behavioral group as well as the lower ending levels.

TABLE 7.10
Changes Over Time in Patients' Symptoms, Communication, and Problem Solving

	Baseline	*16 Weeks*	*16 Months*	*Group Effect*	*Time Effect*	*Time/Group Effect*
Overall Patient Function (GAS)				*F*(1,21)	*F*(2,43)	*F*(2,43)
Supportive	43.7	63.2	55.4			
Behavioral	37.8	50.4	50.9	4.99*	9.18**	0.81
Overall Symptom Rating (BPRS)						
Supportive	1.94	2.06	2.03			
Behavioral	2.06	1.75	2.20	0.00	1.57	2.36
Affective Flattening (SANS)						
Supportive	1.77	1.38	1.73			
Behavioral	2.70	1.84	1.68	1.46	4.57*	2.72
Problem-solution statements				*F*(1,17)	*F*(2,35)	*F*(2,35)
Supportive	0.05	0.09	0.07			
Behavioral	0.01	0.08	0.06	1.03	5.52**	0.70
Nonfacilitating statements						
Supportive	0.27	0.27	0.19			
Behavioral	0.43	0.26	0.13	0.31	10.06**	3.63*
Negative affect						
Supportive	0.78	1.89	2.11			
Behavioral	1.50	0.70	0.70	0.51	0.04	0.82

$^{*}p < .05$. $^{**}p < .01$

It may be that it was the improvements in patient function that stimulated the changes in parent behavior, or it may have been that the patients responded to changes in the parent behavior. With only three measures over 16 months it is difficult to assess the direction of effect. It is quite likely that changes could begin with either patient or parent and be reinforced by corresponding changes in the other family members.

EE AND OUTCOME

The final issue addressed here is the relationship between EE and outcome, specifically the ability of the patient to remain out of the hospital following discharge. Although this was not a major objective of the study, the availability of the data made it possible to address this question. At the outset it was not clear whether EE would be related to patient outcome. First, we modified the standard measures. Second, because this sample is more chronic, it may be difficult to predict relapse. There may be too little variance in outcome. Third, because the components of EE were inversely related to contemporaneous measures of patient function it is not clear how EE should be related to outcome.

Our primary measure of outcome is the number of weeks the patient remained out of the hospital during the 12-month follow-up period. This is not a true survival analysis, but it is a better approximation of outcome than a simple dichotomous relapse variable. Using the traditional classification of families as either high EE or low EE measured both at baseline and at the last assessment prior to discharge and, using an EE classification based on a median split at these two assessment points, we found that EE was only marginally related to outcome and not in the expected direction. For example, using the traditional EE classification at baseline those 17 patients with high EE relatives spent 73% more weeks out of the hospital (39.5) than those patients with no high EE relatives (22.8). This difference was marginally statistically significant ($p = .057$). Eliminating those six patients who were never discharged raised both means but did not change the overall result. Replacing EE with its components, CC and EOI, and controlling for medication compliance, does not change the overall pattern.

After controlling for the patients' overall function (GAS) these differences disappear. Outcome is essentially determined by patient function at discharge and this is not affected by the EE index.

SUMMARY AND DISCUSSION

In this project we were able to shorten both the expressed emotion (Camberwell Family Interview) and communication deviance procedures. Using a 45-minute CFI covering the patient's psychiatric history, irritability, and the patient–respondent relationship, we were able to produce measures of CD, EOI, and CC that were related to comparable measures of interaction taken during conjoint problem solving. These produced a consistent and understandable, if unanticipated, pattern of relationships. The small sample of families included in this study raises the possibility that one or two families might distort the true relationships among these variables. Nevertheless, the consistency and stability over time of these relationships offer support for their validity.

Our examination of the relationships among critical comments, emotional overinvolvement, communication deviance, comparable measures taken during problem solving and patient symptomatology and behavior produced a pattern of results consistent with a more complex perspective of family interaction than provided by the traditional diathesis/stress perspective. It seems that these families are attempting to cope with patient goals and ambitions that, as the family has learned from experience, are not likely to be attainable in the short term. The family's efforts to establish limits and to simultaneously support these young adults interfere with the family's communication and problem solving and lead to greater conflict and criticism. This pattern is stronger among those families with patients who have had long hospitalizations but remain relatively high functioning. Those families with the most experience with the recurrent nature of schizophrenia are undoubtedly the most wary, frustrated, and ambivalent. In addition, patients with the highest functioning and longest history of hospitalization are also the most challenging. Undoubtedly, both factors influence family problem solving and coping. Both the patient's history and current behavior serve to stimulate the familial response.

Both interventions seemed to have a salutary impact on the parents and the patients. We observed a reduction of critical and intrusive comments in family problem solving. The behavioral intervention seemed to produce larger and more sustained changes over time. Most families seem to respond favorably to supportive psychoeducational interventions that give them a variety of information about behavioral management strategies and neither exclude them from the patient's care nor blame them for the patient's difficulties.

Finally, EE did not predict outcome, but this was not surprising given the overall pattern of relationships presented. Expressed emotion is only one aspect of a family's response to patient illness, and in this sample of severely and persistently ill patients those factors that are related to criticism and disruptive communication are also related to better patient function. Perhaps it is the pattern of symptoms among these relatively high functioning patients that explains why they are hospitalized. Perhaps it is the family responding to both its expectations as well as patient behavior. In any case, only a more complex model of family interaction that accommodates the dynamic pattern we see here will help us understand this phenomena.

ACKNOWLEDGMENTS

This research was supported by a grant from the Robert Wood Johnson Foundation. The authors acknowledge the contributions of Dr. Patricia Perkins, MD, Veronica Dooley, Jed Graef, Dana Welch, and the staff of the Evaluation and Training Unit, Rochester Psychiatric Center. In addition we would like to thank the families who participated in the study for their cooperation.

REFERENCES

Andreasen, N. C. (1982). Negative symptoms in schizophrenia: Definition and reliability. *Archives of General Psychiatry, 39,* 784–788.

Bernheim, K. F. (1982). Supportive family counseling. *Schizophrenia Bulletin, 8,* 634–640.

Bernheim, K. F., & Lehman, A. F. (1985). *Working with families of the mentally ill.* New York: Norton.

Blechman, E. (1991). Effective communication: Enabling multiproblem families to change. In P. A. Cowen & M. Hetherington (Eds.), *Family transitions* (pp. 219–244). Hillsdale, NJ: Lawrence Erlbaum Associates.

Brown, G. W., Birley, J. L. T., & Wing, J. K. (1972). Influence of family life on the course of schizophrenic disorders: A replication. *British Journal of Psychiatry, 121,* 241–258.

Cole, R. E., Grolnick, W., & Perkins, P. (1986). *Manual for coding communication and problem-solving in family interaction.* Unpublished manuscript, University of Rochester, New York.

Doane, J. A. (1978). Family interaction and communication deviance in disturbed and normal families: A review of research. *Family Process, 17,* 357–394.

Doane, J. A., Falloon, I. R., Goldstein, M. J., & Mintz, J. (1985). Parental affective style and the treatment of schizophrenia: Predicting course of illness and social functioning. *Archives of General Psychiatry, 42,* 34–42.

Doane, J. A., West, K. L., Goldstein, M. J., Rodnick, E. H., & Jones, J. E. (1981). Parental communication deviance and affective style: Predictors of subsequent schizophrenia spectrum disorders in vulnerable adolescents. *Archives of General Psychiatry, 38,* 679–685.

Doane, J. A., Jones, J. E., Fisher, L., Ritzler, B., Singer, M. T., & Wynne, L. C. (1982). Parental communication deviance as a predictor of competence in children at risk for adult psychiatric disorder. *Family Process, 21,* 211–223.

Dulz, B., & Hand, I. (1986). Short-term relapse in young schizophrenics: Can it be predicted and affected by Family (CFI), patient and treatment variables? An experimental study. In M. J. Goldstein, I. Hand, & K. Hahlweg (Eds.), *Treatment of schizophrenia* (pp. 59–75). New York: Springer-Verlag.

Endicott, J., Spitzer, R. L., Fleiss, J. L., & Cohen, J. (1976). The Global Assessment Scale: A procedure for measuring overall severity of psychiatric disturbance. *Archives of General Psychiatry, 33,* 776–771.

Falloon, I. R. H., Boyd, J. L., & McGill, W. (1984). *Family care of schizophrenia.* New York: Guilford Press.

Falloon, I. R. H., Boyd, J. L., McGill, C. W., Razani, J., Moss, H. B., & Gilderman, M. (1982). Family management in the prevention of exacerbations of schizophrenia. *The New England Journal of Medicine, 306,* 1437–1440.

Falloon, I. R. H., Boyd, J. L., McGill, C. W., Williamson, M., Razani, J., Moss, H. B., Gilderman, M., & Simpson, G. M. (1985). Family management in the prevention of morbidity of schizophrenia. *Archives of General Psychiatry, 42,* 887–896.

Forgatch, M. S. (1989). Patterns and outcome in family problem solving: The disrupting effect of negative emotion. *Journal of Marriage and the Family, 51,* 115–124.

Goldstein, M. J. (1987). Family interaction patterns that antedate the onset of schizophrenia and related disorders: A further analysis of data from a longitudinal, prospective study. In K. Halweg & M. J. Goldstein (Eds.), *Understanding major mental disorder* (pp. 11-54). New York: Family Process.

Goldstein, M. J., Judd, L. L., Rodnick, E. H., Alkire, A., & Gould, E. (1968). A method for studying social influence and coping patterns within families of disturbed adolescents. *Journal of Nervous and Mental Disease, 147,* 233-251.

Grad, J., & Sainsbury, P. (1963). Mental illness and the family. *Lancet, 1*(7280), 544-547.

Hahlweg, K., Goldstein, M. J., Nuechterlein, K. H., Magana, A. B., Mintz, J., Doane, J. A., Miklowitz, D. J., & Snyder, K. S. (1989). Expressed emotion and patient-relative interaction in families of recent onset schizophrenics. *Journal of Counseling and Clinical Psychology, 57*(1), 11–18.

Hatfield, A. B. (1987). Families as caregivers: A historical perspective. In A. B. Hatfield & H. P. Lefley (Eds.), *Families of the mentally ill: Coping and adaptation* (pp. 3-29). New York: Guilford Press.

Hogarty, G. E., McEvoy, J. P., Munetz, M., DiBarry, A. L., Bartone, P., Cather, R., Cooley, S. J., Ulrich, R. F., Carter, M., & Madonia, M. J. (1988). Dose of fluphenazine, familial expressed emotion, and outcome in schizophrenia. *Archives of General Psychiatry, 45,* 797–805.

Holden, D. F., & Lewine, R. R. J. (1982). How families evaluate mental health professionals, resources, and effects of illness. *Schizophrenia Bulletin, 8,* 626-633.

Hooley, J. M. (1985). Expressed emotion: A review of the critical literature. *Clinical Psychology Review, 5,* 119-139.

Jacob, T. (1975). Family interaction in disturbed and normal families: A methodological and substantive review. *Psychology Bulletin, 82,* 33-65.

Jones, J. E. (1977). Patterns of transactional style deviance in the TAT's of parents of schizophrenics. *Family Process, 16,* 327-337.

Jones, J. E., Rodnick, E. H., Goldstein, M. J., McPherson, S. R., & West, K. L. (1977). Parental transactional style deviance as a possible indicator of risk for schizophrenia. *Archives of General Psychiatry, 34,* 71–74.

Jones, J. E., Wynne, L. C., Al-Khayyal, M., Doane, J. A., Ritzler, B., Singer, M. T., & Fisher, L. (1984). Predicting current school competence of high risk children with a composite cross-situational measure of parental communication. In N. F. Watt, E. J. Anthony, L. C. Wynne, & J. E. Rolf (Eds.), *Children at risk for schizophrenia: A longitudinal perspective* (pp. 393-398). New York: Cambridge University Press.

Kane, C. F. (1992). Psychoeducational programs: From blaming to caring. In E. Kahan, D. E. Biegel, & M. Wykel (Eds.), *Family caregiving across the lifespan.* Newbury Park, CA: Sage.

Karno, M., Jenkins, J., de la Selva, A., Santana, F., Telles, C., Lopez, S., & Mintz, J. (1987). Expressed emotion and schizophrenia outcome among Mexican-American families, *Journal of Nervous and Mental Disease, 175,* 143–151.

Kottgen, C., Sonnichsen, I., Mollenhauer, K., Jurth, R. (1984a). The family relations of young schizophrenic patients: Results of the Hamburg Camberwell Family Interview Study I. *International Journal of Family Psychiatry, 5,* 61–70.

Kottgen, C., Sonnichsen, I., Mollenhauer, K., Jurth, R. (1984b). Families' high-expressed-emotions and relapses in young schizophrenic patients: Results of the Hamburg Camberwell Family Interview Study II. *International Journal of Family Psychiatry, 5,* 61–70.

Leff, J. (1976). Schizophrenia and sensitivity to the family environment. *Schizophrenia Bulletin,* 2(4), 560–574.

Leff, J., Berkowitz, R., Shavit, N., Strachan, A, Glass, I., & Vaughn C. (1989). A trial of family therapy versus a relative's group for schizophrenia. *British Journal of Psychiatry, 154,* 58–66.

Leff, J., Berkowitz, R., Shavit, N., Strachan, A, Glass, I., & Vaughn C. (1990). A trial of family therapy versus a relative's group for schizophrenia: Two year follow-up. *British Journal of Psychiatry, 157,* 571–577.

Leff, J., Kuipers, L., Berkowitz, R., Eberlein-Vries, R., & Sturgeon, D. (1982). A controlled trial of social intervention in the families of schizophrenic patients. *British Journal of Psychiatry, 141,* 121–134.

Leff, J., & Vaughn, C. (1980). The interaction of life events and relatives' expressed emotion in schizophrenia and depressive neurosis. *British Journal of Psychiatry, 136,* 146–153.

Leff, J. P., Wig, N., Bedi, H., Menon, D. K., Kuipers, L., Korten, A., Ernberg, G., Day, R., Sartorius, N., & Jablensky, A. (1990). Relatives' expressed emotion and the course of schizophrenia in Chandigarh: A two-year follow-up of a first-contact sample. *British Journal of Psychiatry, 156,* 351–356.

Lefley, H. P. (1987). Behavioral manifestations of mental illness. In A. B. Hatfield & H. P. Lefley, (Eds.), *Families of the mentally ill: Coping and adaptation* (pp. 225–243). New York: Guilford Press.

Liberman, R. P., Falloon, I., & Aitchison, R. A. (1984). Multiple family therapy for schizophrenia: A behavioral problem-solving approach. *Psychosocial Rehabilitation Journal,* 7(4), 60–77.

MacMillan, J. F., Gold, A., Crow, T. J., Johnson, A. L., & Johnstone, E. C. (1986). IV. Expressed emotion and relapse. *British Journal of Psychiatry, 148,* 133–143.

McElroy, E. M. (1987). The beat of a different drummer. In A. B. Hatfield & H. P. Lefley (Eds.), *Families of the mentally ill: Coping and adaptation* (pp. 225–243). New York: Guilford Press.

McReadie, R. G., & Phillips, K. (1988). The Nithsdale schizophrenia Survey—VII. Does relatives' high EE predict relapse? *British Journal of Psychiatry, 152,* 477–481.

Miklowitz, D. J., Goldstein, M. J., Falloon, I. R. H., & Doane, J. A. (1984). Interactional correlates of expressed emotion in the families of schizophrenics. *British Journal of Psychiatry, 144,* 482–487.

Miklowitz, D. J., Strachan, A. M., Goldstein, M. J., Doane, J. A., Snyder, K. S., Hogarty, G. E., & Falloon, I. R. H. (1986). Expressed emotion and communication deviance in the families of schizophrenics. *Journal of Abnormal Psychology,* 95(1), 60–66.

Moline, R. A., Singh, S., Morris, A., & Meltzer, H. Y. (1985). Family expressed emotion and relapse in schizophrenia in 24 urban american patients. *American Journal of Psychiatry,* 142(9), 1078–1081.

Nuechterlein, K. H., Snyder, K. S., Dawson, M. E., Rappe, S., Gitlin, M., & Fogelson, D. (1986). Expressed emotion, fixed-dose fluphenazine decanoate maintenance and relapse in recent-onset schizophrenia. *Pharmacology Bulletin, 22*(3), 633–639.

Overall, J. E., & Gorham, D. R. (1962). The Brief Psychiatric Rating Scale. *Psychological Reports, 10,* 799–812.

Parker, G., Johnston, P., & Hayward, L. (1988). Parental "expressed emotion" as a predictor of schizophrenic relapse. *Archives of General Psychiatry, 45,* 806–813.

Runions, J., & Prudo, R. (1983). Problem behaviors encountered by families living with a schizophrenic member. *Canada Journal of Psychiatry, 28,* 382–386.

Schuldberg, D., Singer, M. T., & Wynne, L. C. (1990). Competence-enhancing communication by parents of high-risk children. *Journal of Family Psychology, 3*(3), 255–272.

Singer, M. T. (1967). Family transactions and schizophrenia: I. Recent research findings. In J. Romano (Ed.), *The origins of schizophrenia* (pp. 147–164). Armsterdam: Exerpta Medica Foundation.

Singer, M. T., & Wynne, L. C. (1963). Differentiating characteristics of the parents of childhood schizophrenics, childhood neurotics, and young adult schizophrenics. *American Journal of Psychiatry, 120,* 234–243.

Singer, M. T., & Wynne, L. C. (1965). Thought disorder and family relations of schizophrenics: IV. Results and implications. *Archives of General Psychiatry, 12,* 201–206.

Strachan, A. M., Leff, J. P., Goldstein, M. J., Doane, J. A., & Burtt, C. (1986). Emotional attitudes and direct communication in the families of schizophrenics: A cross-national replication. *British Journal of Psychiatry, 149,* 279–287.

Strodtbeck, F. L. (1951). Husband wife interaction over revealed differences. *American Sociological Review, 16,* 468–473.

Tarrier, N., Barrowclough, C., Vaughn, C., Bamrah, J. S., Porceddu, K., Watts, S., & Freeman, H. (1988). The community management of schizophrenia: A controlled trial of a behavioral intervention with families to reduce relapse. *British Journal of Psychiatry, 153,* 532–542.

Tarrier, N., Barrrowclough, C., Vaughn, C., Bamrah, J. S., Porceddu, K., Watts, S., & Freeman, H. (1989). Community management of schizophrenia: A two-year follow-up of a behavioral intervention with families. *British Journal of Psychiatry, 154,* 625–628.

Terkelsen, K. G. (1987a). The evolution of family responses to mental illness through time. In A. B. Hatfield & H. P. Lefley (Eds.), *Families of the mentally ill: Coping and adaptation* (pp. 151–166). New York: Guilford Press.

Terkelsen, K. G. (1987b). The meaning of mental illness to the family. In A. B. Hatfield & H. P. Lefley (Eds.), *Families of the mentally ill: Coping and adaptation* (pp. 128–150). New York: Guilford Press.

Valone, K., Norton, J. P., Goldstein, M. J., & Doane, J. A. (1983). Parental expressed emotion and affective style in an adolescent sample at risk for schizophrenia spectrum disorders. *Journal of Abnormal Psychology, 92*(4), 399–407.

Vaughn, C., & Leff, J. (1976). The measurement of expressed emotion in the families of psychiatric patients. *British Journal of Social and Clinical Psychology, 15,* 137–165.

Vaughn, C. E., Snyder, K. S., Jones, S., Freeman, W. B., & Falloon, I. R. H. (1984). Family factors in schizophrenic relapse: Replication in California of British research on Expressed Emotion. *Archives of General Psychiatry, 41,* 1169–1177.

Wynne, L. C., Singer, M. T., Bartko, J. J., & Toohey, M. L. (1977). Schizophrenics and their families: Recent research on parental communication. In J. E. Tanner (Ed.), *Developments in psychiatric research* (pp. 254–286). Sevenoaks, Kent: Hodder ans Stoughton, Ltd.

Wynne, L. C. (1983). A phase-oriented approach to treatment with schizophrenics and their families. In W. R. McFarlane (Ed.), *Family therapy in schizophrenia* (pp. 251–265). New York: Guilford Press.

Wynne, L. C., & Cole, R. E. (1983). The Rochester Risk Research Program: A new look at parental diagnoses and family relationships. In H. Stierlin, L. C. Wynne, & M. Wirsching (Eds.), *Psychosocial intervention in schizophrenia: An international view* (pp. 35–48). New York: Springer-Verlag.

CHAPTER 8

The Family's Organization Around the Illness

David Reiss
Peter Steinglass
George Howe
George Washington University Medical Center

It is a paradox of modern medicine that chronic physical illness is increasingly prevalent across the life span. For children and adults, many recent technical innovations have prolonged the lives of those who suffer severe illness and injury. For many of those afflicted, a sure and rapid death has been replaced by a prolonged life of uncertain duration, filled with serious pain and disability. However, because virtually all of those who are chronically ill or disabled live in families, it is important to think of chronic illness as now more prevalent in families, not just in individuals, and prevalent with increasing frequency across the family's full span of development. We explore the idea that it is the family, as a unit, that is both affected with and challenged by chronic physical disease.

As our work has progressed on the family with chronic illness, we have recognized that this area will be central in the field of family research for three reasons. First, because of its increasing prevalence, chronic illness is less an exotic rarity and more a common component of human and family development. Thus, a complete understanding of child and adult development, as well as a full grasp of the marital and family processes, must take into account both the impact of chronic illness on the family and, conversely, the influence of the family on the biology of the illness itself. Second, a close study of families facing the challenge of severe chronic illness can illumine central issues of family processes that are otherwise hard to observe. For example, we describe later in this chapter how some preliminary family research data in this area may lead us to rethink the processes surrounding dying, death, and bereavement. Third, family research has its pragmatic side, and an understanding of the family with chronic illness is of central importance to clinicians who help such families adapt to the associated stress.

Although our team has been working in this area for over 6 years, we still regard ourselves as just beginning to understand the intersection of chronic physical illness and the family. In this chapter, which should be viewed as an early progress report, we review the main themes emerging from our work to date. However, we recognize this report is not only an update from our laboratory, but is also part of more comprehensive scientific communication: the series of summer institutes designed by the Family Research Consortium to explore the cutting edge of method and theory in family science. As a consequence, we do more in this chapter than simply note our progress. We hope to expose for public scrutiny and critique our basic strategies of work.

The chapter is divided into three main sections. In the first section we present a synopsis of the theoretical perspective we used when we began working with families having chronic illness. In the second section, we describe how we revised this model to take into account the unique experiences of these families. Two research projects based on this perspective are described. The first involved a longitudinal study of families with a member having end-stage renal disease. The second was a qualitative participant-observation study of families engaged in multiple family psychoeducational groups for families with members having chronic physical disorders. Finally, in the third section, we discuss the implications of our research. In this section we summarize our thinking and introduce a new topic: the role of characteristic of the illness itself (e.g., involving or not involving the brain) in a model of family process.

INITIAL PERSPECTIVE

Our work with chronic physical disorders has been heavily influenced by our prior research with both clinical and nonclinical families, especially our studies of families with members having alcoholism (Steinglass, Bennet, Wolin, & Reiss, 1987); and our studies focusing on the problem-solving activities of nonclinical families (Reiss & Klein, 1987). Influenced by family systems theory, one of the goals of this prior research has been the elucidation of properties of whole families that not only distinguish among types of families but also provide clues as to the processes within the family that account for both stability and change of its structures. Toward this goal, we have attempted to construct models of family functioning that see family behavior as the product of two interacting forces—structures that provide developmental (change-oriented) thrust for the family; and regulatory structures that provide stability and patterning to family life over time. The following is a brief overview of the model of family process that has emerged from this work.

We start with the premise that families, in order to serve the immediate and long-term needs of their members, must develop *patterned* structures of transaction both among members, and between members and people outside the family. In considering how such transaction patterns are regulated and maintained over time, we have focused particular attention on two closely related "regulatory structures" that we have termed the *family paradigm* (Reiss & Klein, 1987) and the *family identity* (Steinglass et al., 1987).

The family paradigm refers to implicit emotionally charged conceptions shared by members of the same family. These are conceptions by the family of the social world in which they live: conceptions of its order, equity, coherence, and novelty. Family identity refers to equally implicit conceptions the family has about itself in relation to that social world: conceptions of its own competence, stature, intactness, and durability. These shared conceptions guide and constrain the behavior patterns of the family, setting a stable base for the transactional patterns that provide for the needs of the members.

In the course of our work with families having alcohol abusing members, it became clear that such family structures evolve over time, following a time course we have termed *systemic maturation* (Steinglass et al., 1987). By this we refer to unidirectional changes over time in the family as a unit. Despite the current popularity of developmental perspectives, the concept of systemic maturation is not widely understood. Even seasoned family researchers tend to think of development of individual members within families, individual trajectories that may be tightly or loosely linked depending on both the family and the individuals. In contrast, we have viewed the family itself as a unitary organism with its own developmental phases and transformations. This development is driven in part by the biological maturation of family members. The relationship between systems maturation and individual maturation within families is still unclear although, as we discuss, the study of families with chronic illness is an excellent opportunity to observe relationships of this kind. However, we hypothesize that much of this relationship is reciprocal, with family transactions driving the development of individual members as much as a member's development drives changes in family structure.

The final concept we present here is *developmental distortion.* This refers to the distortion of family structures that support systemic maturation. Such distortions occur when events alter family transactions in such a way that the needs of the family as a group are no longer met, or revisions in family transactions necessary for the next stages of individual development cannot occur. Most frequently this occurs when the demands or needs of one family member come to dictate the pace of family life, superceding the process of systemic maturation. At this point, it is fair to say that family development has become *organized* around an individual-level developmental time course rather than the time course suited to the family as a group. A particularly important issue here is the finding in our research both with chronic medical and psychiatric illness families, that the chronic illness itself (e.g., alcoholism, traumatic physical injury) has the capacity to become such a central organizing principle for family life. When this occurs, we say that the chronic illness and its demands have secondarily produced such a developmental distortion for the family.

To illustrate the interplay between the concepts of family identity, systems maturation, and developmental distortion we turn to some of our work on alcoholism that provided much of the stimulus for the generation of these family systems regulatory and developmental constructs. We approached the task as a two-step process. First we wanted to develop a set of systemic constructs about regulation and development that would hold generally for any family, be it a new heterosexual marriage, a serious gay relationship, or a recent remarriage in a stepfamily. Then we asked the question: In what ways does the presence of chronic alcoholism in one or more family members generate *alcohol-specific* demands that alter both the character of family regulatory processes (identity and paradigm) and developmental processes (distortion)?

Here is how we proposed such a two-step process might look when applied to the early phase of family life when alcoholism surfaces as a major challenge. Ordinarily there are two interlinked tasks that must be addressed in the early phase of any family's life. First, the new family must clarify and redefine its links with past families. For the newlywed couple, these are the families of origin of each spouse. For the gay couple, it might be the families of origin but also might be past lovers. For the stepfamily, it is typically the relationship with previous spouses as well as continuing relationships with children from former marriages. The companion task is for the couple to establish a new or particular sense of identity: to answer the question, "What kind of a new family are we?" In the earliest phase this may often be formulated or experienced as: "How are we different than the previous family of which we were members?"

From the beginning, alcohol can severely distort this early developmental process (Steinglass et al., 1987). When, for example, either member of the new couple had a drinking problem prior to the start of the new family, the more typical redefinitions of links with past families and the nascent identity of the new family are subsumed under a more pressing developmental dilemma: the need to answer the question, "Will we become an alcoholic family?" Our observations suggested that there were three options for the new family. First, the family could vigilantly banish all alcohol or even any exposure to the risk of alcohol. This might be achieved by enforcing abstinence among family members. It could lead the couple to distance themselves from one or both families of origin if either had drinking members, or to break ties with friends who drink. A second option for the family is to allow, consciously or unconsciously, for serious drinking to enter the new family with the risk of alcohol dominating its life. In the latter case, the family is on its way to becoming a true alcoholic family. In the former case, because the family is still so dominated by preoccupations with alcohol, it is fair to term it an early version of a *dry alcoholic family*. Both versions clearly represent developmental distortions.

A third option allows for either moderate social drinking or abstinence. In this option, alcoholic issues are subordinated to the major developmental tasks of this period. It is this option that clarifies most precisely what we mean by systems maturation. When confronted with the risk of alcoholism, say a history of problem drinking in one partner, it is not enough for the individual partner at risk simply to abstain. The development of the relationship depends on the concerted action of both partners to remove the issue of alcoholism from their relationship. Abstinence in the presence of high vigilance by both members leads to the dry alcoholic option described here in which the fear of alcoholism may distort development in ways curiously analogous to the presence of severe problem drinking. Our work has led us to a typology of family structures, contrasting *distinctive* families who protect their transactions from the drinking of one of the members and *subsumptive* families whose development is subsumed by either problem drinking or the fear of it (Steinglass et al., 1987).

APPLICATION TO CHRONIC ILLNESS

These concepts appeared very applicable to the understanding of families living with chronic physical disorder. Earlier researchers had developed models of family reaction to physical disorder (Farber, 1968), but had not attempted to consider the family as a structured and developing unit in this process of adjustment. Our initial thinking emphasized the potential for developmental distortion in the family system as a result of the demands of the chronic illness. An illustration of this application comes from our description of one of the first families with which we worked.

The family consisted of Mr. and Mrs. Saunders (as we call them), a couple in their mid-50s, and their three children—an 18-year-old boy, a younger son, and a 13-year-old daughter. One afternoon, on a broad avenue in Baltimore, MD, Mr. Saunders was carrying out his duties as manager of a grocery store. The place was held up by armed robbers, and, in a vicious departing gesture, they shot Mr. Saunders through the spinal cord, leading to a complete transection and dense paraplegia.

It was the view of the medical staff caring for Mr. Saunders that both patient and family had made an excellent adjustment to their situation. Always a close-knit family, the Saunders were now viewed as a model family because of their capacity to rally around and support this terribly injured man. The insurance companies and rehabilitation training programs also viewed the family's ability to cope as exemplary, and both photographed and publicized the situation.

However, our own evaluation of the family, based on research assessments that included home observations and conjoint family interviews carried out about a year after the shooting, produced a disquieting and very different view of how the Saunders were functioning. Rather than seeing them as a family who had successfully integrated medical care needs into ongoing family life, we found them quite rigidly organized around a single principle: "Let's support father." Particularly salient as a clue here was the spatial rearrangement of the family home we found at the time of our initial home visit. A plan of the upstairs floor is shown in Fig. 8.1.

The cross-hatched areas indicate what changes had been made in response to the illness. On the ground floor, those alterations that had occurred were primarily remodeling changes to make the kitchen and dining areas wheelchair accessible (not reflected in the diagram). In addition, what had formerly been a music room was turned into a room with physical therapy paraphernalia. But otherwise rooms retained their prior functions. On the second floor, however, everything had been dramatically changed. Each of the three children used to have a private room, but now the father had been moved, with his special bed, into the older son's bedroom. An uncle (the mother's brother)—whom we had never heard about despite all the interviewing of this family—had moved in and became very close to his sister; he participated in almost every family activity (we discovered his presence in the family system only by making this home visit). He was occupying another

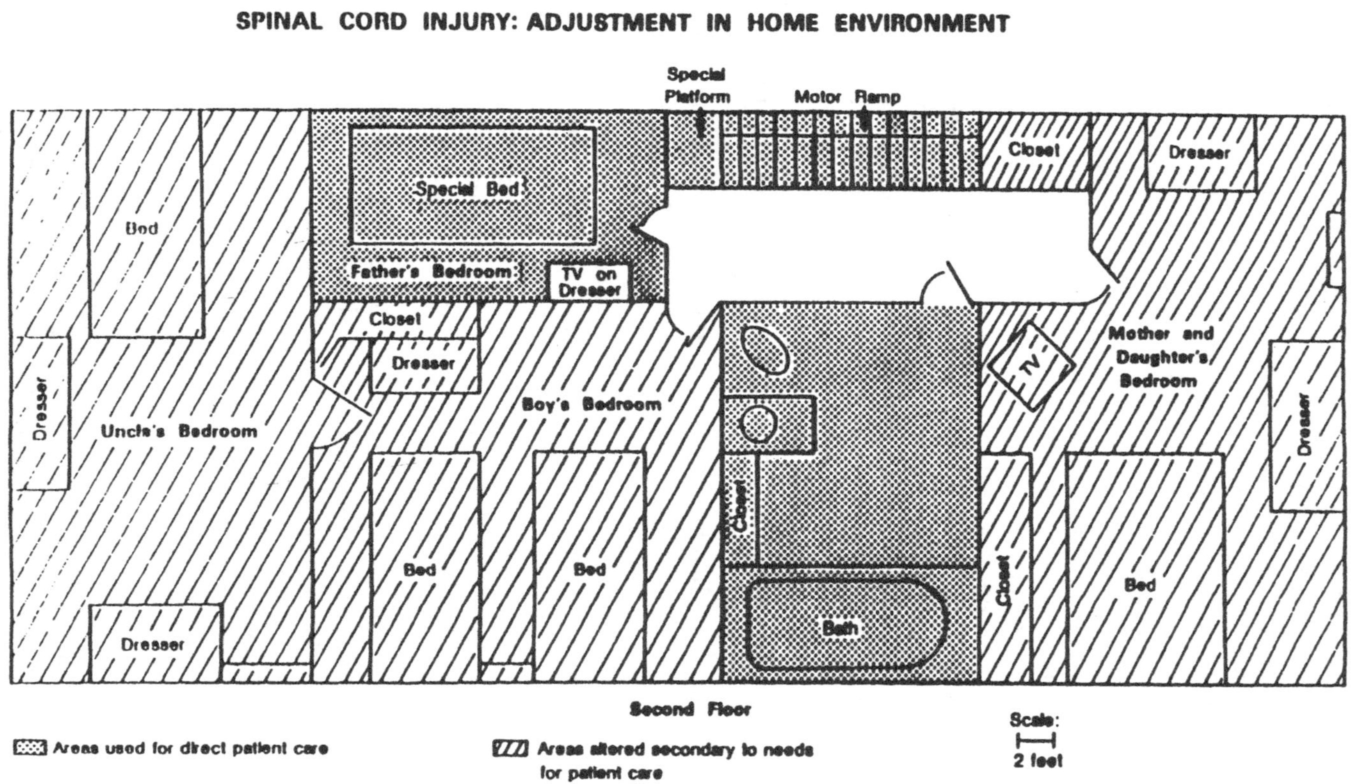

FIG. 8.1 Upstairs floor plan of the Saunders home.

child's bedroom, and the two boys were now sharing the same room. The adolescent daughter was sleeping in the father's old place in mother's bed. Closet and storage space had also been disrupted and reassigned – most telling was that none of the children were now able to keep their clothing in the rooms in which they were sleeping. Nor were there any clear-cut assignments of space for schoolwork or supplies. Instead, these items were cubbyholed in odd places; the main closet and dresser spaces had been assigned instead to medical supplies.

This panorama gave us a sense that the family, organizing around the father's illness, was no longer keeping track of the developmental needs of other members. In fact, the situation appeared quite tragic. Family processes were insensitive to the entire system and its requirements and how individuals fit together as a family. Tending to the illness seemed to have life and death consequences for everyone. The children had to subordinate many of their own needs. For example, both boys were always called upon to move the father in and out of bed or the car. Eventually their own conditions began to worsen; the older son's diabetes got out of control; the other son repeated several grades and had trouble finishing high school; and the daughter became more and more isolated socially.

The family, once highly organized by rules, now viewed the family itself as a tyrant, a disembodied tyrant. Finally, almost inevitably, there was a rebellion. The mother, after 2 years, decided to take the younger son on the first vacation anyone had taken since the injury. The father counter-rebelled, refused to eat, and while his wife was away on vacation, developed serious bedsores and was admitted to the hospital. Despite major efforts, he continued to refuse nourishment, and died. The family managed to regroup, and some follow-up data showed that the older son, at least, did return to reasonably adequate functioning and went into the grocery business.

This case illustrated processes with which we were already familiar. The most conspicuous is the impact of a chronic illness on essential systems development. Clearly, in the Saunders family, this development had become subsumed by Mr. Saunders' disability. More properly, the family's organization around the illness, by subsuming its more ordinary and essential developmental needs, had dramatically skewed (distorted) family life.

However, this case also illustrates other aspects of family process that appeared very salient for families with chronic illness, but that had not been part of our initial model. First, we began to note the impact of a second system, the medical team, on the forms of reorganization engaged in by families. This suggested we could no longer focus on the family as the only social system. Chronic illness often brought the family into regular and intimate contact with medical staff, and these staff members were often members of clinics that functioned as structured systems in their own right. In the Saunders case, this team unwittingly reinforced the family's rigid organization of its resources around the illness. The family's devotion to its patriarch was conspicuously endorsed by the medical staff. As a result, we now believe it important to expand our model to include both social structures, and to develop ways of characterizing the interactions between the two.

Second, it became clear that certain properties of chronic physical disorder were likely to have predictable effects on the family. In the Saunders case it was clear how much Mr. Saunders' impaired mobility served to shape family reorganization. It constrained father's activities at home and was a stimulus to major reorganization of house space that appeared to reflect the underlying social reorganization of the family's transaction. This suggested that our model needed to make explicit reference to important properties of various illness conditions as providing certain patterns of demands on families. As Rolland (1984) pointed out, episodic illnesses like epilepsy are likely to have very different effects on the family than persistent illness such as renal failure; likewise illness with a deteriorating course and fatal outcome, such as some types of cancer, will have a different impact than serious but stable conditions such as paraplegia from traumatic spinal cord injury.

Third, it was apparent that chronic illness placed demands on families that changed over time. These demands appeared to fall into three categories: (a) those related to the onset of a condition, usually putting families into an initial state of crisis; (b) those related to chronic management of the condition; and (c) those demands during the terminal period of the illness. In some families, such as the Saunders, these three situations followed in order, superimposing a cycle of demands on the other developmental tasks of the family. In other families, including those with members having stable and nonprogressive disorders, most of the time the family deals with chronic aspects of the condition.

Finally, we were increasingly impressed by how important the periods of transition between these phases were to these families, in particular how disruptive developmental transitions were to families who were otherwise so rigidly organized around illness concerns and focused on maintenance rather than change issues. Initial longitudinal observations began to suggest the mechanisms by which families relinquished one stage for the next. In the Saunders case, this was reflected in the "tyranny" constructed by the family and its rebellion against what it had itself wrought.

To summarize, our early experiences with chronic physical disorder suggested the importance of the close interweaving of the family system, the medical care community, and the biological properties and changes of the illness itself. Our work now centers on this newly conceived suprasystem, which we have termed the *caregiving system,* and its components. We are interested not only in the relationships among the components of the caregiving system, but on the transformation of this suprasystem across time. As in ordinary family system maturation, we suspect there are phases and transformations of this suprasystem. We have tentatively identified three phases: the acute phase where the caregiving system is organized around the technical requirements of emergency care and rapid and accurate diagnosis; the chronic phase where the system is organized to support both biological and interpersonal maintenance; and a terminal phase which, stimulated by impending or actual death, is focused on comfort and composure. We now describe two research studies that have been based on this perspective.

Study 1: The Caregiving System and Patient Survival

Our first set of data in this scientific venture underscored the importance of the caregiving system and its transformations. The original design of this study, however, did not set out to test these ideas. Instead, we were initially interested in the shared family belief systems we called *paradigms.* Our first question was: How might these shared beliefs, held more or less in common by all members of the family, shape the family's response to the stress of chronic illness? Our findings were not only surprising but took us well beyond an understanding of the impact of family paradigms on the family with chronic illness. Indeed, the findings suggested even more about systems maturation and its linkage with the biology of chronic illness.

Initially we thought that families who experienced mastery and control over the social world, families high on a dimension of paradigm we have called *configuration,* might better meet the challenges of the complex medical and social routines of severe illness. Likewise, families who regarded themselves as a unitary and cohesive group, those high on a dimension we have called *coordination,* would develop more effective collaborative strategies for managing the emotional and practical challenges of illness. Finally, families who were open to the novelty of experience, families high on delayed *closure,* might be sensitive to significant clinical changes in the patient and thus respond early to impending complications in the course of illness. We thought all three of these features of family life would not only lead to better emotional adjustment in the family but contribute to a more benign course of illness. Although we observed families long enough so that almost half our sample sustained the death of the patient, we did not imagine that our variables would predict survival.

Although there are many prevalent illnesses that would be important to study, we picked end-stage renal disease in adults, focusing on patients being treated with hemodialysis, for three reasons. First, the death rate in this illness is fairly constant across the span of illness (about 10%–12% per year). We wanted to study a potentially fatal illness not so much to predict survival time but to have an illness that would constitute a severe stress for the family. Second, despite the heterogeneity of causes of chronic renal disease once the endstate is reached, there is a good deal of biological homogeneity among patients: They all have kidneys that do not work and all of them are at risk for the same consequences of this condition. The major biological heterogeneity comes from the presence of other illnesses, chiefly diabetes. This comorbidity can be easily measured to develop a simple index of biological severity. Third, the treatment of end-stage renal disease, for those patients who are treated by dialysis, is very uniform.

The methods of this study have been presented in detail elsewhere (Reiss, Gonzalez, & Kramer, 1986), so here we present only the highlights. We observed 23 families, following them for 3 or more years to note how they changed over time. To measure configuration, coordination, and closure, we brought three or four family members together in a standard problem-solving situation (Reiss, 1981). Each family was given a set of cards and asked to sort them in any way they wanted. Each member had a desk in front of him or her and was prevented from seeing others by a partition. Some families recognize, sooner or later, that the cards can be sorted according to a pattern. According to previous studies, such families are not smarter or do not have more schooling, nor are they higher in social class. These factors are critical when test situations have time limits, which ours does not. Families who reach this solution are families who believe they can master the setting and, as a consequence search for all the information they possibly can find in acting to achieve the solution. Other families much more casually group the cards by simpler rules. This behavior often reflects a search for the easiest way out of the challenge of the test. Other data suggest an exit of this kind is sought because the family feels threatened by the test situation.

Coordination, in this setting, is shown by whether the family sticks together under a moderately stressful test situation such as this. Do families stay closely paced as they go from trial to trial? All families are required by the tester to lay out the cards two by two. Families who can stick together, trial by trial, are in many respects more tightly woven, integrated, coordinated families. Members in other families pay no attention to each other. Such members do not even talk to each other in this setting, and so members end the trials at very different times.

Closure is measured by several indices reflecting the families' openness to new data on the cards that are displayed later in the task. Early closure families develop a sorting system early in the task and stick with it no matter how disconfirming subsequent data may be.

We also used two other sets of family predictors. The first we call *accomplishment*. This has several components: intelligence of family members, education, occupational status of the patient or principle wage earner, and total household income. These four variables were highly correlated in this sample of families. Thus, we combined them all into one dimension of family accomplishment. This dimension was not correlated at all with any of three measures of family paradigm. Another facet is *intactness* of the family: Is there a marriage? Are there grandparents available to help? How long have the patient and the spouse been married? Indicators of intactness were intercorrelated and statistically unrelated to the paradigm dimensions and to accomplishment.

We added these two variables largely on an intuitive basis. The dimensions of paradigm, although important in our own thinking, did not seem adequately comprehensive to explain much variance in any of the outcome measures. Having these additional results turned out to be a lucky break. Table 8.1 summarizes the design of the study.

Although we included several measures of family functioning and adjustment, it was the survival data themselves that were most striking. Results are summarized in Table 8.2. We found that families who were most coordinated, correcting for any differences in medical severity, had patients who died the soonest. (Delayed closure, as we had predicted, did presage fewer complications.) When we looked at the accomplishment variables, we found a similar surprising pattern. The brightest families with the most patient education, the highest occupational status, and the largest household income did more poorly than the rest. A similar pattern emerged with the intactness variables: More highly intact families had members with lower survival rates.

How did this happen? We reasoned that perhaps it is something about these close families with high levels of engagement in the community who are more successful and able to remain intact. It is possible that these characteristics that predict survival might influence compliance with the complex dialysis regimen. We had a good deal of compliance data; body weight data, reflecting the patient's care in restricting fluid intake; the patient's potassium and phosphorus re-

TABLE 8.1
Time Intervals From Entry Into Study and Variable Measured

Mean Time, mo	*Variables*
−22.3	Time from first diagnosis of renal disease to study entry; no variables measured
−7.9	Time from beginning dialysis to entering study; no variables measured
0	Entry into study
	Demographic variables measured
	Patient: age, occupation, intelligence, marital status, previous marriages, race, sex
	Family: age (mean), No. of persons in current household
	Illness variables measured
	Severity, duration of renal disease, duration of dialysis, patient age (see above)
	Family predictor variables measured
	Problem solving: configuration, coordination, closure
	Accomplishment: intelligence (family mean), education (patient only), occupational status (head of household), income (total household)
	Integration: years married, marital status, family size*
0–9	Noncompliance measured
	Variation in body weight, phosphorus, potassium, nurses' ratings
15–24	Frequency of complications measured
27	First follow-up for death or survival
36	Second follow-up for death or survival

*This variable reflects number of living grandparents.

Source: Reiss, Gonzalez, and Kramer (1986). Copyright © 1986 American Medical Association.

flecting other dieting restrictions and medication compliance; and the nurses' ratings of compliance with several aspects of the dialysis regimen. For coordination, there were no significant relationships, but for the other two dimensions there were strong relationships (see Table 8.3). We found that the more accomplished family members were, the more compliant they were. Nurses' ratings of noncompliance were also lower for these families. The same relationship was found for family intactness and compliance. It is important to note that the variation in compliance measures did not reflect differences between moderate levels of compliance and negligence. Our compliant patients were ritualistic in their compliance. They were fastidious; they never missed a beat; there was a devotion to compliance. It is conceivable that this ritualistic compliance is a mechanism for lessening, not enhancing, chances of survival. Our "noncompliant" patients were, in contrast, perhaps more reasoned. They followed the dialysis regimen for the most part but took occasional holidays from some of the dietary and medication requirements, as well as very occasional holidays from the dialysis itself. This distinction in compliance patterns, first noted by O'Brien

TABLE 8.2
Correlations Between Predictor and Outcome Variables

Variables	Outcome Variables: Alive at 27 mo	Outcome Variables: Alive at 36 mo
Problem Solving		
Configuration	−.17	−.09
Coordination	−.50*	−.41**
Closure	−.09	−.01
Resources-accomplishment		
Intelligence	−.51*	−.65***
Patient education	−.48*	−.41**
Occupational status, head of household	−.16	−.15
Household income	−.46*	−.47*
Intactness		
Years married	−.33	−.64***
Marital status (0 = unmarried, 1 = married)	−.35**	−.48*
Family size	−.46*	−.64***
Other family variables		
Family age, mean of all members in household	.08	−.09
Previous marriages	.31	.21
No. of people in current household	.27	.17

Note: Excludes two patients who died during the first year of the study. $^{*}p < .05$, $^{**}p < .10$, $^{***}p < .01$

Data on household income were missing or unreliable for five families; thus, this analysis used a sample of 18. For other analyses using this variable, household income was estimated from other accomplishment variables, and the sample size was 23.

(1983), turned out to be predictive. High levels of compliance did predict early death.

How do we explain these findings? Three processes seem important to consider here. These involve: (a) the paradoxical vulnerability of "strong" families, (b) the exclusion of the ill member as a last-stage coping effort, and (c) medical compliance as acceptance of exclusion.

The Vulnerability of Strong Families

Why should these strong families be most vulnerable? Let us examine each component of their strength in turn.

Coordination. Recent studies suggest that most families dealing with the first phase of severe illness tend to coalesce around the illness and become more closely integrated and tied together to deal with its pervasive and protean demands (Maurin & Schenkel, 1976; Penn, 1983; Sheinberg, 1983; Steinglass, Temple, Lisman, & Reiss, 1982). However,

TABLE 8.3
Correlations With Compliance Variables of Those Family Variables Significantly Correlated With Complications or Survival

	Noncompliance Variables				
Variables	*SD of Body Weight*	*Highest Potassium*	*Potassium Range*	*Mean Phosphorus*	*Nurses' Ratings*
Problem Solving					
Coordination	−.03	−.11	−.02	−.35	−.21
Closure	.40*	−.19	.17	.22	.29
Resource-accomplishment					
Education (patient)	−.51**	−.24	−.43*	−.29	−.47***
Family intelligence	−.49****	−.37	−.77****	−.31	−.31
Patient	−.23	−.30	−.58****	−.07	−.21
Other 1	−.41***	−.41*	−.60****	−.19	−.26
Other 2	−.51***	−.16	−.62****	−.34	−.31
Income (household)	−.45***	−.13	−.40*	−.36*	−.41*
Intactness					
Years married	−.28	.00	−.38	.06	−.13
Marital status	−.37*	−.21	−.39*	−.16	−.39*
Family size (living grandparents)	−.42*	−.32	−.64****	−.02	−.04

$^{*}p < .10$, $^{**}p < .02$, $^{***}p < .05$, $^{****}p < .01$.

if high coordination, although an effective response to an acute medical emergency, persists, it may make the family more vulnerable in the long run. If family members remain highly engaged with one another and if they focus heavily on the needs of the chronically ill members, independent needs of others in the family go unanswered. The only other study we have found that measured family process and patient survival of chronically ill members reached a similar conclusion. Pentecost, Zwerenz, and Manuel (1976) studied the capacity of patients with renal disease receiving home dialysis to clarify their own wishes, preferences, and choices in a standardized family communication task. Where the family allowed this autonomy and clarity of individual boundaries for the patient, survival was prolonged.

Educational Achievement and Income. Here again the question of family routine may play a central role. Our sample was largely Black. Those families at the lower ends of our education and income dimensions were indeed quite low (for education, 1 *SD* below the mean was 9.6 years of education, or just beyond junior high school, and for total household income, 1 *SD* below the mean income was $5,812). Thus, our measures of accomplishment were comparing two groups of Black families: those in substantial poverty, and those in the high blue-collar range. Stack (1970), in her ethnography of Black family life, suggested that families in the former group make particular use of strong extended kinship and friendship networks as effective mechanisms for dealing with a broad range of calamities to which these families fall victim. Our own sample of Black families, like Stack's was drawn from a relatively stable community in which such bonds may well have matured over time. On the other hand, in line with Howell's (1973) work, our group of lower middle-class families (the higher blue-collar range) may have been more bounded into traditional nuclear units. These smaller groups struggle for self-sufficiency and become highly organized around occupational, school, and community demands. Howell called this "settled living"; the daily rhythm of family life involves the careful integration of a small number of individuals to be maximally responsive, not just to interpersonal needs of family members but to the external demands of work and school. These lower middle-class families, who were at the upper end of the accomplishment factor in our sample, may be more poorly adapted to the enormous demands for changes in patterns of interpersonal support and integration required by severe, chronic illness. (The one datum on extended family we have reported, on the survival of a grandparent, does not seem consistent here: We found that the availability of a living member of this generation was a risk rather than a protective factor. Although this discrepancy must be explored in future studies, it is well to emphasize that Stack reported on the importance of a wide, flexible network of kin and friends in several generations, not just grandparents.)

Longevity of Relationships. This strength is the presence of an official marriage in the family unit, its duration, and the presence of one or more living grandparents. Risk inherent in this structure may be related to a third kind or order. As studies by Cohler and Grunebaum (1981) have shown, the balance between the marital relationship and the relationship between each partner and his or her living parents is particularly delicate. At this phase in the interlocking lifecycles of parents and grandparents, parents are struggling with dual tasks of work and child rearing while grandparents are in the process of partial retreat from the demands of their children and may be preparing to turn tables by anticipating their own needs for support from their offspring. The unanticipated arrival of a devastating illness in one of the marital partners may throw this delicate balance into disarray. When grandparents are still living, the balance between the growing autonomy of a long marriage and the relationship with grandparents may be severely strained as living grandparents re-enter the household of their children as well as re-engage them emotionally. When a member of the household has an acute illness, the presence of grandparents might be supportive. When the illness is enduring, however, this may disrupt a balanced system of relationship between generations. In this connection it is of interest that our sample was approximately divided between families in which there were one or two living grandparents and those in which there were none. Thus, the low end of this dimension is one where there is simply no grandparental generation with which to be in conflict.

Exclusion of the Ill Member as a Last Stage Coping Effort

If our conjecture about the weakness of strong families is correct, we still must explain why death of the patient is a consequence. There are at least two possible explanations. First is that the severely distressed relationship that we believe afflicts these families is itself the mediating mechanism. We know, for example, that distressed relationships can engender immunologic deficiencies in families (Bartrop, Lazarus, Luckhurst, Kiloh, & Penny, 1977; Dura & Kiecolt-Glaser, 1991); they can also place a burden on the cardiovascular system through their capacity to activate the sympathetic nervous system directly (Levenson & Gottman, 1983). However, it is our impression from detailed interviews of these families that they were not suffering severe, conscious distress. Moreover, using distress as an explanation fails to account for why patients in strong families comply so fastidiously with treatment and what role such meticulousness might play in their health.

Indeed, interviews of these families suggest quite a different mechanism: These families, enduring the prolonged disruption of their ordinary routines and relationships, react with an extreme coping mechanism, the reorganization of the family itself. This reorganization often takes the form of excluding a member. Early in the course of illness, the excluded member may be a child, not the patient, whose needs are no longer attended to or who is quite literally shipped out to stay with a relative or friend. In the end, however, the excluded member becomes the patient. In our experience, the exclusion by the family is usually subtle and comes in many forms: family members' anticipatory grief concerning the patient's impending death, their soft but discernible emotional distancing, their exclusion of the patient from family decision making, their reduced involvement with the patient's medical care and crises, and their fashioning of confidences and secrets from which the patient is excluded. In the Saunders family, described earlier, the exclusion of the patient, Mr. Saunders, was seen in the normal vacation departure of Mrs. Saunders with her younger son.

This form of coping through exclusion of a member has been

described in other areas of family life. For example, Boss (1980) described the reorganization of families whose fathers were missing in action but not proved dead. Many of them closed out the father through a variety of social, emotional, and even legal means. Likewise, in families of adult and pediatric cancer patients, many families erect an emotional wall between themselves and the patient, often as a way of protecting the healthy family system that remains (Langer-Bluebond, 1978; Weisman, 1979). We are also suggesting that this mechanism of walling off may be mutual. It is not simply that patients are excluded in such families but they themselves actively participate in the process out of the same protective intent. This intent of course is self-sacrificing but not suicidal in the more ordinary sense of the term.

Langer-Bluebond's (1978) observational studies of pediatric cancer patients clearly demonstrated the active role of the sick children in the distancing and exclusion process, but, with her younger patients, the self-sacrificing motive of this distancing was not clear. This self-sacrificial component of the family process has been reported clearly in another group of chronically disabled patients and their families: narcotics abusers. Stanton (1977) provided dramatic examples of how the family and patient carefully dovetail a series of maneuvers, leading to the patient's death, so that the family is protected from a variety of stresses and the patient actively participates in that protection.

Medical Compliance as Acceptance of Exclusion

If the patient senses and indeed has acquiesced in the exclusion process, what alternatives lie before him or her? Lonely isolation is one; this has been described for cancer patients in the same predicament. However, there is another active group that the excluded patient may join: the social community of the dialysis unit. The work of De-Nour (1983) showed clearly that many dialysis units do function as emotionally charged large groups with their own norms and rules for approval and emotional acceptance of patients. Her work suggested that to be accepted and admired by the nursing staff, the patient must comply with the therapeutic regimen. Thus, compliance may be understood, in part, as a process by which a patient becomes a valued member of the dialysis unit community. This membership may be particularly attractive to patients who have been partially or totally excluded from their families. However, Hartman and Becker (1978) showed that compliance also entails a more somber view by patients of their underlying illness and a vivid anticipation of the serious complications and sequelae that lie ahead. Our noncompliers, those patients from "weak families" and who also survived to our 36-month follow-up, were not uniformly noncompliant. The two noncompliance variables with the strongest association with the family variables and survival were variations in weight and potassium levels that reflect fluctuations in diet. In other words, our noncompliers seemed to experiment with noncompliance, perhaps to see what might happen if they neither fully accepted the gloomy views about their illness nor were heavily invested in securing the admiration of the dialysis community. Thus, our compliant patients may have differed from noncompliers in their steadfast disinclination to experiment and test the limits of their illness. This view of compliance certainly suggests an attitude of resignation consistent with our overall model.

We have provided a detailed interpretation of these data because they seem to provide an insight beyond the specific mechanisms of a family's response to end-stage renal disease. Indeed, they provide a glimpse of the operations and transformations of the caregiving system. These data identify some of the mechanisms that may extend well beyond renal disease. This is a transition, we suggest, that all caregiving systems must make but some enter into it sooner than later. These data suggest that highly coordinated families, particularly those accustomed to success, find the strain of chronic illness particularly unbearable. This, in turn, leads them to begin this transition sooner. The realignment and distancing of relationships between the patient member and the rest of the family may be the major social transformation that ushers in the terminal phase even without a dramatic biological change in the illness. The medical community serves briefly as an alternate family for the patient while the true family begins to plan for a life without its patient member. From this perspective, death may be seen as an integral part of the transformation of the caregiving system. It is not necessarily a failure either of adequate medical care or even of adequate biological resilience of the patient. Rather, it is part of a process by which a beleaguered family system rejuvenates itself in the face of a burden it feels it can no longer manage or endure.

This interpretation is intriguing. The most compelling scientific imperative is to test some of our interpretive speculations with results from direct measures through replication and extension. Our group is currently in the fourth year of an 8-year study to follow an additional sample of these families over an extended period. This project is designed to study the process of exclusion directly, and includes measures of the clinic social system as well.

Study 2: Observing Families in Multiple Family Groups

The study we have just described followed a design commonly used by behavioral researchers. Starting with a clinical case series, it included longitudinal follow-ups to allow for the prediction of survival. A relatively unique aspect of the study involved the use of methods to study each family as a unit. Most research investigating family factors in chronic illness has used reports from single family members in order to describe some aspect of the family. This study actually involved several household members in an interaction, and used data from this interaction to describe family units on various dimensions.

The study we now describe has used a very different set of methods to investigate families as organized units. This study involved the observation of families who had been brought together in a psychoeducational group to discuss the impact of chronic illness on their families. The method of this study is best described as a replicated case study design, with various forms of control imposed across replications, and with participant-observers collecting qualitative data (Yin, 1984). Such methods are more commonly found in anthropology and some branches of sociology, and so may require some explication for readers from other disciplines.

Multiple Family Discussion Groups as Case Study Method

Case study designs fell into disrepute after Campbell and Stanley's (1963) indictment that "such studies have such a total absence of control as to be of almost no scientific value" (p. 6). Many researchers are unaware that these same methodologists later revised their position, and have even themselves begun to elaborate case study designs that allow for increased rigor and control (Campbell, 1975). Yin (1984) has advanced these design issues the furthest of anyone to date, suggesting that a number of techniques such as replication of case studies, analyzing embedded units within cases, and making repeated observations within a case can greatly increase the rigor of the design and the confidence in results.

Yin defined a case study as an empirical inquiry into a contemporary phenomenon in its real-life context, using multiple sources of evidence. The multiple family group intervention that we describe here is in some ways a hybrid of case study and quasi-experimental design, because the investigators do have much more control over the observational context than is possible in pure case study research. The multiple family discussion group (MFDG) is a clinical intervention originally designed as an adjunct to family therapy, recently taking on new life as a major component of programs working with schizophrenia (McFarlane, in press). Steinglass and his colleagues have recently adapted the MFDG format for working with families with chronic medical illness (Gonzalez,

Steinglass, & Reiss, 1987). In this form, the MFDG consists of a brief, time-limited set of discussions, run by leaders who focus the discussion on specific topics in a highly structured format. These discussions are seen as primarily educational, helping families to understand the demands that chronic illness can impose, and allowing several families to share experiences and insights on how to deal with these demands.

In our work, the MFDG has emerged as an excellent base on which to build a partially controlled set of observations of family life. It has a number of advantages that allow for much greater rigor within the case study format. First, the discussion group format can be highly structured, both as to the initial stimulus that begins the discussion and as to the participants who engage in the discussion. A method used in clinical MFDGs, entitled the "group-within-a-group," has been modified so that the composition of interacting parties can be varied systematically. For example, all members with a chronic condition can be put into the center of the room and asked to discuss a particular topic "from the point of view of the patient." At a later date, other family members can be grouped together for other discussions, such as all the members of one family, or all the parents of children with physical disorders. This allows the researcher to study variance across different combinations of people.

Second, the MFDG appears to be experienced by participants as being much more natural than are many interaction research paradigms. Other researchers have attempted to stimulate family interaction through laboratory tasks, or by asking family members to discuss topics of conflict "as they normally would." Alexander (1973) was one of the few other researchers to use the clinic setting as a context for stimulating family interaction for further study. In our experience, the MFDG is particularly suited to this because family members are engaged in the process of trying to discover something about themselves, and are motivated to participate more fully than they might be in more artificial circumstances. In some real senses they take on the goals of the investigators because those goals are consonant with their own. This is a major strength, as we have noted when using other techniques to elicit social interaction that it is easy for family members to feel defensive, distraught, or burnt out, particularly if they are being asked to engage in conflict about painful topics over long periods of time. The MFDG seems to bypass the adversarial nature of this situation. Although the MFDG situation may be considered more naturalistic than many, it is still a context created by the researcher. This allows for much greater control over the setting, but may in its own way distort the behavior of family members relative to the natural patterns of interaction the family engages in at home. The generality of findings from this method, as with any research technique, must be tested.

Third, the group-within-a-group component described earlier provides a very natural way of stimulating family members to discuss their assumptions about their family and their world, while keeping their comments focused in a theoretically relevant area. Thus, it allows for direct access into the belief structures around family identity. Group leaders can prime the pump by asking the small group to discuss something about their common experiences, or can suggest a cognitive framework and watch to see if the group uses this cognitive frame in their discussion. In our experience these probes by the group leader, when given in the context of the inner group, elicit experiences and interpretations by group members that are echoed and re-echoed in the ensuing discussion, naturally amplifying the material that emerges.

Fourth, the MFDG format allows the researcher some control over the makeup of the group. Because we have been interested in some of the more generic aspects of family response, we have elected to create groups that are heterogeneous for type of chronic disorder. This seems to maximize the chances that those topics which become amplified during discussion will be more generic, and less limited to the demands created by particular conditions.

Fifth, the MFDG allows for either qualitative or quantitative data collection. In the early stages of work it made the most sense to us to search for prototypic instances of family thinking and interaction as we went over our videotapes of MFDG sessions. We present examples of such episodes here, as exemplars of the type of qualitative data we have found most useful during this stage of research.

Use of the MFDG as a case study method can be strengthened even more if groups are repeated, and the findings are replicated. Replicated case series are most likely to bear fruit if MFDG procedures are well articulated and carried out in the same fashion from group to group. Thus, an early task for our group was the development of a detailed intervention manual (Gonzalez et al., 1987). The MFDG itself allows for a variety of "internal replications." Because each group involves several families, probes to elicit general patterns of family transaction can be repeated for each family. Longer discussions often include multiple episodes that can be differentiated, allowing for repeated assessment of important variables. We have only begun to explore the complexities of this form of case study research, but our initial experience suggests it holds great promise.

The Present Study

We report here on our experiences with 22 families in six multiple family discussion groups. Each group included 3 or 4 families with members having chronic physical disorders, and as noted earlier, care was taken to ensure that group composition was heterogeneous regarding illness type (Table 8.4 summarizes group composition characteristics).

Patients attended all group meetings, as did other family members 12 years or older. Groups ran for eight sessions, following a highly structured and standardized protocol as outlined in a detailed treatment manual. Critical throughout, however, was the incorporation of a psychoeducational approach to an understanding of the impact of chronic medical conditions on family life, an approach that used our family systems model rather than a psychopathology model in its attitudinal stance toward chronic-illness families. Most important here was the attempt to establish a group atmosphere that encouraged a *nonblaming* review of past family coping efforts and an exploration of new strategies for tackling illness-related family issues. That is, we tried to establish an atmosphere in which the potentially competing needs of illness and nonillness family issues could receive a thorough reexami-

TABLE 8.4
Group Composition of Six Pilot Multiple Family Discussion Groups

MFDG#	*Family#*	*Composition (patient underlined)*	*Patient Age*	*Medical Condition*
1	1	mother, father, daughter	11	genetic liver disorder
	2	father, daughter son	18	Type I diabetes
	3	mother, father, son	46	Type I diabetes
	4	husband, wife	29	congenital heart defect
2	5	mother, father, daughter, daughter	50	scleroderma
	6	husband, wife	67	end stage renal disease
	7	husband, wife	52	stroke
	8	mother, step-father daughter	16	Type I diabetes
3	9	mother, father, son	40	chronic back pain
	10	husband, wife	37	Epstein-Barr virus
	11	husband, wife	54	chronic back pain
4	12	husband, wife	40	congenital hip deformity
	13	husband, wife	33	ankylosing spondylitis
	14	mother, daughter daughter	44	stroke
	15	husband, wife	60	Type II diabetes
5	16	husband, wife	76	advanced cardiovascular disease
	17	husband, wife	60	Parkinson's disease
	18	husband, wife	53	stroke
	19	husband, wife	63	Parkinson's disease
6	20	mother, father, son	50	osteoporosis
	21	husband, wife	35	multiple sclerosis
	22	husband, wife	55	pot-polio syndrome

nation, and problems of developmental distortions secondary to organization around illness concerns could be successfully addressed.

The eight sessions of the MFDG protocol were conceptually further divided into three components–educational, family issues, and affective components–designed to address different aspects of stress and coping with chronic medical illness. The educational component, consisting of the first three sessions, was primarily designed to educate families about the family stresses generic to chronic illnesses and disabilities. The focus here was on the response of the family unit rather than on details of specific illnesses. The family-issues component–the middle three sessions–allowed each family in the group to review and reassess the coping strategies it characteristically used in response to illness demands. The goal here was to help the family examine its pattern of allocation of family resources between realistic illness requirements and the normative needs of family growth and development; the construct of family identity (and its preservation) was used to assist the family in reexamining and reallocating its resources more equitably. The affective component–the last two sessions–was designed to help the family delineate the impact on chronic illness on its emotional life and on evaluating the relative merits of different emotional styles in responding to the illness.

Prototypic Episodes of Family Interaction

We present here transcribed discussion material of three episodes, taken directly from videotapes of MFDG sessions. These episodes have been chosen both because they seem prototypical of the types of issues and transactional styles typically evidenced by chronic medical illness families, and because they illustrate how the two features of the MFDG format we have been emphasizing–the use of the group within a group intervention, and the establishment of a nonblaming atmosphere–help families to more effectively articulate these issues. The themes we illustrate in the MFDG vignettes are: (a) how powerful and tyrannizing an organizing theme chronic illness has become in these families during the chronic phase of illness management; (b) the conflicts that emerge between illness-related and nonillness demands as they impact on the interplay between personal and family identity; and (c) how the researcher's own ideas may be transformed through a sustained transaction with a group of families.

Vignette 1: Nobody Understands or the Transactional Power of Chronic Illness. The first vignette has been chosen to illustrate how, in the MFDG setting, the issue of illness-based family identity is reinforced and sustained. The transcript comes from a discussion carried out by the three patient members of this particular MFDG, and occurs during the initial group meeting. It picks up at the point the first group-within-a-group has been formed, a patient subgroup that has been given the charge to discuss what they see as the "patient perspective" on the impact of illness on family life.

In this particular patient subgroup, one member (Mr. K), 67, has end-stage renal disease, is on hemodialysis, and is accompanied to the group by his wife. A second patient (Mrs. S), 50, has scleroderma and is accompanied by her husband and two daughters. A third patient (Julie D.), 16, has Type I diabetes and is with her mother and stepfather. The transcript picks up at the point the subgroup leader is posing the initial stimulus question to the three patients:

Coleader: Keep in mind as we go through these groups that there are different perspectives. I think we already started to talk about that tonight. We want to particularly have the opportunity to hear from people who have the chronic medical condition—how you feel it affects your life, what particularly for you are the difficulties or how you see the particular aspects for you, and then also how you see the families responding, what you find helpful, and what doesn't work so well.

The other thing I'm going to ask you to do is sort of talk to each other. That's why I kind of wanted to turn you all around. We're going to have all of you talking to each other about the problem, not just talking to me about it. Because we figure the three of you probably know best—

Mr. K: I'm going to suggest something that we'll all agree on.

Mrs. S: What's that?

Mr. K: Other people don't know how it feels, do they?

Mrs. S: They sure don't.

Mr. K: Before I got out of the hospital, they had a patient who was a 22-year-old boy who was on hemodialysis. We had an immediate bond. We didn't have to get acquainted, nothing. Just the fact that we're both doing that, there was a bond there. Yup.

Mrs. S: I feel that way with my doctors. When I go and see my doctors, they have seen scleroderma and have seen the pain. They seem to understand, even though none of them have it. But I do go to a support group for scleroderma. One time there was a speaker who was a psychiatrist or psychologist that also had scleroderma. Boy, that was really helpful.

Mr. K: You all listened to him, huh?

Mrs. S: Everything he said was, nobody knows what it's like to go to a store and have the change fall through your fingers. Not to be able to grasp anything. When somebody else has the same thing, it really is a help.

Julie D: It's easy to get ahold of. When I got the insulin pump, my doctor told me I'd be able to do everything else that any other kid can do, and I can't. I've got something attached to me. I'm not supposed to play close contact sports. I can't jump around or anything for fear that the thing will fall out and break. And it was tough. Now we're playing volleyball in PE, and everybody keeps coming up to me and asking me why I'm not playing. Is it because I don't want to? I just tell them straight out that I can't play close contact sports. If they want to know any more, they can read the book.

I met a girl when I was in the hospital when I lived with my dad who, her blood sugar was too low, and mine was too high. Hers was at the point where, a normal person's blood sugar is between 90 and 100, and her's was going down to like 3 and 5 at night, in comatose states, and they couldn't bring her out of it. I saw her 2 years ago, I guess, when we went to California, and she'd gotten an insulin pump, too. She was doing a lot better. But both of us realized that we had a close bond, because we both knew what it was like.

The doctors didn't realize that I couldn't do things because they didn't have the same thing the matter with them. A lot of times it happens in my family too, with my brother. It's like, I just wish, it sounds horrible, but I just wish he would get diabetes for one day and see how it feels and just go through all the stuff that I've gone through my entire life. He thinks it's so easy.

Coleader: How does he convey that to you that he thinks it's so easy?

Julie D: Just the way, he thinks it's easy for me to take care of myself and easy for me to give my shots and test my blood sugar, and I should do it all the time. The boy is 19 years old, and I'll go into the bathroom to test my blood sugar, and I'll come out with a machine that I have to prick my finger, and he'll lose it. He'll go absolutely crazy. He hates needles. That's how I get even with him. I go after him with a needle. [Laughter]

We suspect that material of the kind contained in Vignette 1 provides clues for future research into the mechanisms propelling families to organize around chronic illness. Here, two ingredients suggest themselves. First, these patients are, at least in this context, defining themselves by their illness. As they introduce themselves to each other, they suggest that their full range of self-experiences are shaped by their illness. Note in this regard how quickly rapport develops among the patients around the starkly simply theme "nobody else knows what it's like." Second, they contend that they alone have legitimacy in defining the illness identity for the family. Even doctors who are not themselves also patients do not know "what it's like." Neither nonpatient family members nor medical professionals are granted the skill or understanding to grasp emphatically the emotional needs of their patient members.

These two ingredients could, we hypothesize, be powerful incentives to a committed and conscientious family to organize around the illness. Clearly, these patient family members are providing no facet of "wellness" for more ordinary, routine or typical transactions. Further, they give no evidence of a willingness to concede to their families that they have been understood, supported, or sustained. Note especially how this aspect of personal identity involves a belief concerning self in relation to others. The comments made here are not of the form "I am X," but rather are of the form "others cannot relate to me because I am X." The interplay between this belief and the shared constructions that other family members might have concerning the illness does not emerge here, but it provides a hypothesis that such experiences and resultant comments by patients are likely to contribute to the family staying focused on the illness and the needs of the patient. This pattern itself can be riveting either because it induces so much guilt or because it provides a pattern of infrequent, variable interval reinforcement. Perhaps this might in some families over time drive members away, but, in most families it is likely to either motivate a redoubling of efforts to reach the patient members, or to produce a high degree of paralyzing ambivalence.

Vignette 2: A Controlled Rebellion. The second vignette is also drawn from a group-within-a-group discussion. But in this case the group is constituted of nonpatient family members (for this subgroup the leaders select one member from each family to form the nonpatient group-within-a-group). This vignette has been chosen because it is a particularly compelling example of the pressures that emerge in these families when normative developmental needs come in conflict with an illness-dominated family identity. In this case, we hear primarily from Debbi S., the 18-year-old daughter of the woman with scleroderma who was one of the patient participants in Vignette 1. The vignette centers on Debbi's attempt to articulate her struggles at getting "air time" within the family for her own developmental needs.

Coleader: I feel a little unfinished with Debbi's point. I think it may be a really important one. I'm not sure this is what you're saying, Debbi, but are you saying that the things that you want to do or have to do are getting confused or are suffering because of the illness—that it's not being seen just as a kid doing what you want to?

Debbi S: I think a lot of it has to do with Helen, my older sister. [Crying] When she was my age, she did things a lot worse, like skipping and stuff like that. I'm not saying I'm perfect. Now, if I do something wrong, it's like total shock. Everyone yells and hollers. If I can't start my car, my dad yells. If I don't get my mom some water, she yells. It's not like that, but it's just like when I wanted to go out, and I wanted a certain time to be in and there's nothing, just you take my time and that's it, and then they get mad when I thought well, there's nobody to say what time I should be in. I just turned 18 and it's like no, this is the time you have to be in, and that's it.

Coleader: From your perspective, what do you think contributes to the difference between how your sister was treated—

Debbi S: Because my mom's sick. And my dad's sick. When my sister was my age, my mom was sick, but she wasn't like she is now. When Helen was my age, it wasn't as bad. Helen's grown up now. She's got two children. Now, I don't want to live my life around my mom's disease. I care about my mom, I know she's in pain and all that, but it's just the way I'm dealing with it. I'm with my mom, I'm home more than anyone. Helen goes to college at night and during the day she works. Helen doesn't see a lot of it. She sees it, but I'm there most of the time dealing with it. I'm not denying her illness or anything. They keep saying I'm denying it. I'm not. It's just that I don't want to live my life around it.

Coleader: Is it coming more to a point of being, is it even worse now that you're about to graduate high school?

Debbi S: Yeah, because I'm seeing I have my life to live now.

Coleader: You're about to leave home.

Debbi S: What am I going to do? Who am I going to be? What am I going to be? I can't live my life around my mom's disease. I know she's in pain, and every day I come home from school she's always, "This hurts, that hurts," and it's not that I don't want to hear it, it's just that one day I just—

Mrs. CVA: It seems almost like more of it's laid on you than on anybody else, because your other sister works and is away at school. You older sister is not there. I understand what you're talking about. I felt like that, too.

Clearly the key statement in this vignette is Debbi's direct challenge to an illness-focused family identity—"I'm not denying her illness or anything. They keep saying I'm denying it. I'm not. It's just that I don't want to live my life around it." In one of the latter sessions of this MFDG, Debbi returned to this theme and even more clearly articulated her awareness of the intensity of the developmental distortions that have emerged in this family. Talking this time directly to her mother, she said, "Just once I want to have a fight between an 18-year-old daughter and her mother, not between a daughter and scleroderma!"

However, we also want to underscore how the MFDG can elicit cognitive and affective material that may not be able to emerge when the family is together alone. In line with our model of family process, the comments by Debbi appear to reflect a stepping outside of the family identity as currently defined. Debbi openly spoke of needs that are in conflict with the medically determined needs of her mother. The very last comment by Mrs. C suggests that this "rebellion" against the family's view of what should take priority is able to emerge because other group members can provide support for the person who is taking the chance. We would also argue that the ability of the group format to create a non-blaming atmosphere allows the "rebellion" evidenced here by Debbi to be a controlled one, and in this sense likely to stimulate a constructive reexamination of nonillness family needs rather than the precipitous and perhaps fatal rebellion experienced by the Saunders family discussed in an earlier section.

This vignette also raises an important question concerning the MFDG as a research tool. Is it possible that the group setting actually elicits this rebellion for some families? If this is so, how can data from such groups support the contention that this is a natural process of family development? This issue is analogous to the problem of measure sensitization as a potential confound (Campbell & Stanley, 1963), but in this case it is very plausible simply because the research method is intertwined with an educational intervention.

Our initial answer to this problem is twofold. First, if we can predict, using our theory, which families are likely to enter into this rebellion as a result of MFDG experiences, and we can predict the path that the rebellion will take, then the MFDG will serve as a way of testing intervention hypotheses. In this case the actions of group leaders are considered to be interventions (analogous to experimental manipulations in other forms of research), and the onus will rest on us as researchers to predict (and not just post-dict) family responses to particular actions by the leaders and the group as a whole. A second answer to this problem lies in the appeal to multimethod approaches. The MFDG case study has strengths and weaknesses, and should be considered as only one useful method in a host of other techniques for studying family process. In this instance the inclusion of delayed-treatment control groups with other forms of data collection would allow us to clarify this issue.

Vignette 3: The Therapist: Researcher Modifies a Metaphor. This vignette is being introduced to illustrate how the research team worked within the group format to generate and refine hypotheses about our chronic-illness model. In designing the group we placed heavy emphasis on the use of metaphors to focus group discussion and illustrate concepts to families. Initially these metaphors were based on our research experiences with dialysis families and our understanding of the chronic illness literature. One of the constructs (metaphors) suggested by this prior research was that of a "family tolerance level" for illness, analogous to individual pain thresholds. Thus, in one of the early groups, when we got to the "education" session, this was one of the concepts the group leader introduced into the group discussion, suggesting to family members that they discuss how much they *as a family* were able to tolerate the demands of the illness. The leader buttressed this concept by making an analogy to individual patients, suggesting that families differ just as individual patients in pain do, some reaching for the aspirin more quickly with others being stoic. These comments came just before the vignette reported here.

Yet, as is seen, it was a construct not itself well "tolerated" by the marital couple to whom it was being applied. What ensued instead was an unfolding cross-family and family-group leader dialogue that led to the framing of a related but nevertheless different construct—that of systemic balancing of individual reactions to illness (individual tolerance levels for illness) as a regulatory mechanism for stabilizing overall family management of the illness.

Thus, this vignette should be read primarily as a window into how the MFDG (a) becomes a vehicle for theory construction in which the emergence of constructs is a process that includes dialogue between researchers and families about the way to most effectively frame (select metaphors) these theoretical constructs, and (b) at the same time affords a setting for hypothesis testing of these emerging theoretical constructs.

We pick up the vignette at the point just after the group leader has introduced the construct of "family tolerance level" to the group. The first family who will be entering the discussion is a cohabiting couple, Bonnie H and Matt H. The female partner is 29 and is suffering from severe, irreparable congenital heart disease. Her partner is currently a full-time student. The second family includes an 11-year-old girl (Annie L) who has congenital liver disease apparently inherited from her father

(Mr. L) who is symptom-free but whose own mother died of the same illness. A major symptom of this disorder is itchiness. The dialogue unfolds as follows:

Coleader: I guess I was wondering about certain behaviors, or things that come from having an illness in the family. The family might tolerate some things and yet other things . . .

Bonnie H: The thing that hit me immediately is with Matt, for instance, day to day living. He's fine. He's willing to do all kinds of things for me, and he does all the housework, that kind of stuff, cooking. He'll bitch about it, but it's always good natured bitching, and we don't fight or anything.

When I go into the hospital, it's like we don't even know each other. He won't come to visit, which has always really upset me. Or, if he does come to visit, it's always, "Well, I've got to go now, dear," the minute he walks in the room. It's like any change in the status quo seems to put a lot of pressure. I don't mean this to attack you, dear.

Matt H: You know that I hate hospitals.

Bonnie H: That's what he says. To me, someone who spends a good part of my time in the hospital, that really is upsetting that someone who I care more about than anything else won't even come visit me or spend time, and I'm stuck in it.

Matt H: Then again, most of the times you go to the hospital, it's not a life-threatening situation.

Coleader: I guess for whatever reasons, there are certain things that you can tolerate well, and there are other things that are more difficult.

Matt H: It's one thing if it's fairly routine. It's another thing if it's serious. If it was ever really serious, she knows that I'd be right there.

Bonnie H: When I was in CCU, you didn't–

Matt H: I was right there at the CCU.

Bonnie H: Because my sister yelled at you.

Matt H: Your sister never yelled at me, I'd slap her. [Laughter] Besides that, what happened after you were out of the CCU? What was it? It was all a bunch of bogus bullshit.

Coleader: It's obviously a hot issue between the two of you. Maybe there's another way to talk about this same issue, but to do it in a way that doesn't . . . I mean if you just go at each other . . .

Matt H: No, this is normal. We're not going at each other. It's just the last three times she's been in the hospital, this hospital right across the street . . .

Coleader: Hear me out. If you talk about it this way to each other, I don't think there's going to be any change either in your appreciation of what the issue is or in either of you feeling any better or any different about it. Therefore, it will be a Mexican standoff. But, so what? You didn't need to come here to go through that again.

Maybe other people can help out with that.

Mrs. L: I've always felt like I had the main—to carry Annie all alone to the doctors. I had to do that, and you had a job. Al didn't have the time that much, but his mother had a liver disease and died at 48. Now we know—And Al bitched, of course, his family's told me about his mother and father. Again, I think he has a very low tolerance for what you did.

Mr. L: I have a very low tolerance for Annie at times. We went on vacation and—

Mrs. L: But your family had to put up with you like that. I know your mother—

Mr. L: I don't think as much as we have, whatever. I do have a low tolerance. I think Nancy realizes that, particularly at nighttime. Our vacations, at the motel (referring to disruptions Nancy causes at night that interfere with Mr. L.'s sleep)—pills.

Coleader: Let's see if we can play this out. Supposing this situation, in order to keep the balance okay for the family as a whole, if you have a very low tolerance (pointing to Mr. L), you've got to have a very high tolerance, (pointing to Mrs. L), and the lower your tolerance is the higher your tolerance has to get until you're just feeling that it's . . .

Mrs. L: Yeah.

Coleader: That's what's been happening, right?

Mrs. L: I think so. And I don't think he'll talk about it. And a lot of it is your mother—I think there's a lot that you've never talked to me about. And it started when she was born, and I know it's hard. You close up, and you see it as a geologist. We're so different. I think, and I feel, or I feel like I feel too much, and you're very practical and scientific and don't feel anything.

Mr. L: That's not really true.

Coleader: That reminds me sort of what Greg was saying. Everybody has their own individual issues around why they might not tolerate one thing more than another.

Mrs. D: But it doesn't make it any easier.

Bonnie H: It's a balance, and that's right. That's how I feel. You're taking the balance of the whole illness sort of on your shoulders. I feel it's all on my shoulders.

[Multiple conversations between Mr. & Mrs. L]

Mrs. L: I am not blaming you. It could have been anything. Somehow, we've got to work out something to deal with it.

Mr. L: It's an ongoing thing.

Coleader: The question may be for the two of you, and for these other issues also, especially the ones that people feel most deeply about, this question of whether there's a way to even define the issue so that it isn't something that feels as if it's only going to be resolved if one person takes the blame. I think as long as it feels as if one person does all, I don't see how any reasonable person would go ahead with a discussion on that kind of level. There would be a lot of activity, but nothing resolved. Between the two of you, if the issue always gets framed that there's a hero and villain of the piece, in this case, I guess a heroine and a villain, it's unlikely that you're going to get very far with that kind of discussion.

Matt H: It's not that she's thinking I'm the villain or I'm thinking she's the heroine. It's just . . .

Bonnie H: It's a hard situation.

Matt H: The hospital has screwed us so many times. Sure, there's been a couple of times when they've been right. But the times they've been wrong, they have really screwed us and tattooed us. Like, they kept her in over the Super Bowl. [Laughter] The circumstances were she's got a spot on her lungs that's always showed up in the X-rays. It has been there for 12 or 13 years. She goes in, they X-rayed her. It was a new doctor. The doctor says, "You've got a spot on your X-ray on your lungs. It might be pneumonia. You can't leave for 3 days." All he had to do was go downstairs and look at her old records which were down there, and he refused to do it. So, she ended up spending Super Bowl weekend and all that crap sitting in the hospital, and, after 3 days, they said, "Oh, we made a mistake. We checked your records downstairs, and it was okay." They've done that to us three times.

So, I get pissed off at the hospital, and it always brings it up. So it's really not between us two . . .

Bonnie H: What I'm saying in answer to you though, is how do we even approach it so we can even discuss it? It is a hot issue. It's not like I'm trying to approach it like he's a villain or I'm a heroine. It's just, we can't even seem to get to where we can talk about it. If I say, "Gee, this bothers me," he'll deny that there's a problem, and it's the same kind of situation. Some things you just can't even get near to talk about.

This vignette suggests how the MFDG format allows for the introduction and reworking of theoretical constructs about medical illness and the family. Perhaps most important here is the way families themselves become partners in this theory construction process. The researcher (group leader) has introduced the construct, the families have reacted to it in a way that makes it clear that modifications are in order. The therapist then modifies the concept not for any specific family but as a general concept. Commenting no further on variation among families in their tolerance levels, he turned instead to discuss variation *within* families. A new construct is developed—that there is an inverse relationship in tolerance differences among members of the same family; if one member is very intolerant of illness, then another must be excessively tolerant.

The vignette also shows how the MFDG format allows a testing of this new construct. As this new concept evolved in several clearly specifiable steps, the families progressively affirm it. This affirmation was only, to a modest extent, cognitive. More dramatic was the evolving affective and interactional patterns within and among families which seemed to give much more weight to the affirmation.

Parenthetically this episode also highlights yet another stage of the process of family "rebellion" against illness—one of the core constructs of our model. In the functional version of family rebellion, as the desires and needs of other family members are aired (assisted by the nonblaming atmosphere established in the MFDG) and family/illness conflicts emerge, these are rapidly followed by attempts at *renegotiation.* As family members broaden the scope of the family identity to include once again explicit attention to the needs of members other than the patient, such exchanges become much more frequent. In this case the MFDG becomes a setting for problem solving and conflict resolution, and the transactions among family members while in the group can be described in terms of such processes. Conflict and its resolution become a natural part of the process of reorganization.

It is clear that Bonnie H did not attend to this as a family-level concept, but immediately took up the issue of how tolerant the other members of the family could be. That is, she focused on an individual-level concept of tolerance, and used it to discuss what she wanted and was not getting from her partner. This suggests as a hypothesis that during the conflict resolution stage of reorganization, the interpretation that family members make of each other's actions may be influenced by a tendency toward blame and focusing responsibility for change on one another. This is congruent with other research on family conflict (Bradbury & Finchman, 1990).

THE NEXT STEP IN STUDIES OF THE CAREGIVING SYSTEM: THE ROLE OF BIOLOGICAL FEATURES OF THE CHRONIC ILLNESS

Our research observations and data are beginning to suggest guidelines for both understanding and helping families with chronic illness. More immediately they have allowed us to sharpen our hypotheses concerning the important processes that these families experience. Specifically, the data we have reported suggest the following general picture:

1. There seem to be several transactional mechanisms that initiate the reorganization that families go through during various transitions; this includes the initial reorganization around the illness during the acute phase, the transition from the acute to the chronic phase, and the period as families pass into the terminal phase.

2. In the initial reorganization, families may contribute to the constriction of family identity by focusing attention entirely on the illness, to the detriment or even total exclusion of competing nonillness family issues. The patient may contribute to this process by constricting his or her personal identity through strict focus on the illness, and demands that others in the family attend here exclusively as well. The medical care team may contribute by regarding the family as accessory nursing staff whose sole mission is to alleviate the suffering of the patient.

3. The transition from the acute to the chronic phase may lead to developmental distortion if this constriction is not eased. Successful resolution of this dilemma entails the initiation of processes that help the family, first, air its nonillness developmental issues; and second, adjudicate a more balanced distribution of family resources between illness-related and nonillness family priorities. Because the family's illness identity is often so firmly entrenched, the initiation of this process often requires a temporary rebellion of one or more family members against the illness. This rebellion often occurs when the family becomes aware of the suffering of other members. This may take the form of recognizing the needs of an adolescent to become more autonomous, as in Vignette 1, or attending to the distress of an overburdened caretaker as in the case of Mrs. L in Vignette 3. It is possible that MFDGs serve as settings for moderated rebellion, and may even act to prevent more dramatic and fatal rebellion such as that in the Saunders family.

4. Because the MFDG may provide a good setting for "controlled rebellion" in the chronic phase it may be a very useful intervention with two potentials. First, it may be an important therapeutic tool. Second, randomized, controlled clinical trial of this intervention can provide critical tests of our model: Reductions in family distress and prolonged patient survival should occur in those families that can be helped to balance illness and developmental needs.

5. The transition into the terminal phase may be accompanied by processes of exclusion as we hypothesized from the renal dialysis study. Such exclusion may be more likely in families that are more at risk for

disruption by chronic illness, such as those that are more tightly coordinated.

An important unanswered question concerns the role of the nature of the illness itself. We raised this issue in noting the destructive impact of a paralytic illness on the Saunders family. A number of researchers have recently suggested that the impact of chronic illness depends less on the specific nature of the illness than on the amount of burden it imposes on the family (Pless & Perrin, 1985; Stein & Jesosp, 1982). According to this view, the nature of the illness itself need not be a significant factor in a family model. Other researchers have taken the position that symptom patterns and disabilities specific to an illness are likely to mold the individual and family response to that illness in particular ways (Howe, Feinstein, Reiss, Molock, & Berger, 1992). We approached this question by studying a sample of adolescents with a variety of chronic illnesses. We turn to that study now to illustrate the issues involved.

In order to determine the impact of biological characteristics of illness we need to make sure that we are not confounding a general characteristic in which we have an interest with the characteristics of a specific illness. For example, we asked the question whether illnesses that affect the brain might have more impact on family processes than those that do not. In order to answer a question of this kind we must not only sample subjects and their families but also sample illnesses. The best strategy is to pick several illnesses in each of the two categories: neurological and non-neurological. The illnesses within each category should be somewhat different from each other in presenting symptoms, prognosis, and clinical course in order to assure that the common thread among them is that they are either all neurological or non-neurological. Further, there need to be enough patients (and their families) in each specific illness group so that we can be certain it is not just one or two of the illnesses in each category that are contributing to the difference between the two. For example, we should be able to test whether it is only one particular neurological illness that accounts for the differences between the overall category of neurological illness and that of non-neurological illnesses. Finally, where possible, all illness groups should be comparable on major factors that might impact on our outcome measures such as race, gender, and social class.

Given these stringent sampling requirements for examining the effect of biological features of illness, it is not surprising that almost no published studies have used this strategy (Howe et al., 1992). We began our study with chronically ill adolescents reasoning that we might see the impact of illness on their families and on their own adjustment most clearly at this developmental stage. With regard to the family, we reasoned that the parents and siblings would have been exposed to years of the experience of illness and should be showing major impacts if there were any. With regard to adjustment, we reasoned that this period of development puts major academic and social demands on youngsters and those with significant adjustment difficulties will be clearly apparent during this period. We selected 80 adolescents and their families with neurological illness approximately evenly divided into four groups: cerebral palsy, an illness with visible disabilities and often conspicuous speech and motor defects; epilepsy, an episodic illness invisible except at the time of a seizure; hydrocephalus, which for our patients only rarely had visible stigmata; and spina bifida which, in most of our patients, had conspicuous impairments of lower extremities as well as other disabilities. For comparison, we studied 85 adolescents without neurological abnormalities approximately equally divided into four groups: severe vision impairment due to congenital conditions; cystic fibrosis; diabetes; and arthritis. As a comparison group we studied 49 adolescents who had received acute care at the same hospital that treated our chronically ill adolescents. The three groups did not differ significantly on age or gender of child, income, and family structure (one- vs. two-parent families). Parents of the non-neurological group were better educated and those of the control group were younger. There were some differences that were not significant but showed trends: with the comparison group having slightly more Blacks and lower socioeconomic status (SES) ratings. As expected, the neurological group showed lower IQ scores. All adolescents with chronic conditions had endured their illness for many years and some since birth or infancy. A complete description of project methods may be found in Howe et al. (1992).

In assessing the impact on families of variation in illness characteristics, we followed two complementary strategies. The first was to examine the relationship between illness categories on measures of both competent and pathological adolescent functioning. Here, where we find significant deficits in adjustment, we can search systematically for family factors that may either mediate or moderate these effects of illness. Equally important, we can ask whether the impact of the illness on the family is direct or mediated by the secondary deficits in development with which it is associated. Ultimately, longitudinal data is critical for analyses of this kind. A second strategy is to examine the relationship of illness categories with family process, whether or not the illness seems to produce significant maladjustment in the teenagers. Here we can ask an additional question: For those illnesses where there is no indication of adjustment difficulties do the same family factors that promote good adjustment in our healthy controls also operate in families of the chronically ill? Our case study and observations in the multiple family group, for example, suggest that good adjustment in the ill member may be achieved at the expense of overall family development as well as the adjustment success of other members.

Table 8.5 reports findings derived from the first of these two strategies. We are currently completing analyses suggested by the second strategy and report them elsewhere. We examined a broad span of measures of adjustment. These included the Child Behavior Checklist (Achenbach & Edelbrock, 1983) for the primary caretaker (almost always the mother); the Child Depression Inventory (CDI; Kovacs, 1985) for the child; a measure we devised of initiative, self-directed behavior and social and work skills; the Autonomous Functioning Index (Sigafoos, Feinstein, Damond, & Reiss, 1989), which was filled out in its entirety by the child; and an extensive, tester-administered battery of academic achievement (Woodcock & Johnson, 1977).

Table 8.5 shows that adolescents with illnesses that involve the brain were more likely to show behavior problems and deficits in autonomous functioning than were controls, even when demographic differences among the groups were partialed out. Almost all of these differences remained when IQ was partialed out as well. Table 8.5 also shows sizable deficits in academic competence in the neurological group. Here differences in the math subscale were preserved after IQ effects were partialed out. Adolescents in the non-neurological illness group showed little or no impairment in psychosocial functioning. In addition, mea-

TABLE 8.5
Results of Analyses of Covariance, Including Adjusted Means

	Neurological	*Non-neuro*	*Control*	*Effect for Group F*	*Effect for Sex F*	*Effect for Interaction F*
Psychological Symptoms						
Child Behavior Checklist	57.45	54.18	53.30	5.35*	7.49*	1.83
Child Depression Inventory	8.05	6.56	6.77	1.41	3.24	<1
Autonomous Behavior						
Autonomous Functioning Index	179.21	193.20	203.53	6.10**	1.87	<1
Child report of work experience	4.62	4.99	6.24	7.26***	<1	2.42
School Achievement						
Woodcock-Johnson	39.78	54.33	63.20	20.12***	<1	<1

$^*p < .05$, $^{**}p < .01$, $^{***}p < .001$.

Note: Reproduced with permission from Howe, Feinstein, Reiss, Mollock, and Berger (1992).

sures of self-esteem and peer relationships, using the patient as informant, showed no differences among the three groups. As Table 8.5 shows, the CDI also showed no differences. We wondered if the relatively good scores of our ill children on these measures reflected an acceptance of their illness after living with it for many years. These data are consistent with other published data (Howe et al., 1992) as well as results reported in this volume (see chapter 3). These data center our efforts in model building on diseases that involve the brain. These illness are likely to have a particularly significant impact on the family either directly or secondarily through the associated lags in adolescent development. Because they may pose such a challenge to family development, the family's response to them may be especially important in moderating the impact of brain involvement on development in these youngsters. In this regard, these illnesses may have important parallels with another brain-involving chronic illness: schizophrenia (see chapter 7).

Taken together, these newly emerging findings, along with those we have reported in previous sections, lay the groundwork for the development and testing of a model of the caregiving system: the intersection of illness, patient, family, and caregivers. This model has stimulated several lines of investigation by our group beyond that reported here. For example, in our current longitudinal study replicating our pilot work with renal patients, reported earlier in this chapter, we are studying the development of relationships between patients and the staff of the dialysis unit parallel with alterations in the relationship between patients and their families. Also, we have just completed a study searching for those aspects of brain-involving illnesses that affect development and which of these might have an impact on family process. In the data we have just reported it is notable that the impact of brain involvement on IQ had almost no role in our findings because group differences persisted after the effects of IQ were partialed. At present we are concentrating our attention on subtler alterations in attention, perception, and memory. These may not influence IQ scores but they might alter the ill children's relationship with their families as well as account for their patterns of adjustment difficulties.

ACKNOWLEDGMENTS

Many people have contributed to this work. We wish, in particular, to acknowledge the assistance of Carl Feinstein, Sherry Davis Mollock, Sandra Gonzalez, Carol Reisen, Karen Berger, Ann Sigafoos, Jane

Jacobs, and David Palmiter. Portions of this chapter reprinted from Reiss, Gonzalez, and Kramer (1986).

REFERENCES

Achenbach, T. M., & Edelbrock, C. (1983). *Manual for the child behavior checklist and revised child behavior folder.* Burlington, VT: University of Vermont.

Alexander, J. F. (1973). Defensive and supportive communications in normal and deviant families. *Journal of Consulting and Clinical Psychology, 40,* 223–231.

Bartrop, R. W., Lazarus, L., Luckhurst, E., Kiloh, L. G., & Penny, R. (1977). Depressed lymphocyte function after bereavement. *Lancet, 1,* 834–836.

Boss, P. G. (1980). The relationship of psychological father presence, wife's personal qualities and wife/family dysfunction in families of missing fathers. *Journal of Marriage and Family, 42,* 541–549.

Bradbury, T. N., & Finchman, F. D. (1990). Attributions in marriage: Review and critique. *Psychological Bulletin, 107,* 3–33.

Campbell, D. T. (1975). Degrees of freedom and the case study. *Comparative Political Studies, 8,* 178–193.

Campbell, D. T., & Stanley, J. C. (1963). *Experimental and quasiexperimental designs for research.* Chicago: Rand McNalley.

Cohler, B. J., & Grunebaum, H. U. (1981). *Grandmothers and daughters: Personality and childcare in three generation families.* New York: Wiley.

De-Nour, A. K. (1983). Staff patient interaction. In N. B. Levy (Ed.), *Psychophrenology: II. Psychological problems in kidney failure and their treatment* (pp. 117–132). New York: Plenum.

Dura, J. R., & Kiecolt-Glaser, J. K. (1991). Family transitions, stress and health. In P. A. Cowan & E. M. Hetherington (Eds.), *Family transitions.* Hillsdale, NJ: Lawrence Erlbaum Associates.

Farber, B. (1968). *Mental retardation: Its social consequences.* Boston: Houghton-Mifflin.

Gonzalez, S., Steinglass, P., & Reiss, D. (1987). *Family centered interventions for the chronically disabled: The 8-session multiple family discussion group program. Treatment manual.* Washington, DC: University Rehabilitation Research Treatment Center.

Hartman, P. E., & Becker, M. H. (1978). Noncompliance with prescribed regimen among chronic hemodialysis patients: A method of prediction and educational diagnosis. *Dialysis Transplant, 7,* 978–989.

Howe, G. W., Feinstein, C., Reiss, D., Molock, S., & Berger, K. (1992). *Adolescent adjustment to chronic illness: 1. Comparing neurologic and nonneurologic conditions.* Manuscript submitted for publication.

Howell, J. T. (1973). *Hard living on clay street: Portraits of blue collar families.* New York: Doubleday.

Kovacs, M. (1985). The child's depression inventory (CDI). *Psychopharmacological Bulletin, 21,* 995–998.

Langer-Bluebond, M. (1978). *The private worlds of dying children*. Princeton, NJ: Princeton University Press.
Levenson, R. W., & Gottman, J. M. (1983). Marital interaction: Physiological linkage and affective exchange. *Journal of Personality and Social Psychology, 45*, 587-597.
Maurin, J., & Schenkel, J. (1976). A study of the family unit's response in hemodialysis. *Journal of Psychosomatic Research, 20*, 163-168.
McFarlane, W. R. (in press). Family psychoeducational approaches in the treatment of the psychotic disorders. In A. S. Gurmon & D. P. Kniskern (Eds.), Handbook of family therapy (2nd ed.). New York: Brunner/Mazel.
O'Brien, M. E. (1983). *The courage to survive: The life career of the chronic dialysis patient*. New York: Grune & Stratton.
Pentecost, R. L., Zwerenz, B., & Manuel, J. W. (1976). Intrafamily identity and home dialysis success. *Nephron, 17*, 88-103.
Penn, P. (1983). Coalitions and binding interactions in families with chronic illness. *Family Systems Medicine, 1*, 26-36.
Pless, I. B., & Perrin, J. M. (1985). Issues common to a variety of illnesses. In N. Hobbes & J. M. Perrin (Eds.), *Issues in the care of children with chronic illness* (pp. 41-60). San Francisco: Jossey-Bass.
Reiss, D., & Klein, R. (1987). Paradigm and pathogenesis: A family-centered approach to problems of etiology and treatment of psychiatric disorders. In T. Jacob (Ed.), *Family interaction and psychopathology: Theories, methods and findings*. New York: Plenum.
Reiss, D., Gonzalez, S., & Kramer, N. (1986). Family process, chronic illness and death: On the weakness of strong bonds. *Archives of General Psychiatry, 43*, 795-804.
Rolland, J. (1984). Towards a psychosocial typology of chronic and life threatening illness. *Family Systems Medicine, 2*, 245-282.
Sheinberg, M. (1983). The family and chronic illness: A treatment diary. *Family Systems Medicine, 1*, 16-25.
Sigafoos, A., Feinstein, C., Damond, M., & Reiss, D. (1989). The measurement of behavioral autonomy in adolescence: A preliminary psychometric study of the autonomous functioning checklist. *Adolescent Psychiatry, 15*, 432-462.
Stack, C. B. (1970). *All our kin: Strategies for survival in the black community*. Hagerstown, MD: Harper & Row.
Stanton, M. D. (1977). The addict as savior: Heroin, death, and the family. *Family Process, 16*, 191-197.
Stein, R. E., & Jessop, D. I. (1982). A noncategorical approach to chronic illness. *Public Health Reports, 97.4*, 354-362.
Steinglass, P., Bennet, L. A., Wolin, S. J., & Reiss, D. (1987). *The alcoholic family*. New York: Basic Books.
Steinglass, P., Temple, S., Lisman, S., & Reiss, D. (1982). Coping with spinal cord injury: The family perspective. *General Hospital Psychiatry, 4*, 259-264.
Weisman, A. D. (1979). *Coping with cancer*. New York: McGraw Hill.
Woodcock, W. J., & Johnson, M. B. (1977). *The Woodcock-Johnson psychoeducational battery*. Hingham, MA: Teaching Resources.
Yin, R. K. (1984). *Case study research: Design and methods*. Beverly Hills, CA: Sage.

Author Index

Page numbers in *italics* denote complete bibliographical references.

Subject Index